Jesus in Twentiet~~h~~
Literature, Art

Jesus in Twentieth-Century Literature, Art, and Movies

Edited by Paul C. Burns

UBC Studies in Religion: 1

continuum

NEW YORK • LONDON

2007

The Continuum International Publishing Group Inc
80 Maiden Lane, New York, NY 10038

The Continuum International Publishing Group Ltd
The Tower Building, 11 York Road, London SE1 7NX

www.continuumbooks.com

Printed in the United States of America

Library of Congress Cataloging-in-Publication Data

Jesus in twentieth-century literature, art, and movies / edited by Paul C. Burns.
    p. cm. — (UBC studies in religion ; 1)
  Includes bibliographical references.
  ISBN-13: 978-0-8264-2840-0 (hardcover : alk. paper)
  ISBN-10: 0-8264-2840-1 (hardcover : alk. paper)
  ISBN-13: 978-0-8264-2841-7 (pbk. : alk. paper)
  ISBN-10: 0-8264-2841-X (pbk. : alk. paper)
  1. Jesus Christ—In literature. 2. Literature—20th century—History and criticism. 3. Jesus Christ—Art. 4. Jesus Christ—In motion pictures. I. Burns, Paul C. II. Title.

PN57.J47J47 2007
700'.48232—dc22

2007015995

Contributors

Daphna Arbel, PhD (Hebrew University)
Associate Professor, Biblical and Early Jewish Literature at the University
of British Columbia

Paul C. Burns, PhD (University of Toronto), BLitt (Oxford University)
Associate Professor Emeritus, Early Christian Studies at the University of
British Columbia, and Founding Faculty Tutor at Quest University
Canada

J. Robert C. Cousland, PhD (University of St. Andrews)
Associate Professor, New Testament and Classical Studies at the University
of British Columbia

Robert A. Daum, PhD (University of California at Berkeley)
Diamond Chair, Hebrew Bible and Rabbinic Literature at the University of
British Columbia

F. Peter Ford Jr., PhD (Temple University)
Coordinator for the Program in Christian-Muslim Relations at Mekane
Yesus Theological Seminary in Addis Ababa, Ethiopia

Ross Labrie, PhD (University of Toronto)
Professor Emeritus, Department of English at the University of British
Columbia

Dietmar Neufeld, PhD (McGill University)
Associate Professor, New Testament Studies at the University of British
Columbia

Alan F. Segal, BHL (Hebrew Union College), PhD (Yale University)
Ingeborg Rennert Professor of Jewish Studies, Barnard College, Columbia
University

Katherine Sirluck, PhD (University of London)
Senior Instructor, Department of English at the University of British
Columbia

Steven Taubeneck, PhD (University of Virginia)
Associate Professor, Department of Central, Eastern, and Northern European
Studies at the University of British Columbia

Contents

Illustrations   ix

Introduction   1

Modern Uses of Biblical Exegesis

1. Imagining Jesus Then and Now: Nino Ricci's *Testament*
   by Dietmar Neufeld   19

2. Transformation of Biblical Methods and Godhead in
   Norman Mailer's *Gospel*
   by Paul C. Burns   37

Antithetical Treatments of Marxism

3. José Saramago's *Kakaggelion*: The "Badspel" according to
   Jesus Christ
   by J. Robert C. Cousland   55

4. *The Master and Margarita* and Bulgakov's Antiauthoritarian Jesus
   by Katherine Sirluck   75

Romantic and Freudian Applications of Sexual Love

5. The Existential Turn: Refiguring Christ from Kazantzakis
   to Scorsese
   by Steven Taubeneck   109

6. D. H. Lawrence's Risen Jesus
   by Ross Labrie   127

Jewish Treatments of the Crucified Christ

7. "Ben-Yosef Is a Jewish Son": Jewish Portrayals of Jesus—
   Dialectic Reclamation of Presentation and Transformation
   by Daphna Arbel   139

8. Crossing Cruci-fictional Boundaries: Transgressive Tropes in
   Chaim Potok's *My Name Is Asher Lev*
   by Robert A. Daum   155

A Muslim Life of Christ
9. ʿAbbās Maḥmūd al-ʿAqqād's *The Genius of Christ*:
   An Innovative Muslim Approach to Jesus
   by F. Peter Ford Jr.   175

Treatments of Christ in Two Recent Movies
10. Christology in the Dark: *The Da Vinci Code* and *The Passion of
    the Christ*—What They Tell Us about American Religion Today
    by Alan F. Segal   211

Bibliography   223

Illustrations

The following illustrations fall between pages 146 and 147

William Holman Hunt: *The Light of the World*, 1853

Georges Rouault: *The Passion*, 1944

Marc Chagall: *White Crucifixion*, 1938

Yellow Crucifixion, 1943

Resistance, 1940s

Exodus, 1952–1966

The Soul of the Town, 1945

Self-Portrait with Wall Clock, 1947

Introduction

The figure of Jesus continues to captivate the attention of authors and artists in this modern, so-called secular, post-Christian era.[1] There have been numerous investigations of this interest in other phases of modern culture. Film treatments, in particular, have received a range of critical, academic assessments.[2] Some of the themes in these critical studies have parallels to issues in this study. A significant common theme is the increasing interest in the Jewish identity of Jesus and his immediate milieu. There are, however, some distinctive features of written narratives, which deserve their own study. Moreover, themes in twentieth-century Jewish art illustrate significant shifts in Jesus as an emblematic Jew. In the final essay, this study returns to a discussion of the implications of the treatments of Jesus in two recent popular movies.

The literary examples in this study include the three genres of novel, biography, and gospel. While these genres do overlap, the differences in their respective histories and expectations are important for this study. Most of the examples are novels, by Nino Ricci, Norman Mailer, José Saramago, Chaim Potok, Nikos Kazantzakis, Mikhail Bulgakov, and a novella by D. H. Lawrence. The novel is an evolving modern genre with a focus on patterns of consciousness, developing self-understanding, and motivations in the principle characters. A dynamic feature of the modern novel is the integration of the roles of the principle character and the narrator and hence the interpreter. Both Mailer and Saramago use Jesus as the principle character and as the narrator. In this development of the genre, James Joyce had played an important role with the developing protagonist providing the language, images, and perspectives as the narrator. Potok's Asher Lev develops the "call" to be an artist with strong parallels to Joyce's *Portrait of the Artist as a Young Man*. In Potok's novel and its sequel, however, there emerges a resolution to the struggle between artist and community, which is, tentatively, more positive.

1

To interpret their characters and their options, modern novelists may appeal to significant cultural perspectives of existential anxiety, or Marxist protest against the economic and class exploitation, or Freudian emphasis on the defining role of erotic experience, or the Romantic search for authenticity and harmony with nature. Several of the contributors to this volume develop their historical perspective from one or other of these themes. Dostoyevsky is used to interpret both Kazantzakis and Bulgakov. Dostoyevsky's polarization between personal experience of faith and institutional orthodoxy has been very influential among various approaches to Christian existentialism. Some modern writers sharpen this polarization by invoking Nietzsche's critique of the enervating themes in Judeo-Christian culture. As a result of these divergent cultural perspectives on human experience, there develops a variety of alternative models of the human person in the modern novel. Many of these cultural constructions appear in the texts under consideration here. The emphasis on the personal experience, perspectives, and motivations of the principle character makes the novel a truly characteristic genre of modern Western culture. Due to the different cultural perspectives employed by these novelists, different models for the human Jesus are to be found in these texts.

For the purposes of investigating novels that deal with the "Jesus figure," the traditional genre of the "Life of Christ" is important. These "Lives" have a long and constructive role within various schools of Christian spirituality.[3] From the Middle Ages to the modern period, they were designed to support the devotional meditations of those who sought to imitate some theme or aspect of Jesus. These texts were employed not to replace the canonical Gospels but to make them more personally and culturally relevant to the devout reader. Often they would be written by and for members of different religious orders who would emphasize the distinctive charism of that community. Sometimes they would also make use of some elements of contemporary biblical scholarship. In the eighteenth and nineteenth centuries, some members of the Enlightenment such as Hermann Samuel Reimarus appropriated this traditional devotional genre to present portraits of Jesus entirely devoid of the miraculous and the supernatural. This engendered intense controversy, which had immediate detrimental effects on the respective careers of Strauss and Renan.[4] Their two Lives of Jesus have influenced several of the texts under consideration in this study. These works primarily seek to explore the human Jesus without reference to the Christian belief in the divinity of Christ. This study includes an essay on a twentieth-century Life of Jesus composed from the perspective of a believer. This believer, however, is not a Christian. 'Abbās

Maḥmūd al-'Aqqād is an orthodox Muslim. In the concluding essay, by Alan Segal on two recent popular movies, we return to the implications of Christ's divinity as they are expressed through a "high" or a "low" Christology.

Although gospels deal with the life of Jesus, they differ in significant ways from "Lives" and novels. The canonical Gospels purport to have been written by eyewitnesses, and they construct their accounts from the perspective of those who have come to believe in the resurrection of Jesus. These Gospels, attributed to Matthew, Mark, Luke, and John, were not the only ones produced within the early Christian community, however. There were others often attributed to one biblical figure or another, such as the *Proto-Gospels of Thomas* and *James*, the *Gospels of Thomas, Mary Magdalene, Philip*[5], and the most recent discovery, fragments of the *Gospel of Judas*.[6] Scholarship in the last generation has been devoting increasing attention to these texts, with attempts to identify their original communities and their agendas. This scholarship, as we will see, has had an impact on some of the authors examined in this study, especially Nino Ricci and Dan Brown. By calling their works "Gospels," these ancient and modern writers may be claiming an equal or alternative authority to the canonical Gospels. Such assumptions or claims have provoked controversy among early and contemporary Christians. Two of the most recent texts in this study are by Mailer and Saramago, who both invoke the distinctive term "Gospel" in their titles. Although Ricci does not use the term explicitly, he certainly constructs his narrative around four distinctive "voices" who were participants and observers in the events they are recounting. All three, Ricci, Mailer, and Saramago, in their own ways disparage the texts and the motives of the evangelists. The implication is that they are producing a competing version.

Before addressing the contexts and theses of each of the contributors, I will supplement their respective historical perspectives by acknowledging a major impulse for this investigation. In an important study entitled *Jesus through the Centuries: His Place in the History of Culture*, Jaroslav Pelikan examines the creative intersections between dogmatic formulations and cultural expressions in literature, art, and music from the early church through the twentieth century.[7] Pelikan is particularly insightful in his evaluations at critical junctures of Christian Trinitarian and christological thought in the fourth and fifth centuries, the Middle Ages, and the fractious disputes of the Reformation. He carries his investigation through the periods of the Enlightenment and Romanticism, but perhaps his most general and hence least effective chapter is his discussion of the twentieth century. Here he highlights the increasing sensitivity to global perspectives and versions of Christ in African and in Chinese artistic renderings. But in his more recent sequel, *Mary through the Ages*, Pelikan devotes specific chapters to the Jewish context of the biblical treatment of Mary and also includes an important chapter on the extensive treatment of Mary in Islam.[8] In several ways Pelikan has prepared the way for this study, especially for the examples from twentieth-century Judaism and Islam.

To expand on Pelikan's cursory treatment of patterns in twentieth-century Western Christianity, perhaps we can invoke his perceptive appeals to artistic examples in order to demonstrate the dramatic paradigm shifts in the modern era. The pre-Raphaelite painter William Holman Hunt first produced his iconic *The Light of the World* in 1853. This presents a serene Jesus figure in a pastoral setting gently knocking on a door slightly overgrown with a vine, ostensibly inviting the person within to open up to mercy and forgiveness. Jesus is carrying a lantern, which sheds light and warmth around him and dispels the surrounding evening dusk. In dramatic contrast to this peaceful pastoral encounter of Jesus with the individual, there are the dark, fragmented paintings of Georges Rouault in the first half of the twentieth century. In his *Passion* of 1944, for example, Rouault invokes the suggestion of the sacred in stained glass windows by inserting curved black lines in many of his paintings. But here those heavy black lines accentuate the darkness, brokenness, and death provoked by the experiences of war. Within these dark canvasses there is often a flash of color, so light continues to penetrate the darkness but in a very different context than in the nineteenth-century version.

This dramatic shift from the gentle encounter with Jesus in nineteenth-century pastoral images to the identification of Jesus with the darkness, fragmentation, and death of the modern human condition is also reflected in traditions of systematic Christian thought of the twentieth century. There have been a number of creative attempts to sharpen the interpretations of Jesus as the "representative" human who experiences a developing self-awareness and experiences suffering, abandonment, and death. At the same time, Christian theologians were attempting to explore Jesus as "transformative" of the human condition on both personal and communal levels.[9] Systematic Christian theology, with its increasing interest in the humanity of Jesus Christ, does not seem to have had any direct influence on the creative artists and writers represented in the essays in this volume. The one possible exception is Kazantzakis. One of the many cultural influences at work in his creative imagination may have been the emphasis on the humanity of Jesus in Western Christian piety and theological thought, which he might have encountered during his Paris sojourn. This would not have endeared him to the leadership of the Greek Orthodox Church of his day.

This project began with discussions among colleagues who teach in a program on "Religion, Literature, and the Arts" at the University of British Columbia. We took our interests to a panel discussion of a regional meeting of the Society of Biblical Literature in May 2004. There we found a receptive audience and the encouragement to proceed. We were urged to print plates from the symbolic and "narrative" art of Chagall; we were challenged to find a contribution on modern Islamic treatments of Jesus. This volume is our response to that enthusiasm. To facilitate coherence in the collection, I have grouped most of the essays in pairs, with each pair focusing on a general theme. Some historical background on the specific themes is provided within the respective groupings. Thus, the collection opens with essays on two novels, one each by Ricci and Mailer.[10] They happen to be the most recent publications in our collection but, in very different ways, they each deal with "Modern Uses of Biblical Exegesis." The second cluster deals with "Antithetical Treatments of Marxism" in novels by Saramago and Bulgakov.[11] The third group deals with "Romantic and Freudian Applications of Sexual Love" in a novel by Kazantzakis and a novella by Lawrence.[12] The next section deals with "Jewish Treatments of the Crucified Jesus" in paintings by Chagall and in a novel by Potok.[13] The next chapter is a study of the *Life of Christ* by a Muslim writer, and the final chapter is a discussion of audience responses to the treatments of Jesus in two films: *The Passion of the Christ* and *The Da Vinci Code*.

Uses of Scriptural Exegesis by Ricci and Mailer

In the modern period there are many ways to read a sacred text. Since the 1980s members of the Jesus Seminar have captured public attention with their use of a wide range of ancient texts, some of which have been dramatically recovered only in the twentieth century, in order to reconstruct the historical Jesus and his milieu. Since Ricci is fascinated by this work, the first essay will explore the traditions and methods of this school and demonstrate how Ricci imaginatively constructs his sympathetic and realistic version. Within a Jewish yeshiva, even in New York, treatments of the Hebrew Bible differ from the social-historical analyses of members of the Jesus Seminar. The yeshiva's members recite a text in Hebrew and then test the meaning of a passage by invoking parallel episodes and personalities from other passages in Scripture. Mailer, whose maternal grandfather was a rabbi, would have known this practice. Mailer is aware of at least some of the noncanonical sources, but he is much more interested in his own version of this biblical "intertextuality."

Dietmar Neufeld uses Ricci's own acknowledgment about his interest in the Jesus Seminar on the last page of his novel as the key for his essay. Neufeld provides an informative and insightful sketch of three important stages of the so-called quest for the historical Jesus. This approach has dominated modern New Testament studies ranging from Reimarus through Strauss and Renan to Schweitzer and on to the new or "third" quest by members of the Jesus Seminar. Under the influence of these scholars, Ricci uses, without distinction, the evidence of the canonical Gospels as well as Q and the *Gospel of Thomas* and other early apocryphal texts. This effort of historical reconstruction is evident in Ricci's orthography of proper names for characters and places, a sense of the original topography of the region with its terrain, wilderness, distances, routes, and extensive demographic variety. The same scholarly resource provides important background on the practices of healing his Yeshua had learned in Alexandria and applies in several episodes in the novel. The most significant contribution from this scholarship is the understanding of strained relations between various social groups of the period in Israel. There is definitely tension between the Roman occupiers, with their fortresses, armies, and vigilance, and the resident Jewish population. Ricci relates this tension to the issue of the paternity of Yeshua. Miryam was the victim of rape by a Roman soldier. The same context accounts for the rebellious perspective of the Judas figure, who is presented as a loyal confidant of Yeshua, anticipating his portrayal in the recently published *Gospel of Judas* rather than as the betrayer of the canonical Gospels. Miryam of Migdal emerges as a homely young follower jealously protective of Yeshua. Her understanding of the discovery of the kingdom within suggests the influence of the Gnostic texts, which have attracted the attention of recent scholars. From the Jesus Seminar, Ricci derives the painful internal frictions of the Jewish population: between traditional Jews and sectarian Samaritans, between urban temple elites and rural peasants of Galilee, between men and women. Ricci exploits these tensions to invest many stages of his narrative with sudden, extreme acts of violence: the unthinking treatment of the young rebel, Ezekias; the rape of Mary; the brutal deaths of the parents of Simon, the final witness; the senseless death of victims on the cross. Against this threatening background the Jesus figure emerges as a person with insight and wisdom. With an appreciation for the familiar tendency to reinvent Jesus according to one's cultural and personal parameters, Neufeld presents the contours and nuances of Ricci's Yeshua.

The portraits of the other figures in Ricci's reconstruction are each very imaginative and intriguing. Ricci has replaced the four evangelists with voices of his own choice: Judas (his Yihuda of Qiryat), Mary Magdelene (his Miryam of Migdal), Mary (his Miryam), and a pagan shepherd (his Simon of Gergesa). Rather than four roughly parallel narratives, Ricci has each tell one stage of the story from his or her own perspective, with Simon taking over the final stages leading up to the death on Calvary. This method entails some repetition, but it permits divergent assessments of persons and events. Ricci invests each with a striking personality and motivation. Judas is intensely distrusted by Mary Magdalene; on the other hand, he is befriended by Simon, who exonerates him from his traditional role of betrayer. The homely Mary Magdalene has a possessive and somewhat fanciful relation with Jesus. Striking and intriguing as these personalities and relationships are, they tend in this novel to compete for interest with the main character.

In my essay, I argue that Mailer also demonstrates familiarity with ways of dealing with biblical texts but that he does so in ways very different from the approach of Ricci. Mailer relies heavily on the canonical Gospels themselves for his evidence, with some allusions to the Essene community, although he too seeks to carve out an independent narrative but by using the subject himself as the narrator. Mailer's narrative employs a method of biblical exegesis standard in Judaism from the period of the temple through rabbinical traditions to the present day. Persons and events are interpreted from the perspectives of previous biblical texts. Mailer shows his mastery of this technique, though he subverts the conventional God and Satan polarity with his own personal theodicy of a morally compromised and inadequate divine power who, Mailer claims, is competing for attention among other divinities. Mailer does construct this compromised deity within the formal creedal parameters of the Nicene equality of Father and Son. His subversion of the basic tenet of Nicene Christianity provides the central dynamic of this novel. That paternal relationship is revealed, as in the Synoptics, at the baptism in the Jordan. It is not the Divine voice, however, that offers the identification in Mailer's novel but rather Satan, immediately after the baptism, during the encounter in the desert. The power of his novel, such as it is, rests on the psychological implications of this dysfunctional father/son relationship.

Antithetical Uses of Marxism by Saramago and Bulgakov

Marxism has provided an alternative analysis of the struggle between good and evil within categories that are primarily economic and political.

Two of the major novelists examined in this study present interpretations of Jesus within starkly contrasting evaluations of the Marxist version of reality. Saramago, an avowed Marxist, subverts the traditional Judeo-Christian opposition of God and Satan. Bulgakov, by contrast, employs his understanding of Jesus to offer a highly imaginative indictment of the Communist state of the USSR. Both writers employ the figure of Jesus within the opposition of God and Satan to provide highly dramatic versions of the human dilemma within these contrasting worldviews.[15]

J. Robert C. Cousland reviews some of the personal background of Saramago and the basic themes and structure of the novel in order to argue that the author has satirically reversed basic values of the Christian gospel to propose a Marxist reinvention of the gospel message. Cousland concludes that Saramago has provided an ideological gospel, which he intends to be more humane but which, in Cousland's assessment, is destructively tragic.

Saramago was born and raised in Portugal in impoverished circumstances. He joined the Communist Party and retains to this day a worldview derived from a saying of Marx: "If the human being is shaped by his circumstances then it is necessary to shape those circumstances humanely." Cousland argues, convincingly, that Saramago makes extensive use of characters and episodes in the canonical Gospels and the extensive range of apocryphal literature from early Christianity to construct an uncanny but chilling satire of the Christian gospel. Saramago reconstructs a wide range of the characters and episodes of the Gospel traditions, and he invests much of this with a perverse satirical perspective. He suggests that the foreskin of the circumcised Jesus can be found as an object of veneration in a chapel; he observes that it would be very difficult to administer a paternity test to God. After a mysterious annunciation scene, Jesus is born in a cave near Bethlehem; he grows up in the family of Mary and Joseph. After the death of Joseph, he wanders off and comes under the influence of the mysterious Pastor. Pastor is presented as the ideal shepherd who is always looking out for the good of the flock, killing only the aged and the sick for the good of the others. He never takes one for himself. Then in a reversal of "the binding of Isaac" in Genesis, Pastor severs his relationship with Jesus after Jesus takes a lamb to sacrifice to God. This God demands blood and sacrifice to satisfy his bloodlust. This theme dominates the divine agenda, since Jesus is granted a vision of the future followers that is full of the blood and destruction of the Crusades and the Inquisition. Without his mentor Pastor, Jesus again wanders off and uses Mary Magdalene as prostitute and confidant.[16] Jesus comes to realize the dire implications of this divine mission and desperately attempts to avoid them by conspiring to set up his own death. He realizes the futility of this escape only on the cross, when he becomes painfully aware that he has been tricked. In a much more malicious scene than Mailer's account of God's mocking Jesus walking on water, Saramago's God laughs during this final tragic episode on the cross. Then in a chilling example of Saramago's powers of subversion of the original Gospel text, he says that men forgive this god because he does not know what he has done. Cousland demonstrates that the Marxist Saramago has designed Pastor as the ideal communist who does everything for the common good, whereas the god figure is a self-centered, manipulative, and destructive force. This central polarity ultimately replaces the good news of the Christian gospel with the tragic view that all life ends only in death. Cousland's concluding assessment is succinctly summarized in his title, "Saramago's *Kakaggelion*" or "Badspel."

In contrast to this tragic perspective, Bulgakov retains many of the traditional features of the New Testament polarization of good and evil. Katherine Sirluck provides a close reading of Bulgakov's text by pointing out its dense range of personal and literary parallels. Just as Neufeld has provided a survey of modern New Testament studies, Sirluck offers an informed overview of some cultural themes in Western Christian and Russian literature. She applies this to Bulgakov's dense allegory and concludes that the Russian author has affirmed the reality of Jesus as a spiritual force for those who appropriate him in their own guilty collusion with coercive human authority.

God and his son Yeshua represent good, while Satan/Woland and his minions are evil. Evil and Satan are the dominant forces in this narrative, with their control of all the social institutions of the Soviet state. This control is exercised through the police, psychiatric clinics, and the censorship of all publications. The tyranny of the state is reflected in the Russia of Stalin and in the role of Pilate within the Roman Imperial bureaucracy. Much against his better nature Pilate passes judgment against Yeshua. This echoes Bulgakov's own experience as a White Russian medical officer who failed to intervene to defend murdered innocent Jewish civilians. In the novel Margarita had betrayed her husband and agreed with Satan to play the role of hostess at his macabre ball. However, the death of Yeshua is not the end; the sins of Pilate and Margarita are not the end. Bulgakov has a somewhat unorthodox view of salvation, which has strong roots in his predecessor Dostoyevsky. The power of Yeshua continues to operate not through the institutional church with its canonical texts and sanctioned rituals, but in the memory and imagination of people who need and seek forgiveness. The power of the goodness of Yeshua strikes a resonant response within the goodness that remains innate in every human being. In time even Pilate will resume his conversation with Yeshua. Margarita's compassion for Frieda and a frightened child becomes the foundation for her continuing journey out of the darkness of Moscow toward a rainbow, suggesting the sign of the universal covenant revealed to Noah. Sirluck enables the reader of Bulgakov to appreciate the power of the narrative within its dense political, literary, and religious allusions.

Romantic and Freudian Applications of Sexual Love in Kazantzakis and Lawrence

Some modern Jesus narratives focus on sexuality as a necessary condition for full human experience. This focus has been heightened within some of the traditions of nineteenth-century Romantic quests for wholeness and value. This pursuit has certainly been sharpened by the clinical analytic theories of Freud. Suggestions of sexual intimacy between Jesus and Mary Magdalene are as old as the *Gospel of Philip* and, perhaps, the *Gospel of Mary*.[17] Some modern novelists, such as Kazantzakis and Lawrence, feature different types of sexual intimacy. Mailer, surprisingly, excludes it; Ricci restricts it to the fantasies of Mary.

Steven Taubeneck employs the intellectual resources of Kazantzakis to argue, persuasively, for the refashioning of Jesus into an "embattled seeker" of freedom in the universal struggle between the competing claims of spirit and matter. He is seeking for the authentic, existential resolution in his reconstructed figure of Jesus. To demonstrate the inherent tension in his conception, Taubeneck shows how the first paragraph of the novel moves from an idyllic, Romantic view of the natural setting to something much more troubling and even sinister. He reviews Kazantzakis's fascination with the critical thought of Nietzsche; Kazantzakis translated some of Nietzsche's works into Greek and made Nietzsche the focus of his thesis. In the break with conventional accommodations of the human struggle between spirit and body, the Greek novelist ultimately, according to Taubeneck, moves much closer to Dante, whose *Divine Comedy* Kazantzakis had also translated into Greek. Thus, the triumph of the human spirit is ultimately the choice for the ascetic ideal. The pivotal section of the temptation on the cross occurs in the biblically significant chapters 30 to 33. With a telling comparison to Kierkegaard's psychological study of Abraham in the face of the divine command to sacrifice his son, Taubeneck presents at length the temptation to consider the sensual, domestic option first with Mary Magdalene and then with Martha and Mary. But Jesus opts for the spirit and the ascetical ideal. Kazantzakis inserts a significant adjective into his version of Jesus' last words: "He uttered a triumphant cry." Taubeneck also offers an insightful assessment of Scorsese's film version. Although faithful to the text in many ways, Taubeneck argues that Willem Dafoe's portrait contains many elements of a 1960s hippie figure within a commune of groupies. Taubeneck concludes his discussion of the novel and the film with the challenge that "a fully plausible, existential Christ still waits to be imagined."

Ross Labrie demonstrates that Lawrence chose to focus on one stage of the traditional life of Jesus. While Bulgakov, too, had emphasized one stage—namely, the confrontation with Pilate and the resulting death on the cross—Lawrence chose the life of the resurrected Jesus. Labrie argues that Lawrence's objective is to develop an intensely vital version of the resurrected life to replace what, in his view, is the vague ethereal apparition of traditional Christianity. Lawrence develops his case in two stages, through the metaphor of the fighting cock and his version of the Egyptian fertility myth of Isis. Both Jesus and the cock begin as tethered or bound victims, the cock by a rope and Jesus in his burial cloths. Lawrence has Jesus awaken from a life constricted by an anemic, ascetic objective to embrace an energetic, sometimes violent life. Both the cock and Jesus are set free to fight and to triumph. Lawrence is influenced by Blake's and Nietzsche's repudiations of the passivity of conventional Christianity. His Jesus is introduced to a single sexual encounter with the priestess of Isis. The agenda here is not so much erotic as a fulfillment of the Romantic quest for wholeness, unity, and value in response to a deep, vital, unconscious, instinctual urge. The consequence seems to produce a heightened awareness enjoyed in solitude, for the relationship with Isis is not a continuing one. Labrie develops a profound contrast between this mythic characterization of love, experienced in consciousness, with the central biblical theme of charity expressed actively in a reciprocal relationship between God and humans and, by extension, between humans.

Jewish Treatments of Jesus

The horrors of the Holocaust, which haunt the second half of the twentieth century, might make this an inauspicious time for Jewish interest in the Jesus figure. In fact, it was a convention for many Jews to refer to him, contemptuously, as "that man." But Jewish artist Marc Chagall has painted a number of striking images of Jesus on the cross. Jewish novelist Chaim

Potok has portrayed the tension within a Hasidic family and community when one of its members becomes an artist and paints his own version of the crucified Jesus.

Daphna Arbel examines the significance of Chagall's initiative within the traditions from eighteenth- to twentieth-century Jewish academics, writers, and artists. She provides an informative and insightful history of Jewish scholarly assessments of Jesus, from the dismissive "that man," to the "Jew among Jews," to Martin Buber's "elder brother." The dominant focus here is the exploration of the Jewish context of the historical Jesus, which has some interesting parallels with the "quest" recounted by Schweitzer and other scholars up to the present day. She also deals with a range of creative developments in Jewish literature and poetry from the beginnings of the twentieth century, where Jesus is constructed to express modern Jewish concerns and aspirations. For the critical years of the Holocaust, writers such as Elie Wiesel invoked the figure of Jesus on the cross. In the reconstruction after the war and the struggle to establish the state of Israel, Jesus was identified with earlier Jewish leaders against the Seleucid and Roman occupiers as an embodiment of Jewish courage and hope. Within this evolving understanding, Arbel selects a number of Chagall's paintings for her perceptive interpretation. For detailed analysis of themes of "suffering and hope" in Chagall's work through 1945, she selects *White Crucifixion* (1938), *Yellow Crucifixion* (1943), *The Martyr* (1940–1944), and *The Crucified* (1944). For the emergence of themes of "renewal and hope" in works after World War II, she examines *Resistance* and *Resurrection* (1948) and *Exodus* (1952–1966). She concludes with themes of Chagall's inner search in *The Soul of the Town* (1945) and *Self-Portrait with Wall Clock* (1947). The figure of Jesus is always depicted in Jewish dress and often with a prayer shawl and a Torah scroll and surrounded with images evocative of the pogroms and the Nazi agenda. Arbel points out that whereas Chagall has Jesus identify with the destruction and death of the Jewish people, his Jesus does not represent the redemptive figure of Christian faith. Yet in so many of the representations, the Jesus figure on the cross possesses dignity, and the use of the biblical symbol of light in several examples certainly suggests hope for the future. She concludes that for Jewish creative writers, poets, and artists like Chagall, Jesus becomes an icon upon whom they project a variety of personal and communal concerns and aspirations.

Robert A. Daum develops a thesis by which he explores the dynamic tension within Potok's novel, but he questions the validity of the binary confrontation of the core symbols to represent Judaism in relation to

Christianity, particularly in the generation after the Holocaust. Asher's parents are trying to recreate the values and practices of Hasidic Judaism in Brooklyn. The father is often away to assist the fractured community in Europe and elsewhere. The mother is anxious and fragile because of his absences and because of the murder of her brother during similar missions. Their son grows up within this intense form of Judaism, but he has an innate talent and drive to become an artist. In passing, Daum notes parallels with the tensions between the artist and communal culture in James Joyce's *Portrait of the Artist as a Young Man*. To assist the talented young member of his Hasidic community, the rebbe intervenes to encourage the boy's ability with the hope that he will remain an observant Jew. During his sojourn/exile in Europe, Asher pursues his dream and is captivated by Michelangelo's *Florentine Pietà*. After much personal tension, he produces his own version of that core Christian symbol. But he dramatically transposes the content. For the central figure of the dead Christ, he places his own anxious mother. He replaces the two flanking figures with himself and his father. In several passages throughout the novel, the character distinguishes himself from Marc Chagall, hence the title of the novel. Asher has transformed the key symbol of the suffering Christ into the suffering Hasidic Jew. Here Daum questions the legitimacy of the Hasidic Jew as the core symbol of the multifaceted Jewish identity. He also acknowledges the uses of representational art in the Jewish tradition despite its aniconic perspectives. He even cites other examples of Jewish treatments of Jesus within medieval and modern Jewish writing and art. He does not dispute the central role of the crucified Christ for Christianity. Daum concludes, however, that the simplicity of the binary replacement undermines the complexity of modern Jewish experience and Jews' interpretations of their reality.

An Islamic Life of Christ

In the current tension between Christians and Muslims, it is important for Christians, and for Westerners generally, to acknowledge the significant role of Jesus within Islam. In ways that may surprise many contemporary Western readers, 'Abbās Maḥmūd al-'Aqqād provides a sensitive, discursive Life of Christ. So as we near the end of our survey of twentieth- and twenty-first-century narrative treatments of Jesus, we return to a very traditional religious perspective.

F. Peter Ford Jr. translated al-'Aqqād's text from Arabic to English in 2001. In his essay he provides an informative introduction to the career of al-'Aqqād, a survey of the treatments of Jesus in Islam, and an analysis of this Life of Christ. This version respects the evidence of the canonical Gospels, as well as some features that have emerged in modern European studies of Jesus. The appealing narrative by Renan encouraged al-'Aqqād to develop a romanticized version of Jesus; some Western biblical commentaries provided him with some background information; Dostoyevsky's dramatic *Grand Inquisitor* inspired al-'Aqqād to consider a potential return of Jesus in his final chapter. He follows the Gospels' accounts of Jesus' birth and public ministry with teaching and miracles. Al-'Aqqād remains faithful to observant Muslim beliefs about the status of Jesus and his mission. He affirms the virgin birth and Jesus' status as divine messenger and Messiah. To protect Islamic monotheism, Jesus is not divine; he is a messenger, possibly the greatest of them except for Muhammad. To maintain the Muslim tradition, this Jesus does not die on a cross but instead, following a sectarian Islamic tradition, ends his days in India. Ford's purpose is to assist a modern Western audience to understand and appreciate the deep religious respect Muslims have for Jesus.

Jesus in Two Recent Movies

In his discussion of *The Passion of the Christ* and *The Da Vinci Code*, Alan F. Segal examines the respective appeals to two sides of America's current religious identity. He identifies the first as a coalescence of evangelical Christians and conservative Roman Catholics, and the second as more liberal and secular believers with a tendency toward cultural assimilation. Both films attracted considerable attention. Segal explains the appeal of Gibson's film to the first group, although he observes that the account of Christ's suffering is influenced as much by the nineteenth-century visionary Anna Katharina Emmerich as by the Gospels. He relates Dan Brown's novel and the subsequent movie to liberal believers and others who enjoy a conspiracy story about Christianity, regardless of the lack of any coherent objective evidence. In working out his perceptive analysis of the emerging bifurcation of American religion, Segal reintroduces critical theological perspectives of "high" and "low" Christology. High Christology begins with the divinity of Christ, who stoops to accept the human condition. Low Christology, on the other hand, begins with Jesus in the human condition with spiritual aspirations for something beyond. Segal illustrates how the first operates in *The Passion of the Christ* and the second functions in *The Da Vinci Code*. He goes on to argue that each proposes a different model for salvation. High Christology is directed toward the ultimate "resurrection of the body." Low Christology, in its current cultural manifestation, assumes the "immortality of the soul."

The purpose of this study is to present a context for discussing the continuing treatments of Jesus by creative writers and artists in our culture. This will provide not only an opportunity to explore competing versions of humanity, but also to engage in a responsible discourse that crosses conventional boundaries of our culture. From these examples, it is evident that in our times a wide variety and, sometimes, competing models of Jesus have emerged. In some, at least, perspectives of religious faith, biblical scholarship, and critical theology can be effectively engaged.

This project would not have been possible without the participation of this wide range of colleagues, and to each of them I am very grateful. Along the way others have provided encouragement, advice, and support. Included among them are David Evans, Hanna Kassis, Paul Mosca, Shirley Sullivan, and Roger Wilson. Right from the initial workshop in 2004, Rabbi Dr. Yosef Wosk has encouraged and supported the inclusion of artistic examples in this project. Without these contributors and supporters, this project would be not have been possible.

NOTES

1. For a traditional discussion of the separation of modern Western culture from institutional Christianity, consult O. Chadwick, *Secularization of the European Mind in the Nineteenth Century* (Cambridge: Cambridge University Press, 1975). For a current evaluation from a social-historical perspective, consult H. McLeod, *Secularization in Western Europe: 1848–1914* (Basingstoke: Macmillan and New York: St. Martin's Press, 2000).

2. For studies of films by New Testament scholars, consult A. Reinhartz, *Scripture on the Silver Screen* (Louisville, KY: Westminster John Knox, 2003); W. R. Telford, "The New Testament in Fiction and Film: A Biblical Scholar's Perspective," in *Words Remembered, Texts Renewed: Essays in Honour of John F. A. Sawyer*, ed. J. Davies, G. Harvey, and W. G. E. Watson (Sheffield: Sheffield Academic Press, 1995), 360–94; and R. Walsh, *Reading the Gospels in the Dark: Portrayals of Jesus in Film* (Harrisburg, PA: Trinity Press International, 2003). For studies from a more theological perspective, consult L. Baugh, *Imagining the Divine: Jesus and Christ Figures in Film* (Kansas City, MO: Sheed & Ward, 1997). For a historical survey from *King of Kings*, to *Life of Brian*, *The Last Temptation of Christ*, and *Jesus of Montreal*, consult Richard Stern, *Saviour on the Silver Screen* (New York: Paulist Press, 1999). Two of the novels in this study have been adapted to popular film versions. Martin Scorsese produced his version of Kazantzakis's *Last Temptation* in 1988; Russian Television had a recent successful serial version of Bulgakov's *The Master and Margarita*.

3. See the evangelical F. W. Farrar, *Life of Christ* (London: Cassel, 1874); the Catholic A. Goodier, *The Public Life of Our Lord Jesus Christ: An Interpretation*, 2 vols. (London: Burns, Oates, and Washbourne, 1930) and *The Passion and Death of Jesus Christ* (London: Burns, Oates, and

Washbourne, 1933); and the popular H. Daniel-Rops, *Jesus and His Times*, 2 vols. (Garden City, NY: Image, 1958).

4. See D. F. Strauss, *Das Leben Jesu* (Tübingen, Germany: C.F. Oslander, 1836); and J. E. Renan, *Vie de Jésu* (Paris: Culman Lévy, 1864). Strauss's publication led to his dismissal from Tübingen and undermined his attempt to secure a position at Zurich in 1839. Renan was dismissed from his position at the Collège de France in 1865, the year after the publication of his book.

5. For a current edition in English and informative discussion, consult B. D. Ehrman, *Lost Scriptures: Books That Did Not Make It into the New Testament* (Oxford: Oxford University Press, 2003); and Ehrman, *Lost Christianities: The Battles for Scripture and the Faiths We Never Knew* (Oxford: Oxford University Press, 2003).

6. See R. Kasser, M. Meyer, G. Wurst, *The Gospel of Judas* (Washington, DC: National Geographic Publications, 2006).

7. J. Pelikan, *Jesus through the Centuries: His Place in the History of Culture* (New Haven, CT: Yale University Press, 1985). This book was reprinted with a new preface in 1999.

8. J. Pelikan, *Mary through the Ages: Her Place in Culture* (New Haven, CT: Yale University Press, 1996).

9. For a concise but comprehensive overview of eleven approaches to the study of Jesus Christ in the modern period, consult J. A. Fitzmyer, *Scripture and Christology: A Statement of the Biblical Commission with a Commentary* (New York: Paulist Press, 1986). For an example of a discussion on the developing human psychology of Jesus, consult K. Rahner, "Dogmatic Reflections on the Knowledge and Self-Consciousness of Christ," in *Theological Investigations* 5 (Baltimore: Helicon, 1966), 193–215. For discussions of the humanity of Jesus encompassing all people, consult K. Barth, *The Humanity of God* (Richmond, VA: John Knox, 1960); E. Schillebeeckx, *An Experiment in Christology* (New York: Crossroad, 1981); W. Pannenberg, *Jesus: God and Man*, trans. L. L. Wilkins and D. A. Priebi (Philadelphia: Westminster, 1968). For liberation theology, consult J. Sobrino, *Christology at the Crossroads: A Latin American Approach* (Maryknoll, NY: Orbis, 1978). For an informed overview of patterns in systematic treatments of the humanity of Jesus in the twentieth century, see, e.g., E. Johnson, *Consider Jesus: Waves of Renewal in Christology* (New York: Crossroad, 1990). For an adaptation of traditional christological themes to a postmodern cultural perspective, see R. Haight, *Jesus Symbol of God* (Maryknoll, NY: Orbis, 1999); and Haight, *Future of Christology* (London: Continuum, 2005).

10. N. Ricci, *Testament* (Toronto: Anchor Canada, 2003); and N. Mailer, *The Gospel according to the Son* (New York: Random House, 1997).

11. J. Saramago, *O Evangelho Segundo Jesuys Cristo* (1991); ET, *The Gospel according to Jesus Christ*, trans. G. Pontiero (New York: Harcourt Brace, 1994); M. Bulgakov, *The Master and Magarita*, trans. M. Ginsberg (New York: Grove, 1995).

12. N. Kazantzakis, *The Last Temptation of Christ*, trans. P. Bien (New York: Simon & Schuster, 1960); and D. H. Lawrence, *The Man Who Died* (London: Martin Secker, 1931).

13. C. Potok, *My Name Is Asher Lev* (New York: Knopf, 1972).

14. A. M. al-'Aqqād, *The Genius of Christ*, trans. and ed. F. P. Ford Jr., Studies in Contemporary Philosophical Theology (Binghamton, NY: Global Publications, 2001).

15. It could be argued that "class conflict" informs the social setting constructed by Ricci in his recent novel. There certainly are clashes on several levels. Violent episodes dominate each section of the narrative. Judas is depicted as a member of a rebel group determined to oppose Roman occupation. In this collection this novel is located among those deeply responsive to current academic studies of the Jesus Seminar. Marxist critical perspectives may very well influence some members of this circle, but for the sake of this study Ricci's work has been placed there.

16. See the next section for a discussion of the role of sexuality in some of the modern treatments of Jesus.

17. See, e.g., the *Gospel of Philip* 32: "There were three who always walked with the Lord: Mary his mother and her sister and Magdalene, whom they called his lover. A Mary is his sister and his mother and his lover." See, again, 55: "Wisdom, whom they call barren, is the mother of the angels, and the consort of Christ is Mary Magdalene. The [Lord loved Mary] more than all the disciples, and kissed her on the [mouth many times]. The other [women/disciples saw] . . . him. They said to him, 'Why do you [love her] more than all of us?' The Savior answered and said to them, 'Why do I not love you as I do her?'" See also the *Gospel of Mary*: "Peter said to Mary, 'Sister we know that the Savior loved you more than the rest of women. Tell us the words of the Savior, which you remember." See also Levi's rebuke of Peter and defense of Mary near the end of the surviving fragments.

1 | Imagining Jesus Then and Now

Nino Ricci's *Testament*

Dietmar Neufeld

Miryam of Migdal wistfully comments, "Thus it was that everyone who heard him or laid eyes on him formed an image of him, and believed him a holy man or a madman, a heretic or sage, with deepest certainty. Yet I who was among those closest to him, who'd been embraced by him and had walked with him by the lake, could not say what it was that formed him, and indeed as the days passed and the weeks and the years, only knew him less. So he seemed like a glimpse I'd had of something that I could not put a name to, and which always slipped from my gaze before I had a chance to know it, like the great bird I had seen as a child when I traveled into the mountains and imagined a god."

Nino Ricci, Testament 223–24

Setting the Stage

"Then as now, however things are remembered, it is certain it won't be how they actually were"[1] (454). Ricci's Yeshua, a man of contradiction, ambiguity, vulnerability, and nuanced complexity, still asks, "So, tell me, what else are they saying about me?" A famous set of passages in the Gospels records Jesus asking his disciples a similar question: "'Who do people say that the Son of Man is?' And they said, 'Some say John the Baptist, but others Elijah, and still others Jeremiah or one of the prophets.' He said to them, 'But who do you say that I am?' Simon Peter answered, 'You are the Messiah, the Son of the living God'" (Matt. 16:13–16; cf. Mark 8:28; Luke 9:19). It is clear from these passages that Jesus was seen by his contemporaries in many different ways.[2]

Perceptional differences about an important historical figure are not unusual, and they point to a human propensity for noticing or discerning details about events in unique ways. Consequently, Jesus was seen and imagined differently by different people. Some saw him as a prophet, others as a holy man, others as John the Baptist returning from the dead or Bacchus come to life to bless crops and cure infertility.[3] Still others saw him as a dangerous radical deserving of capital punishment. John 21:25 records that "there are also many other things that Jesus did; if every one of them were written down, I suppose that the world itself could not contain the books that would be written." Implicit in these words is the invitation for each generation to imagine anew the deeds and words of Jesus.

True to form, every generation since the time of Jesus has had the impulse to reinvent Jesus, to make him understandable. Each reinvention has been done for its own reasons: to undergird personal belief, escape the traditions of dogma and ecclesial influence, legitimize political agendas, maintain boundaries and structures in rigidly stratified societies and religious groups, silence other narratives not in agreement with the received view, modernize a figure hopelessly mired in cultural trappings no longer part of the postmodern human experience, deconstruct gender inequities, or address ethical issues driving contemporary experience. Jesus has been portrayed as a rebel and revolutionary, rationalist, liberal Christian, sentimentalized wonderer preaching a universalized message of love, apocalyptic visionary, gadabout and party animal, egalitarian encouraging inclusive meals without regard for gender and socioeconomic divisions, and a peasant Jewish cynic. Jesus has continually been undressed, dressed, and redressed in the clothing that reflects the spirit of a particular period, with its concerns, aspirations, and values. Pelikan observes that one of the best ways to capture the mood of any age is to pay attention to how it portrays Jesus. He illustrates the truth of this observation by noting how Jesus and other biblical characters were adorned and clothed in the art of Renaissance Europe. For example, the guards at the tomb of Jesus are attired in the armor of the Swiss Guard in the *Madonna of the Book* by Sandro Botticelli (1483). This Florentine painting resembles its society, and Mary in the crucifixion scene wears a brocade Florentine gown. The story of Jesus is recaptured through the cultural lenses of the day. Jesus, Pelikan argues, becomes a mirror of each age, as each period reflects its concerns and its issues onto Jesus and reads from that Jesus a support for its concerns.[4]

The point is that historians, or any interested persons for that matter, are not detached and isolated technicians of the past who merely present the past with the greatest possible semblance of how it actually was. According to Braun, the historical past does not just sit there in self-evident categories of persons, events, and activities ripe for the plucking, but are selectively picked from items in records regarded as the most significant (text, artifact, epigraph). The past is a pliable construct subject to the shaping of the historian, who imposes a complex set of value judgments on the evidentiary data relative to his or her own social location. The facts that emerge are then counted as important, assigned a status, and tied into a coherent interpretative pattern of meaning by converging models (interdisciplinary lenses) that offer explanatory consistency to the evidentiary facts.[5] Moreover, according to Braun, the constructive activity of selection, judgment, and assigning meaning is rooted in the social, institutional, and disciplinary environments that provide the motivations and intellectual apparatus of the historian.[6] While some have perceived the negotiation of Jesus' past in terms of the concerns of postmodern historiography as invalid and destructive, Braun says that "the historical Jesus would hardly exist as a figure of continuing interest, most certainly not in the reshapable and displaceable forms he has taken on in the history of Jesus research, apart from the social-political and intellectual warrants for his existence that are inherent in the modern discourse about the historical Jesus."[7]

Quests for the Historical Jesus

Attempts have been made to mitigate the effects of one's social, cultural, and religious environment on one's understanding of Jesus. The so-called quests for the historical Jesus were intended to investigate the life of Jesus untrammeled by dogmatic, personal, and cultural prejudices. The first phase began with H. S. Reimarus (1694–1768). Under the influences of the German enlightenment, Reimarus wanted to discover who Jesus was by entirely rational means, that is, by historical research unfettered by dogmatic considerations or ecclesiastical control. This stage found its culmination in the magnum opus of A. Schweitzer, *The Quest of the Historical Jesus: Critical Study of Its Progress from Reimarus to Wrede.* Schweitzer was, of course, critical of sentimentalized perceptions of Jesus that had stripped him of his revered status and, at the same time, he attempted to restore the perception of the overwhelming historical greatness of this figure.[8] Jesus was Jewish to the core, apocalyptic in orientation, and a prophetic genius who raged against the injustices of his day—totally irrelevant to and unlike modern man. The so-called Lives of Jesus were nothing more than reflections of the faces of those who sought him and were therefore void of any historical validity. Schweitzer concludes poetically: "He comes to us as One unknown, without a name, as of old, by the lake-side, He came to those men who knew Him not. He passes by our time and returns to His own. The historical Jesus will be to our time a stranger and an enigma."[9]

Stage two of the quest was represented by the work of Bultmann who, under the influence of German liberal theology and the Tübingen school, came to the conclusion that it was impossible to know much about Jesus historically because the early church's perceptions of Jesus were shaped by its agendas of preaching, propaganda, instruction for the catechumen, and rescuing Jesus from the vagaries of time without firm evidence about who he was or what he taught and did. The main object of his study became the early church and not Jesus. Bultmann's famous dictum, "I do indeed think that we can know almost nothing about the life and personality of Jesus, since the early Christian sources show no interest in either," basically determined the tone of this stage of the quest.[10]

While the third stage, known as the "new quest" or "third quest," involved a renaissance in the study of the historical Jesus, nevertheless some expressed residual skepticism. For example, Bornkamm, in evaluating past attempts at full-face portraits of Jesus, comments pessimistically:

> Why have these attempts [to write a life of Jesus] failed? Perhaps only because it became alarmingly and terrifyingly evident how inevitably each author brought the spirit of his age into his or her presentation of the figure of Jesus. In point of fact, the changing pictures found in innumerable lives of Jesus are not very encouraging, confronting us as they do now with the enlightened teacher of God, virtue, and immortality, now with the religious genius of the romantics, now with the teacher of ethics in Kant's sense, and now the protagonist of social theory. These are the different pictures that emerge, depending on who's writing the story.[11]

The pessimism of Bornkamm, however, has been mitigated by a variety of proposals competing for the most appropriate model by which to understand Jesus, with the promise that the essential elements of Jesus' life are recoverable. One group of contemporary scholars (Martin Hengel, John Meier, E. P. Sanders, Ben Witherington III, and N. T. Wright) continues the so-called "third quest" in the belief that "the historian of the first century . . . cannot shrink from the question of Jesus."[12] They are more or less united by the conclusion that Jesus was first and foremost a Jew and that he must be positioned within his Jewish world in order to be understood. They emphasize that he was an apocalyptic prophet who announced the coming of the kingdom of God.[13] While optimism informs the work of these questers, considerable disagreement nevertheless continues to exist about which of the extracanonical Gospels count as historically valid, whether Jesus was or was not an apocalyptic sage, whether his sapiential outlook came from within the ambit of Jewish wisdom or that of the Greek, whether he regarded himself as a messiah, whether he was resurrected, and how much of what is recorded in the Gospels about what he said and did he actually said and did. In many ways, the real Jesus continues to cast a silhouette eternally shrouded in the mists of the past and continues to invite imaginative retellings of his life.

Writers such as Marcus Borg, John Dominic Crossan, Burton Mack, and other members of the Jesus Seminar also continue in the tradition of the "new quest." What unites them is their insistence that understanding the Hellenistic world and the Roman Empire that ruled Palestine in Jesus' day is absolutely essential to understanding Jesus. Some authors have even preferred to stress the Roman and Hellenistic framework over and against the Jewish. This has led to proposals that see Jesus not as a Jewish prophet but as a teacher of wisdom, a sage with greater similarities to the philosophers of the Cynic school than to any purely Jewish model. These authors also insist that Jesus was not an apocalyptic or eschatological teacher; in the words of Crossan, Jesus found his own voice and "began to speak of God not as immanent apocalypse, but as present healing."[14]

Crossan's methodological stance and inventory of texts are informed in part by his long association with the Jesus Seminar and by years of painstaking research. Both he and the Jesus Seminar take seriously a number of extracanonical materials arranged by chronological stratification and independent attestation.[15] For the words of Jesus, the *Gospel of Thomas*, discovered in 1945 at Nag Hammadi in Egypt, and the Sayings Gospel Q are crucial. The *Gospel of Thomas* comprises 114 loosely organized sayings attributed to Jesus that are not set in a narrative framework. The Sayings Gospel Q consists of the "double tradition" material, that is, that which is present in both Matthew and Luke but not Mark. However, Q may also contain material that is preserved only by Matthew or only by Luke as well as material that is paralleled in Mark (called Mark/Q overlaps).[16] Scholars believe that these written collections of sayings ascribed to Jesus appeared perhaps as early as two decades after Jesus' death. The New Testament Gospels were composed during the last quarter of the first century by third-generation authors on the basis of folk memories preserved in stories that had circulated by word of mouth for decades. The written Gospels were then copied and recopied, modified, corrected, augmented, and edited by numerous storytellers for a half century or more before achieving their final written forms.

Of particular importance since 1985 has been the work of the Jesus Seminar. Using an interdisciplinary lens with models and insights based in studies of honor and shame in ancient Mediterranean societies, of peasant societies, of political systems, of economic systems, and of medical anthropology, the Jesus Seminar has made significant strides in describing the social context of Jesus and his followers. In the working out of this context, it has made decisions about the words and deeds of Jesus but also, on the basis of these conclusions, what he was essentially as a historical person. The working out of who Jesus was historically finds its expression in a number of historical premises that are arguably contentious and open to contestation. One of the driving features of the Jesus Seminar is to move beyond the authorized and canonical texts that received ecclesiastical approval in the fourth century. Earlier studies of the historical Jesus dismissed them with the hasty assumption that they were nothing more than fanciful elaborations of the authentic gospel and came from a much later period. Moving "beyond the holy four" is the recognition that the early Christian community cherished a rich diversity of texts and traditions about Jesus. Traditions about Jesus are complex and are betrayed by the incredible richness of the materials at our disposal. Studying these texts "disclose[s] to us how Christian communities gathered, arranged, modified, embellished, interpreted, and created traditions about the teachings and deeds of Jesus."[17] With this presupposition in place, an inventory of the principle texts required for understanding the early Jesus traditions is established: *Signs Gospel, Gospel of Thomas, Secret Book of James, Dialogue of the Savior, Gospel of Mary, Infancy Gospels of Thomas and James, Gospel of Peter, Egerton Gospel, Oxyrhynchus Gospels 840 and 1124, Secret Gospel of Mark,* and the Sayings Gospel Q, along with others.[18]

Jesus Then and Now

Nino Ricci makes no secret of his indebtedness to the work of the Jesus Seminar, current feminist research on the Marys in the Gospel tradition, and revisionist historians on the life of Judas Iscariot. While admitting his *Testament* to be a work of fiction that does not purport to be an "accurate historical representation of the figure of Jesus," he nevertheless has "made every effort to work within the bounds of historical plausibility, based on

what is known to us of the time and place in which Jesus lived."[19] Ricci
continues, ". . . in my research I have drawn on many sources, including
the work of the Jesus seminar and of other contemporary scholars who
have tried to arrive at an understanding of the historical Jesus."[20] In an
interview shortly after the release of *Testament*, Ricci commented that the
"Jesus Seminar helped provide me with a map for making my way
through the minefield of Jesus studies, applying reason, methodology, and
a spirit of critical inquiry—though I found it had no shortage of critics
and detractors—to a field too often marked by dogma and irrationality."[21]

Ricci traces the original seed of inspiration for *Testament* to one of the
first books he owned, a picture Bible called *The Guiding Light*. Its stories of
marginalized men and women and miracles from a gently illuminated
Jesus made purchase on his imagination. But as he matured, that first idyllic connection with Christianity yielded to a complicated one "that saw
him pass from post-Vatican II Catholicism to born-again evangelism and
finally to a last, desperate phase with Norman Vincent Peale."[22] While by
early adulthood he could no longer call himself a Christian, "neither, by
any means, could he say that he'd got free of Jesus, who seemed far too
powerful a figure to rid himself of by so simple a thing as loss of faith."[23]
So like Yihuda of Qiryat (Judas Iscariot), Ricci found that there "was in
Yeshua that quality that made one feel there was something, still, some bit
of hope, some secret he might reveal that would help make the world over.
Tell me your secret, I had wanted to say to him, tell me, make me new. And
even now, though I had left him, I often saw him beckoning before me as
towards a doorway he would have had me pass through, from darkness to
light" (122). In light of this, Ricci recounts that by the time he reached his
twenties he had conceived the idea of doing a fictional treatment of the life
of Jesus, to reconcile his sense of the power of this figure with some of the
more problematic aspects of the Christian tradition.[24]

So it was during Ricci's university days that he found a way of holding
on to Jesus by "reinventing him, seeing him no longer as a figure of faith
but of history, on the one hand, and of myth, on the other."[25] This new
way of reading the life of Jesus revealed to him that the Gospels were
themselves patchwork texts written by real people in a real time and place
and that they showed abundant evidence of their human composition: in
their divergent, often contradictory points of view, and in their many
gaps, anachronisms, and evidences of editorial tinkering. What emerged
from this re-envisioning of the Gospel tradition for Ricci "was a double
sense of Jesus, as a real figure of vitality and brilliance and contradiction
on whom had been overlaid, however, a mythic Jesus of apocalypse and

divinity, who in the pattern of death and rebirth relived every ancient fertility myth from the stories of Thammuz and Marduk of ancient Sumeria and Babylonia to the Egyptian Osiris and the Orpheus and Adonis of the Greeks."[26]

Personally obsessed with the figure of Jesus, Ricci, "like a magpie began to gather up bits of lore and fact on the subject . . . and to acquaint himself in a fairly unsystematic way with the vast array of Jesus retellings, from Ernest Renan's *La Vie De Jésus* . . . through to *Jesus Christ Superstar*."[27] What he found is that these retellings were not able to cast off the mantle of divinity that covered the traditional Jesus. What seemed interesting to him was the idea of a Jesus entirely human who was a visionary, a rebel rouser and radical in his thought and behavior, who would have continued relevance for today. Here he found the Jewish historian Josephus immensely useful to contextualizing the story of Jesus. Josephus helped Ricci to understand the political, religious, and economic turmoil that was endemic to the cultural ferment of first-century Palestine. It was a place of many sects, associations—voluntary or otherwise—and guilds (Pharisees, Sadducees, Qumran, Zealots, Sicarii) embroiled in conflict not only with each other but also with Rome, the despised occupier. Messianic figures arose, made claims, garnered followers, but then were hunted down and killed by the Romans or their client kings. Josephus also compellingly revealed the brutality of the Roman regime that eventually led to the destruction of the city of Jerusalem and the temple in 70 CE.

Ricci was aware of early traditions that Jesus was the bastard son of a Roman soldier. While early Christians dismissed these traditions as malicious rumors designed to discredit them, the canonical Gospels nevertheless exhibit some discomfort with the issue of Jesus' paternity. Matthew records that upon Joseph's hearing of Mary's pregnancy he immediately wishes to dismiss her in order to mitigate the shame that would come his way. Mark 6:3 records the reaction of a crowd offended at the audacity Jesus shows in his teaching. They raise the issue of Jesus' paternity by commenting, "Is not this the carpenter, the son of Mary and brother of James and Joses and Judas and Simon, and are not his sisters here with us?" Once Ricci started thinking in terms of Jesus' bastardy, he began to see a new way of understanding Jesus' teaching: "his privileging of the marginalized, his defiance of convention, his emphasis on the inner person rather than on the outward forms of religious observance."[28] The theme of Jesus' paternity is picked up throughout the story; not only does it haunt the mother of Jesus but also Jesus himself until he finally confesses it in the open in the home of Joseph of Arimathea. While at Joseph's home, Zadok, a well-dressed temple official, begins handing out slurs designed to impugn the reputation of Jesus before his host. Offhandedly he questions Jesus' geographical and paternal origins: "'. . . though I hear the man isn't a Galilean at all but a Jerusalemite, at least on the mother's side. On the father's side it's not clear.' Zadok looked Jesus in the face then for the first time. 'Who was he, your father,' he said. 'I might have known him.'" (408). Eerie silence greets the comment, with the host eventually apologizing profusely for the insulting way in which Jesus was addressed in his house. Jesus, however, comes out of the closet on the paternity issue: "'It was my mistake to come here,' he said now, 'and to bring shame to you. But it's not because of what I've taught or what I've done but because of something I can't change, which is that I don't have any father but my God, and I am a bastard'" (409). This admission is hard on Simon, and he questions whether Jesus "had made a mistake, since Jesus could never be a savior for the Jews, being a Bastard. And he'd kept turning the matter over in his head and still had to think that Jesus had cheated them, and got his power not from their god but from the devils, and so had been cast down in the end" (422).

Ricci also accepts the likelihood that much of what is recorded in the Gospels about what Jesus says and does is not from him directly. He acknowledges the conclusion of the Jesus Seminar that 82 percent of the sayings of Jesus recorded in the Gospels did not come from him.[29] Ricci is convinced that the early period was also about reinvention and imagination so that each age is left the task of rewriting the story of Jesus. Captivated by the question of the identity of this man from Nazareth, Ricci provides a compelling reimagining of a figure free from the mythic vagaries of early portrayals. He provides four testimonies from four very different people who knew Jesus: Judas, a Jewish rebel who did not betray Jesus; Mary Magdalene, a chaste young woman and follower of Jesus who jealously defends him; his mother, who was raped by a Roman soldier; and Simon, a pagan shepherd who follows Jesus to Golgotha. The author couples his fanciful story of Jesus as a mere mortal becoming myth with a realistic depiction of political and ethnic intrigue of the era.

In Ricci's imagination, this mythicizing of Jesus began immediately: "Rumor and reputation became coconspirators; increased reputation amplified the gossip about him and gossip in turn augmented his reputation. Small events begat big stories so that eventually you couldn't tell the difference between the things that actually happened and what had been made up" (360). Indeed, Miryam, Jesus' mother, has great difficulty sorting rumor from truth: "Tales of his healing spread and, soon enough he gained a reputation as a healer and even a worker of wonders, though I imagined He did little more than apply ointments and salves. . . . In the end, I hardly knew what to make of all the reports I had of him" (296). Similarly, Simon of Gergesa, observing Jesus from a distance teaching on the beach and moving to shoals nearby, swears that Jesus was "standing right on the lake, which some said he could do. I'd heard it told that once he'd hiked himself straight across the water from Capernaum to Tarichea, just walking along like that as if it was nothing" (319). Fabricated tales attract and take on a life of their own so that, in the words of Simon:

> I couldn't tell the difference any more between things that had actually happened and what we'd made up. I'd been that way as a boy—I'd hear a story about some piece of wonder or magic and then it was as if I was the one who'd witnessed the thing, I saw it so clearly. The truth was you could meet a lot of people who were like that, sensible people otherwise but who, when it came to wonders, couldn't have told you what they'd seen with their own eyes, or only heard about, or invented whole cloth. That seemed the way so many stories got spread. (360)

Accordingly, Ricci's idea in *Testament* was to try to look at the figure of Jesus in purely human terms. Ricci accepted that some actual historical figure is to be found behind the myth of Jesus as it was handed down. What he tries to envision is what Jesus might have been like, stripped of interpolations and inventions of the later Christian tradition and the early church's vested interest in that tradition. What sort of person could have been responsible for the teachings that have come down to the modern world? Ricci's stripped-down Jesus reveals himself to be "at heart a teacher—not a mystic, not a cultist, not even a healer per se, but merely what he had presented himself to me [Yihuda] as from the start, someone with a few plain truths he wished to impart to people" (93).

While Ricci acknowledges his debt to the Jesus Seminar, he insists nevertheless that he "has made every effort to work within the bounds of historical plausibility" (457). For Ricci, the "holy canonical four" do not hold privileged place. He unashamedly makes use of the Gospels that did not make it into the canonical tradition. The *Gospel of Thomas* and the Sayings Gospel Q are important to Ricci's reconstruction, especially regarding Jesus' kingdom talk. For example, Miriam of Migdal learned from Yeshua of things "that were not taught in the assembly house even to the men and finally couldn't be taught at all in the way we understand teaching, but could only be discovered in oneself" (137). She noticed that he often spoke of God's kingdom, "and people imagined he meant to make himself king of Israel, or that the end of days was at hand, or that we must wait until death for the kingdom to come to us" (137). She discovered that the

kingdom of God "was neither one thing nor the other, not a place outside
of us that we must travel to like some far province or city but rather inside
us in the way we looked at things, and so always there for us to bring
forth" (149). Yihuda of Qiryat also observed that the kingdom "was of an
entirely unpolitical nature, a philosophical rather than physical state,
requiring no revolution" (47). Yihuda admits that in the beginning he
"lacked the patience to follow [Yeshua] in his logic, particularly as
regarded his god's kingdom, despite developing many analogies and stories to explain the nature of this kingdom; yet each seemed as obscure as
the next, nor was it clear if the place was in heaven or on earth, or if it had
a governor or was ruled solely by God" (46).

Preoccupied with a similar question on the nature of God's kingdom,
the *Gospel of Thomas* records Jesus saying:

> If your leaders say to you, "Look the (Father's) kingdom is in the sky," then
> the birds of the sky will precede you. If they say to you, "It is in the sea,"
> then the fish of the sea will precede you. Rather, the kingdom is within
> you and it is outside of you. When you know yourselves, then you will be
> known, and you will understand that you are children of the living father.
> But if you do not know yourselves, then you live in poverty and you are
> the poverty.[30]

Both Miriam and Yihuda eventually discover that Yeshua's notions
were not of the sort that could be reduced to simple principles: "rather,
they had to be felt, as it were, and lived out, so that it was only the experience of them that could bring you understanding" (46). Indeed, comments Yihuda, "over time I came to see a wisdom in his approach, and the
folly of putting into words notions that by their very nature, like God himself, must exceed our understanding" (49).

Ricci clearly departs from the traditional views of Yihuda as villain and
betrayer and portrays him as friend, confident, and beloved of Jesus.[31] The
author of the Gospel of Matthew portrays Judas clearly as a traitor: "But
woe to that one by whom the Son of Man is betrayed! It would have been
better for that one not to have been born" (Matt. 26:24). Luke depicts him
under the possession of the devil: "Then Satan entered Judas called Iscariot, who was one of the twelve; he went away and conferred with the chief
priests and officers of the temple police about how he might betray him to
them" (Luke 22:3–4). Not to be outdone, the author of the Acts of the
Apostles records that after his heinous deed, "this man acquired a field
with the reward of his wickedness; and falling headlong, he burst open in
the middle and all his bowels gushed out (Acts 1:18). With the recent
release of the *Gospel of Judas*, however, a very different character sketch

emerges of Judas. He is not the consummate betrayer but a confidant of Jesus with privileged access to the mysteries of the kingdom—a loyal servant who in the end emerges an honorable friend of Jesus.[32]

Yihuda, similarly, becomes a devoted friend and follower of Jesus—a rebel who eventually shares the road with Jehoshua (32). Here Ricci exploits recent scholarship about the social unrest and the economic, political, and religious turmoil that created tensions between the Roman occupier and the occupied. As one of the occupied, Yihuda was committed to the overthrow of Rome via agitation, intrigue, surreptitious spying, and infiltration. One day he sees Yeshua and is strangely drawn to him. A series of events slowly but surely draws the two of them together in an indissoluble bond. Yeshua's appearance was no more than a "wraith against the dawn, walking with that strange light-footedness of the very thin and the very frail that makes them look almost lively and spry even when they are at death's door" (9). Appearances are deceiving, however, because Yihuda was impressed with the fearless compassion Yeshua exhibited to Ezekias, a victim of the senseless brutality so characteristic of this age. Ezekias was a young recruit of the Sicarii, an informant in the court of Herod Antipas, who had been found out, tortured, and was being dragged off to the fortress at Macherus. While Yihuda, as a fellow rebel, did not know how to react given that this Ezekias could give him away, Yeshua braves the cohort of soldiers, heads off to the well for a scoop of water, and brings it to the prisoner (10). Moreover, observes Yihuda, for this Jewish holy man, purity is not an issue of concern as it is for the crowd. No one touches Ezekias for fear of contamination, yet Yeshua does not hesitate but shares with Yihuda "the contamination of Ezekias' death." He tended to him and "made him seem human again" (22, 29).

In the course of conversations, Yihuda discovers that Yeshua was an acolyte of the prophet Yohanan, who had been arrested by Herod Antipas, killed, and his followers dispersed. Yeshua is now on the run and hiding from the soldiers. This made Yeshua's gesture of kindness to Ezekias all the more compelling. Yihuda comments, "So we were both of us outlaws, it seemed, joined in that way if no other" (22). Yihuda's interest in Yeshua is considerably sharpened as he observes how Yeshua deals with a Phoenician woman's possessed daughter. Yihuda discovers that Yeshua enjoyed renown as a healer, though not without questions about his authenticity (28). His tender manner with the young girl calls to Yihuda's mind Yeshua's caring offer of water to Ezekias. While there was nothing miraculous about the healing of the girl, Yihuda claims that the

> incident affected me deeply. The vision of that young girl's face, called back, it
> seemed, from some precipice as if indeed by a kind of magic, had seared itself

into my mind. . . . Yeshua held true throughout to the plainest and simplest of
observations and gestures, and in so doing had brought about improvement
that, if not permanent, had at least the great virtue of being honest. (30)

Throughout *Testament*, questions are raised about how Jesus heals, where
he acquired his skills, and under whose power he works. Zadok wonders
whether it is known that the "Galilean was a great magician . . . who went to
people's graves at night and raised them from the dead" (408). Jerusalemites
would not have accepted as authentic stories of Jesus' healings because they
"couldn't imagine someone from Galilee doing such a thing, and then it was
almost every day for them that some charlatan came along to the city claiming this or that" (403).

Earlier in *Testament*, as Yihuda is telling his story, he notes the transformation that had taken place in Yeshua from a primitive, beggarly waif to a
sophisticated teacher in the style of the Greeks: he was "changed in appearance now, fair and well-groomed and well-fed so that he seemed almost
Greek, and changed, too, in his manner, with an air of authority" (25). He is
surrounded by rough-looking Galileans speaking in muted Aramaic while
Jesus engages in a lively debate with him about the customs of the city in
Greek (25–27). Yihuda is also surprised that though Yeshua had been an
acolyte of Yohanan, he had not bought into the notion of an imminent end
of days but rather "seemed to think more in the manner of a Greek than a
Jew, finding recourse for his arguments in logic rather than scripture. . . . As a
child he had lived in Alexandria" (26). Yeshua presented himself as an itiner-
ant teacher, but not one who resembled the teachers that Yihuda had studied
under in Jerusalem; their "minds were like windowless rooms circumscribed
on every side by law, while Yeshua's was curious and quick" (31).

Ricci's Yeshua finds a linguistic home in the social context of the Greek
philosophers of Alexandria. He is a purveyor of wisdom who speaks in riddles,
chreiai, designed to confound the intellectually arrogant, the aristocracy and
their pride of wealth, those who maintain gendered structures, the religious
elite, and the powerful political brokers of Rome. As such, he is a consummate
boundary transgressor building strange fires under the familiar. Yihuda sees
both his deeds and speech bordering on the reckless, especially his open com-
mensality and group formation. He encourages and welcomes women. Yihuda
speaks of the women: "There were several of them who hovered around Yeshua
like the Greek furies, and whom I could hardly tell apart—were in fact not
much more than girls—were a source of considerable tension . . . because
he treated them with a measure of parity with the men and suffered them
to be among his intimates" (44). He champions the poor but also sits down
with the tax collectors; he disarms his enemies with kindness.

Simon of Gergesa, a pagan shepherd, picks up the story in its final stages. At this stage in the narrative, Ricci deliberately begins to use the conventional names for Jesus and Judas. This convention is intended to push the unfamiliar, contextualized story into the realm of the familiar for modern readers. Simon observes that Judas and Jesus have a special bond: "You couldn't imagine two men more different than Judas and Jesus, one a rebel and the other for peace, one rude and hardly willing to give you the time of day and the other one taking in every beggar who came by, but still you could see that they were connected, even more than if they'd been alike" (378). Judas on several occasions, at great risk to his own life, tries to dissuade Jesus from going to Jerusalem, because he is convinced that he will be killed: "I had to betray all my oaths to tell you what I did. Don't let it be for nothing" (374). All of it seems to no avail as Jesus and his followers continue resolutely onward to Jerusalem. Judas angrily bursts out at one point, "I came back to save your lives, but Jesus doesn't seem to mind giving them up. If that's what you want, then you can march off to your deaths the lot of you, for all the good it'll do anyone" (382). In the end as Simon is reminiscing about the death of Jesus and who may have been complicit in his death, it turns out not to have been Judas who betrayed Jesus, despite the suspicions about him, but Aram: "They had not gathered that it was Aram who'd betrayed Jesus and assumed it was Judas, since his was the name they'd made out during the charges—I ought to have set them straight then but didn't want to admit I'd knelt there beside Aram while he'd sealed Jesus' fate in that courtyard—it looked as if he'd been the one, in the end, that they'd just taken to the gate and let go" (435).

Using Simon's voice, Ricci raises fundamental questions about how the crucifixion came to be so layered with meaning as time progressed. Simon muses about what happened to Jesus' followers after his execution. They were quiet and in hiding for some time, confused by what had happened and afraid they'd be next. But as time went by and nothing happened, they began to become more emboldened, banding together to keep up his teaching. The truth of Jesus' bastardy and crucifixion, difficult as they were, appeared not to have come out. It was the shock of Jesus' death "that started twisting them, and that they had to strain to make sense of the thing, and that in time, with someone like Jesus, things got distorted" (453). Simon notes that "for every little thing he did when he was alive some story gets put in its place, and if he'd lanced somebody's boil it turned out he'd saved a whole town, and if there were fifty in a place who'd followed him, now it was five hundred" (453). Even more so did the rumor mill grind out stories about his death:

> Then there was the story that went around that the morning after Jesus was killed, Mary and Salome went to the grave and his body was gone. . . . Somehow the story got skewed, or maybe it had happened that the group had taken Jesus' body by mistake. But eventually it got told that he'd been raised from the dead and walked out of the place, and there were people enough to come along then to say they'd met him on the road afterwards looking as fit as you or me. (453)

Conclusions

In Ricci's world, imagination has a purchase on truth. Imagination powerfully "carves out a reality, not uncritically, of things both seen and unseen. With imagination he stretches beyond the sensually verifiable, and reaches or creates a social context and figure that he feels should exist, and which satisfies a longing which seems to him reasonable."[33] Creative imagination—the combination of sensation, opinion, and fact—helps Ricci to create works of great literature. It is something that is vividly in his mind, and through words he tries to bring it to his audience in *Testament*. Storytellers must have the capacity to feel something before they try to convince others of what they write. Miriam of Migdad discovers this principle for herself. She notices that notions must be felt and lived out in order to reach true understanding; otherwise they remain inert. An imagination so exercised is able to take images not immediately before the eyes and present them in such a way that they can be seen with our eyes as if they were immediately present.[34] Authors must possess vision, that is, "those things through which the images of things not present are so brought before the mind that we seem to see them with our very eyes and have them before us."[35] Imagination must play a role in creative thinking. And so, the Jesus of Ricci's imagination and Simon's imagination formed a rich, multilayered story that produced something beautiful: "It was as if some curtain had been pushed aside in my head and I had a glimpse of something I understood but couldn't have put into words, like some beautiful thing, so beautiful it took your breath away, that you saw for an instant though a gateway or door, then was gone" (455). Ricci states "that he (Ricci) let himself be led by instinct, imagination, and his own intuitive sense of what might best shed light on the character of his protagonist."[36]

Paula Fredrickson once accused Marcus Borg of imposing twentieth-century values onto a first-century setting, noting that Jesus was a Jew of his time rather a left-leaning liberal of ours.[37] In some ways, the same criticisms have been leveled against Ricci by conservatives in the church who see the Gospels as accurate records divinely protected by the hand of God during the process of selecting and recording the story of Jesus. Certainly the Jesus Ricci ends up with "is a man of contradiction and ambiguity, capable of great wisdom but also of arrogance, a man of peace who was yet perpetually combative; Ricci also ends with a Jesus who is entirely human yet visionary, revolutionary and radical in his thought, and who indeed added something new to the world that continues to have relevance to this day."[38]

While Ricci's *Testament* stands in the tradition of reinventing Jesus, Ricci has nevertheless approached his task with methodological rigor, critical insight, and creative flair. Ricci's Jesus emerges as paradoxical yet powerful. Simon of Gergesa muses at the novel's end:

> However things get remembered, you can be certain it won't be how they actually were, since one man will change a bit of this to suit his fancy, and one a bit of that, and another will spice it to make a better story of it. And by and by the truth of the thing will get clouded, and he'll simply be a yarn you tell to your children. And something will be lost then because he was a man of wisdom, the more so when even someone like me, who when I met him didn't know more than when the crops came up and how many sheep it took to buy a bride, had come to understand something of him in the end. (455)

In stitching together a story of Jesus with a bit of this and a bit of that, then spicing it with imagination, Ricci gives shape to a historical figure who emerges from the shadows to challenge the traditions and dogma of today, yet all the while remaining tantalizingly mysterious, open to yet another recasting of his life.

NOTES

Epigraph. N. Ricci, *Testament* (Scarborough: Doubleday, 2002).

1. Ibid., 454.

2. Even his name, Jehoshua, testifies to differing perceptions about Jesus. The disciples of Jesus, known for not wasting words, addressed Jesus by the shortened Yeshua, which made him seem common. It was Yohanan, after he had been baptized by Jesus, who named him formally Yehoshua, as was his practice (Ricci 2002: 26).

3. Ibid., 91.

4. See J. Pelikan, *Jesus through the Centuries* (New Haven, CT: Yale University Press, 1999).

5. W. Braun, "Social-Rhetorical Interests," in *Whose Historical Jesus?*, ed. W.E. Arnal and M. Desjardins (Waterloo, Ontario: Wilfrin Laurier University Press, 1997), 92.

6. Ibid., 92–93.

7. Ibid., 93.

8. A. Schweitzer, *The Quest of the Historical Jesus: Critical Study of Its Progress from Reimarus to Wrede*, trans. W. Montgomery (London: A & C Black, 1910), 274.

9. Ibid., 403.

10. R. Bultmann, *Jesus and the Word* (London: Charles Scribner's Sons, 1958), 14.

11. G. Bornkamm, *Jesus of Nazareth*, trans. I. McLuskey, F. McLuskey, and J. M. Robinson (New York: Harper & Row, 1960), 13.

12. N. T. Wright, *Christian Origins and the Question of God: The New Testament and the People of God* (Minneapolis: Fortress, 1992), 468.

13. Ben Witherington III, "The Wright Quest for the Historical Jesus," *Christian Century* November 19–26, 1997, 1075–78.

14. J. D. Crossan, *The Historical Jesus: The Life of a Mediterranean Jewish Peasant* (San Francisco: HarperSanFrancisco, 1991), xii.

15. These include, among others, the *Gospel of Thomas, Egerton Gospel, Gospel of the Hebrews*, Sayings Gospel Q, *Didache* 16, *Cross Gospel, Gospel of the Egyptians, Dialogue of the Savior, 1 Clement, Barnabas*, Shepherd of Hermas, *Apocryphon of James, Gospel of the Nazoreans, Gospel of the Ebionites*. See N. T. Wright, *Jesus and the Victory of God* (Minneapolis: Fortress, 1996), 47–62; and Crossan, *Historical Jesus*, 427–66.

16. See J. S. Kloppenborg, *Excavating Q: The History and Setting of the Sayings Gospel*. Minneapolis: Fortress; New York: Citadel, 2000).

17. R. J. Miller, *The Complete Gospels* (Sonoma, CA: Polebridge, 1992), 3.

18. Ibid., 4–5.

19. N. Ricci, *Testament* (2002), 457.

20. Ricci, *Testament*, 457. Subsequent references to this work will be given as page numbers in the text.

21. Interview from Ricci's Web site: "On Writing *Testament*," http://ninoricci.com.

22. Ibid.

23. Ibid.

24. Ibid.

25. Ibid.

26. Ibid.

27. Ibid.

28. Ibid.

29. R. W. Funk and R. W. Hoover, *The Five Gospels: What Did Jesus Really Say?* (New York: Macmillan, 1993), 5.

30. H. Koester and T. O. Lambdin, "The Gospel of Thomas," in *The Nag Hammadi Library in English*, ed. J. Robinson (San Francisco: Harper & Row, 1978), 128.

31. See W. Klassen, *Judas: Betrayer or Friend of Jesus?* (Minneapolis: Fortress, 1996); D. Van Biema, "A Kiss for Judas," *Time*, February 27, 2006, 37; and J. M. Robinson, *The Secrets of Judas: The Story of the Misunderstood Disciple and His Lost Gospel* (San Francisco: HarperSanFrancisco, 2006).

32. See R. Kasser, M. Meyer, and G. Wurst, trans., *The Gospel of Judas* (Washington, DC: National Geographic Publications, 2006).

33. Watson, Gerard, "Imagination and Religion in Classical Thought" in *Religious Imagination*, ed. J. P. Mackey (Edinburgh: Edinburgh University Press, 1986), 35.

34. Ibid., 38–39.

35. Ibid., 39.

36. Ricci, "On Writing *Testament*," http://ninoricci.com.

37. P. Fredrickson, "Did Jesus Oppose Purity Laws?" *Biblical Review* 11 (1995): 23.

38. Ricci, "On Writing *Testament*," http://ninoricci.com.

2 | Transformation of Biblical Methods and Godhead in Norman Mailer's *Gospel*

Paul C. Burns

"Your Father," said the Devil, "is but one god among many. . . . You would do better to consult the breadth of his rages; they are unseemly for a great god. . . ."
"That is not so," I was able to answer.
The Devil replied, "He is not in command of Himself!"
Norman Mailer, The Gospel according to the Son 48–49

Since the publication of *The Naked and the Dead* in 1948, Norman Mailer has startled readers with his choices of subject matter and even more with his raw and often disturbing perspective. In his novels and essays, Mailer challenges prevailing opinions in the United States on issues such as war[1] and political leadership[2] as well as treating in a provocative fashion familiar American symbols such as Marilyn Monroe and Gary Gilmore.[3] He explores these subjects in unexpected and even troubling ways. In *The Gospel according to the Son*, published in 1997, forty-nine years after his first major novel, Mailer appears once again to have shifted his subject, his interpretive lens, and his writing strategies.[4] He does this to explore the figure of Jesus Christ, but he does not probe the various popular images of Jesus Christ in contemporary American religious culture. Instead, he seems to be turning consistently and sympathetically to the foundational texts of the canonical Gospels and incidentally revisiting some aspects of the literary culture of his own family's Jewish roots, which he seems to have avoided since his first novel.[5] Although his title could be dismissed as a catchy phrase coined by some publicist, Mailer's formulation demonstrates that not only does he understand the formal titles of the canonical Gospels, but that he intends to exploit the traditional understanding of Jesus as Son of God. However, he explores this relationship of Father and Son not within the theological perspectives of the Nicene Creed but rather in a dysfunctional psychological context. The political and social setting of his novel, as well as the tone of language, the episodes, and the personal relationships, illustrate Mailer's knowledge of the form and the structure of the Gospels. He also imitates the type of intertextuality familiar in the foundational texts of Christianity, which employ passages and themes from the Hebrew Scriptures to interpret later persons and events. In the application of such intertextual methods and conventions, however, Mailer presents his own idiosyncratic and disturbing understanding of the deepest personal relationship presented in the Gospel tradition, namely, the relation of the Son to the Father. What makes the relationship problematic is Mailer's construction of the character of the Father.[6]

Upon its publication in 1997, Mailer's *Gospel* was greeted by many polite but perfunctory reviews.[7] Two were sharply critical, arguing that Mailer's attempt to find a level of hieratic language to capture the physical and mysterious possibilities of the original Gospels was a dismal failure.[8] One lengthy review by Frank Kermode, however, was genuinely enthusiastic about the book.[9] Kermode's enthusiasm should not be a surprise, since he has been a major contributor to integrating literary approaches to biblical scholarship.[10] In Mailer's novel Kermode recognizes a creative writer who has not only dealt with the characters and themes of the canonical Gospels, as some other writers have done, but has also attempted to employ the very episodes, to copy the tone of the original language, and to apply the uniquely Gospel method of intertextuality.

I propose to explore Mailer's use of such techniques in his *Gospel* and to pose a question about the compatibility of the two genres of novel and gospel. First, on physical and social settings, people and events, we can trace several parallels between Mailer's novel and the canonical Gospels. Second, many similarities also exist at the level of narrative technique, such as quality of diction and extended use of intertextuality. But there are differences as well, because Mailer's own selection of textual allusions leads to quite different interpretations of Jesus' character and his relation to God. Third, with regard to the identity of the narrator, there are major differences. Unlike the narrator of each of the canonical Gospels, Mailer makes Jesus, the principle subject, into his narrator. This feature locates the focus of attention on the complex inner experience of his Jesus. This allows Mailer to present, immediately, both the cognitive and affective experience of his subject. Thus, Mailer focuses on persistent doubts, troubling confusions, an impulse to kindness, and a pervading sense of inadequacy in his central figure. This psychologically conflicted character is a strikingly different portrait of Jesus from that provided by the narrators of the Gospels attributed to Matthew, Mark, Luke, and John. A generation or two after the actual events, these narrators looked back through the defining events of the death and resurrection of Jesus to select, organize, and interpret the experience of their main character for a community of believers. The religious perspectives of these narrators provide, at the very least, a stability and a confidence to their Jesus that is profoundly absent in Mailer's version.

At this point the conventions of the modern genre of the novel contrast profoundly with the assumptions inherent in the canonical Gospels. In their current form and use within the Christian church, the Gospels are the works of believers after the resurrection looking back to recount and to interpret the events and teachings of the mysterious figure Jesus and the plan for human salvation he shares with his Father. The modern novel changes that critical relationship between author and subject in order to make the subject himself into the creator and narrator of his own interpretative account. We see a similar phenomenon in several other modern treatments of the Jesus figure that recast the material through the perspective of an actor who is to play the part of Christ, such as in Nikos Kazantzakis's *The Greek Passion* or Denis Arcand's film *Jesus of Montreal*. Other novelists retell the story in different ways. Nino Ricci employs four participants in his narrative: Yihuda of Quirat, Miryam of Migdal, Miryam the mother of the Jesus figure, and Simon of Gergesa.[11] José Saramago retells the gospel story through the perspective of an unidentified narrator.[12] Mailer, like only a few others, attempts to retell the story from the perspective of the main character. In this study, we will examine the consequences of such a subject-narrator in content, techniques, and the ultimate character of the narrator.

The Setting

Since he replicates the settings from the canonical Gospels, the geographical, social, and political contexts of Mailer's novel are quite familiar. Thus, for example, Bethlehem is the place where Jesus was born; Nazareth, the location of his childhood and adolescence. Galilee, the Jordan, and the towns of Capernaum, Magdala, and Tiberias are all sites Jesus visits. The climax of his travels is Jerusalem, and key events are located around the temple, in the house of Caiaphas, and on Golgotha. Other place names are mentioned without any clear sense of physical location, such as Bethsaida, Caesarea Philippi, and Jericho. Mailer makes one error in geography by describing Decapolis as simply a "pagan city" (93) when it was actually a league of about ten Hellenistic cities situated to the east of the Jordan. His text leaves the impression that Mailer did not have actual experience in these various sites. There are no references to the physical experiences of temperature, quality of light, sounds, or smells of this terrain. We may surmise that most, if not all, of Mailer's descriptions of the physical settings in this novel have been derived from written sources and his own creative imagination.

The social and political setting in Mailer's novel reflects accounts in the canonical Gospels. Mailer exploits the basic polarization between the Jews and Romans as well as the numerous factions among the Jews themselves. He distinguishes the identity and the values of the Galileans from those of the urban classes, including both priests and Pharisees. For the political climate, Mailer presents a realistic version of Jewish hostility to Roman emblems in the environs of the temple, issues of jurisdiction, and the clever maneuvers between Pilate, the Roman procurator, Herod Antipas, the Roman appointee as king of Samaria, Idumea, and Galilee, and Caiaphas, the Jewish high priest. Mailer does not mention the Sadducees or the archaeological evidence for the impressive architectural contributions of Herod. In other ways, however, Mailer adds features to the complex setting of his novel. He expands the descriptions of the desert and the environs of the temple where critical events and discoveries occur. He also amplifies the description of Tiberias with memories of Jews who were buried there after a war with the Romans in order to dramatize Jewish animosity toward the Romans (181). To the Jewish groups mentioned in the Gospels he explicitly adds the community of the Essenes. All of these expansions of the Gospel versions are based on his own imaginative reconstruction with perhaps some awareness of literary treatments in Josephus and in modern scholarship on the Dead Sea Scrolls and Qumran. Mailer does not develop any implications of the textual evidence of the scrolls.

The Language

One of the surprising features of this novel is the diction and tone of the language Mailer employs. In contrast to his other novels, there is no raw, graphic language or preoccupation with sex and violence. Instead, the language attempts to reflect the tone of many modern serious English translations of the Gospels. Mailer attempts to replicate the simple yet dignified tone of the originals. He strives to express the simple, concrete circumstances of many of the Gospel episodes. Some of his imaginative amplifications are successful, as in the case of Jesus' learning to work as a carpenter with Joseph:

> After a time, I could make use of iron, and was able to work with my tools upon woods from many lands: maple, beech, oak, yew, fir, lime, and cedar. Oak we would select as framing for a door, and maple which was supple, for beds, keeping cedar which was sweet smelling, for chests. Wild olive, being very hard was for tool handles. (24)[13]

Much later, during the passion, Jesus makes a jarring comment on the roughness of the wood and workmanship of the cross! (227–28)

Mailer combines this simplicity of language and observation with respect and dignity. He retains the convention of initial capitals for names, pronouns, and possessive adjectives designating God. When Jesus uses scriptural texts in speaking to God, he uses the archaic forms of respect: "Thee," "Thou," and "Thine." Although Mailer does employ the uppercase for proper names and titles of Jesus, there are occasions when the pivotal title "son" is not capitalized. This is a telling indication of Mailer's treatment of this central but conflicted relationship.

All the characters who provide the personal context for the Jesus of the novel have antecedents in the canonical Gospels: God, Joseph, Mary, Peter, James, John, Judas, and Mary Magdalene. On the one hand, Mailer retains some of the basic relationships to be found in the canonical texts. For instance, he does not seriously develop or exploit the relationship of Jesus with Mary Magdalene. On the other hand, he replaces the role of John as "the beloved disciple" with Judas, and he expands and reinterprets the roles of Judas and Satan. By far the greatest difference in all of these relationships is a shift to an emphasis on the personal perspective of the narrator in the novel. This shift alters the nature of all the relationships and cloaks them with the basic uncertainty of that figure.

The Chronology

Mailer's chronology itself does not appear to reflect any particular symbolic meaning such as that employed in the Gospel of John, which structures many of the episodes around a single journey up to Jerusalem, the climax of the mission of Jesus. The forty-nine chapters or episodes of Mailer's novel fall into roughly three major sections and a concluding chapter. In each section the issue of the identity of Jesus is raised. Although Mailer follows many conventions of the canonical Gospels, his treatment of this central issue is dictated by conventions inherent in the genre of the novel. He begins with an excerpt from the Gospel according to Mark dealing with the baptism in the Jordan and the divine proclamation of the status of Jesus as "the beloved son" (1:1-11). Mailer's narrator then presents an abrupt disclaimer about the validity of the canonical Gospels and undertakes to retell the whole story from a different and, implicitly, more truthful perspective.

The first section up to chapter 10 deal with the birth, childhood, and adolescence of Jesus. Three major sections deal with the adult or "public" life of Jesus: the encounter with Satan in the desert (chs. 11–14), three days of teaching and miracles in Jerusalem (chs. 29–41), and the trial, passion, and crucifixion (chs. 42–48). The final scene in heaven occurs in chapter 49. This sequence is reasonable and coherent but, unlike the Gospel of John, does not appear to contain any special symbolic meaning. In the section on Jesus' childhood, the special identity of Jesus is explained to him by Joseph but then seems to have been mysteriously suppressed. Only in the desert, after the baptism in the Jordan, is the divine sonship asserted and explained, and not by God, as in Mark, but by Satan. Mailer uses this episode to present God as severely limited in power and in goodness. Through the experiences of teaching and dealing with appeals for miracles, Jesus struggles to understand the meaning of his relationship to this problematic figure of God. Then in the passion and death, as we shall see, the limitations of this relationship are definitively exposed. The final chapter presents the resurrection and Jesus in heaven "at the right hand of the Father." His basic relation as son to the Father is formally retained but painfully unresolved.

Intertextuality

Within his imaginative reformulation of the life of Jesus based on this central problematic relationship, Mailer employs a very conventional methodological strategy. Mailer reproduces features of the interlinguistic and intertextual character of the canonical Gospels. He occasionally imitates the habit of the writers of the canonical Gospels in explaining key Hebrew and Aramaic terms for their Greek audience.[14] In a similar way Mailer exploits the complexity of the original languages on at least one occasion when he connects the Greek term "Christ" to the Hebrew term "Messiah." He, however, works in reverse, pretending that his speaker is moving from Greek back into Hebrew. Moreover, unlike his biblical models, his narrator also adds a sociological comment: "Christ being the word for Messiah in Greek, a language that many of the elevated in Jerusalem liked to use" (29).

Mailer, more significantly, employs the texts of the Hebrew Scriptures to explore the meaning of persons and events in his narrative. Early in his novel, Mailer has Jesus outline the kind of education in the Scriptures he had received as a boy. Jesus says that by the age of eight he could "read the language of the old Israelites" (20). He knew the Torah and the Prophets: "We also studied Genesis, Exodus, Leviticus, Numbers and the book of Deuteronomy. We read the prophecies of Elijah, Elisha, Ezekiel and Isaiah" (20–21).

Just as the canonical Gospels make considerable use of the Pentateuch, the Prophets, and Psalms,[15] Mailer employs some of the same parallels but also creates dramatically different interpretations by applying passages from Kings, Maccabees, the Song of Songs, and Job. Mailer's Jesus as narrator is not content with vague allusions to passages, because he seeks to identify the book in each case, without chapter or verse, and then quotes the passage. This general technique, adapted from the four Gospels, produces some very startling interpretations of the events in the novel.

Encounters with Satan and with Mary Magdalene

In two expanded encounters, first with "Satan in the desert" and then with the "woman caught in adultery," Mailer's idiosyncratic use of texts from Hebrew Scriptures is evident. In the defining encounter with Satan, issues fundamental to the novel are presented. It is Satan, not God, who declares that Jesus "is not a prophet but indeed the Son!" (19). Then, with the use of specific passages in the Hebrew Scriptures, Satan offers his view of a God with limited power and understanding who has "no right to command complete obedience from His People" (50). He then quotes a passage from Isaiah 3:16–24 on "the haughty women of Zion" and the utter destruction that awaits them. When Jesus interjects with the conventional explanation that this reference to women is really a metaphor for the whole people, Satan dismisses it: "'No,' replied the Devil, 'He pretends to speak of the nation of Zion. But it is women he belittles'" (51). Then the Devil quotes selections from an extensive passage at Ezekiel 16:9–43 full of lurid details of the "cleansing of the fallen woman": "Tell me that your Father is not filled with an adoration of women. Which he hides from himself! For he hates their power to entice Him" (52). Aspects of this por-

trait of God will reappear in the final scene in heaven, although with attitudes toward women somewhat emended. Satan presents the Father as "but
one god among man" (48). God has only limited divine power and goodness: "Your Father is but one god among many. You might take account of
the myriad respected by the Romans" (48). The Devil goes on to describe
limitations in the character of God:

> You would do better to consider the breadth of His rages; they are unseemly
> for a great god. They are swollen and without proportion. He issues too many
> threats. He cannot bear anyone who would dispute with Him. . . . He is not
> in command of Himself." (49)

At the conclusion of this long encounter with Satan in the desert, a
traditional Christian use of Isaiah 9:5–7 is invoked. As he makes his way
out of the desert and back to Nazareth, Jesus recalls the passage: "Unto us
. . . a child is born, unto us a son is given; and the government is upon his
shoulders; and his name shall be called wonderful, counsellor, the mighty
God, the everlasting Father, the prince of peace" (56). The traditional
implications of this passage for the identity of Jesus are not asserted with
any confidence. But Mailer's Jesus feels a vague sense of loyalty to this
God, even though he is a somewhat disturbing and limited figure. Jesus
has a sense that he is being called to do something. His response is bewil-
derment and befuddlement, not awe and commitment to a mission.

In another telling confrontation in the novel, Mailer employs a passage
from the Hebrew Scriptures to exploit a potentially salacious interest in
women and sexuality. In the scene of "the woman caught in adultery,"
identified in the novel as Mary from Magdala, Jesus engages her accusers
quite vigorously. The gravity and the excitement of the encounter are
enhanced by a passage from 2 Kings 9:27–39 on the dramatic death and
trampling of the body of Jezebel (175–76). Mailer recalls other passages
from Proverbs and Ezekiel that have powerful warnings against seductive
women. His Jesus experiences a moment of repressed lust. He goes on to
recognize both the general sinful condition of all people and a basic goodness in Mary. So Jesus decides not to condemn her. He questions her about
her future, but she interrupts him simply yet firmly: "If you do not condemn me, do not pass judgment" (180). In a very real sense she ends up
with the last word. Jesus is struggling with uncertainty in himself about
his identity and his role. This encounter suggests an exchange between
Jesus and Mary Magdalene with the balance tilted in her direction. Given
Mailer's interest, even obsession, with violence and sex in other writings,
he surprisingly attributes no sexual relationship to these two.

This is but one example of how the relationships between Mailer's Jesus and those whom he pardons or heals differ greatly from those in the canonical Gospels. Each request for healing or forgiveness in the novel provokes uncertainty in himself about the source and limit of his power.

Miracles

Unlike the Lives of Jesus that appeared in the nineteenth century,[16] Mailer does not dismiss the miracle stories of the canonical Gospels but recasts many of them. In contrast to the accounts in the Gospels, however, in Mailer's novel they become occasions for psychological self-doubt in Jesus. In several episodes Jesus even uses scriptural texts in order to underscore his fundamental uncertainty about the source and extent of his power. The actual choice of scriptural parallels continues to be startling.

Mailer presents a series of miracles from the traditions of the canonical Gospels. The first example is from John, but others principally follow Mark. The final one, however, is moved out of the original order so that Mailer concludes with an evaluation of the Father's attitude toward Jesus. Mailer's list includes the following: the production of wine at Cana (John 2:1–12); the cure of a leper (Mark 1:40–45); the raising of the daughter of Jairus together with the cure of the woman with a hemorrhage (Mark 5:21–43; Matt. 9:18–26; Luke 8:40–56); the multiplication of the loaves and fish (Mark 6:30–44; Matt. 14:13–21; Luke 9:10–17; John 6:1–13); the cure of a blind man (Mark 8:22–26); and the walking on water (Mark 6:45–51). Mailer does respect the restrained style of the miracle accounts in the canonical Gospels. In those Gospels, the miraculous event itself is subordinated to a dialogue or gesture between a person making a request and Jesus. Once that occurs, Jesus uses a word or gesture to accomplish the miracle, with little or no emphasis on the surprising event itself. But Mailer's restrained treatment of many of the same miracles is designed for quite a different purpose. Although God assures him that "when you believe in Me, miracles will be in your hands, your eyes, and your voice" (66), Mailer's Jesus remains profoundly unsure of his power and his relation to the Father. He faces a number of the traditional miracle episodes with a singular lack of confidence in any outcome. Later, in his confrontation with the Pharisees, he seems to accede to their view that "there are no miracles in man's hand" (185). The dramatic failure or cessation of the miraculous power in Mailer's Jesus occurs, as we shall see, on the cross.

An early example of this uncertain approach to requests for a miracle of healing occurs with a leper. Jesus is initially perplexed about what he can do, but then he remembers a passage from Exodus (4:1–9) in which God helps Moses to recognize that he has been given miraculous powers (75). Jesus then surmises that God is addressing him through that text and follows the identical procedure by putting his hand on the chest of the victim, who is then cured.

In the double episode dealing with the daughter of Jairus and the woman with the hemorrhage (96–99), Mailer's Jesus reacts quite differently from the accounts in the Synoptic Gospels (Mark 5:21–43; Matt. 9:18–26; Luke 8:40–56). First, at the very outset of this episode, Mailer's Jesus responds to Jairus's request with the rather surprising observation that faith and loss of faith are closely related. He returns to this same combination of faith and unbelief in the cure of the blind man (183) and the blessing of the cup at the Last Supper (199). This seems to negate the fundamental assumption of faith as the basis for cures and miracles in the canonical Gospels. He agrees to Jairus's request to help his daughter, but when the woman with the hemorrhage touches him and is healed, he is immediately assailed by doubts about the limits of his power. Has this unexpected act used it up? He still approaches the child and hopes that she is merely in suspended animation and not actually dead. He is once again directed by a scriptural passage from 2 Kings (4:4–37) about how to conduct this miracle. That passage refers to Elisha, who raises the child of the Shunammite woman to life by lying on him. Mailer's Jesus, however, decides not to lie on the little girl, just in case she fails to wake up. This fundamental state of uncertainty about the nature and extent of his power is reflected as well in many of the other miracle stories in the novel.

Mailer treats the multiplication of the loaves and fish by an odd reduction of the event itself. He begins by noting again his criticism of the "exaggeration" that characterizes the accounts in all four Gospels. Then Mailer has his Jesus put a little crumb of bread and fish on each of the five hundred tongues. After this, Mailer's Jesus speculates that each morsel became enlarged in each person's mind. Mailer concludes that "this was a triumph of the spirit rather than an enlargement of matter" (116). In the very next episode this reductionism to some psychological wish fulfillment seems to be challenged by God in a way that casts their relationship in a very uneasy light. As he was walking on the water, Jesus says, "I could hear my Father's laughter at my pleasure" (117). But the tone of the laughter abruptly shifts, and God's laughter becomes puzzling, even disturbing: "Then came a second wave of His laughter. He was mocking me. For I had concluded too quickly that there was no extravagance in His miracles" (117).

This episode picks up the uncertainty and self-doubt that are consistent throughout the miracle accounts in the novel and certainly affect Jesus' approach to his teaching. Jesus decides to begin his teaching at the synagogue in Nazareth, prompted by a basic uncertainty and uneasiness: "Since my tongue was hardly the equal of my hands when they worked with wood, I thought to begin where some, at least, would know me" (63–64). He decides to begin with the ringing summons at the beginning of the Gospel of Mark: "Repent, for the Kingdom of God is at hand. The end is near" (1:14–15). But Mailer's Jesus lacks conviction, and his words are greeted only by a polite silence. There is none of the energy and wrath reported in the Gospel of Luke where the people rose up and cast him from the city (4:16–30). Mailer's Jesus uses this opportunity to distance himself from the account in Luke. Later Mailer's Jesus offers his account of the Sermon on the Mount in Matthew 5–7. He includes his version of the Beatitudes, the parable of the light, revisions of the law, and the text of the Our Father (111–15). But the whole passage is presented as an uneasy effort on the part of Jesus to convince both himself and his listeners that they should love God more. His motive for this discourse is stated at the outset:

> But they did not love my Father enough. I should have known that. But then, I did not love Him enough, not enough. . . . I must put away all doubt. I must convince all who listen of my love for Him. (111)

This uneasiness and uncertainty also affects most but not all of his personal relationships.

Joseph, Mary, and Others

Jesus' relationship with Joseph is, in some ways, the most effective one in the novel. Joseph is an older man and was a widower before marrying Mary. He taught Jesus the skills of the carpenter with knowledge of the quality and function of different kinds of wood. It is Joseph who first informs Jesus of his unusual birth (9) and of his connection with the line of King David (15). At age twelve Joseph tells him about his true father, but Jesus seems to suppress that information: "An even greater weight was upon me. That was Joseph's story concerning my true father. I could hardly see myself as the Son" (21). He becomes the victim of a great fever at that time. Only after the death of Joseph, when Jesus is thirty years old, do Joseph's words come back to him and disturb the peace he had found as a carpenter:

> Soon I was distraught. His great secret came back to me. If I knew again that the Lord was my Father, I hardly knew in what manner; He was still far from

me. Whenever I thought that He would soon appear, He did not. I was in need of new wisdom. (27)

Jesus then goes to John the Baptist. After considering his faults, he is baptized in the Jordan. At the baptism many of the features in the canonical Gospels are reported except for one critical difference. Mailer's Jesus reports the descent of a dove, a vision of millions of souls, and a voice that acknowledges that God knows him and that He will send him on a mission (34). There is no proclamation about the status of Jesus as "the beloved Son." As we have seen, Satan declares that key identification during the encounter in the desert.

In contrast to his relationship with Joseph, Jesus' relationship with Mary is very problematic. Mailer reports most of the traditional episodes that involve Mary, such as the annunciation, birth, visit to the temple, marriage at Cana, attempt to get the attention of Jesus on his public mission, and appearance at the foot of the cross. He also adds a scene in heaven before the throne of God. In each instance, this relationship is strained by misunderstandings between Mary and Jesus. Mary is described as "modest," "vain," and "with a will graven in stone" (59). Like Joseph, she is a member of the Essenes. She believes that Jesus too should be content to be an Essene, and she does not think him fit to be a preacher (59). In his encounter with John the Baptist, Jesus can accuse himself of no more than disrespect toward his mother and some lustful thoughts (33). He hopes that the miracle at Cana might appease her. As he departs on his journey, he leaves with "staff, a cloak, my sandals and her tears" (62). This modification of the canonical Gospels implies that these tears were not a sign of affection but of frustration. Later, when Mary comes to get his attention, she adopts the same argument from the Pharisees expressed in the canonical tradition and says that he should not be performing miracles on the Sabbath. When Jesus claims that those who do the will of God are his mother and brothers, he does not intend to exclude Mary. He later regrets this comment, since Mary did not understand and it made her cry (90). Later he visits Nazareth in order to apologize to Mary, but his apology seems to have been ineffectual (99 and 105).

He remains uneasy about his relationship with his mother. Only at the cross does he seem to feel close to her. He laments, "Now, and too late, I have understood her love ... and belonged to her again" (226). At this point he confides her to the care of Timothy, not John. This is part of Mailer's attempt to distance his account from that of the canonical Gospels. In Mailer's final episode in heaven, Mary appears with Jesus "at the right hand of the Father." Although Mailer presents the scene in conventional scriptural language, the relationship between Jesus and his mother remains cool and distant. Jesus says of her, "My mother is much honored. Many churches are named for her; perhaps more than for me. And she is pleased with her son" (240). The references to the numbers of churches and the faint echo of the Father's words in the canonical versions are both ironic. Thus, even in heaven there is no resolution in the tension between son and mother.

Since Mailer distances his version of Jesus from the canonical accounts, he minimizes the relationship of Jesus with those followers associated with canonical texts and the church. Hence Matthew, Mark, Luke, John, and Peter tend to fade into the background. Judas, however, emerges with a unique and important relationship with Jesus. Judas is presented as the one disciple with an independent social analysis. Jesus feels that he can learn from Judas much about social issues. Judas, born among the rich, had become angry with the divisions between rich and poor. He fully understands the power structures among both Jews and Romans. He empathizes with the ordinary merchant class. When discouraged, Jesus asks Judas why so many Jews want nothing to do with him. Judas claims that they are not vitally concerned about "the end of the world and entrance into another realm" (136). The merchant enjoys a smaller, more stable world, where he can enjoy little triumphs.

Judas uses "Yeshua," the Aramaic form of Jesus' name, perhaps as a sign of affection. Yet he says that he does not believe Jesus' message of salvation. He remains with him because of the possible egalitarian impact of that message, which might make the poor feel more equal to the rich (137). Jesus seems to appreciate Judas' realistic assessment of the social context, but he continues to search for his own vision of the future. He concludes, "I loved Judas. In this hour I loved him even more than Peter" (139). Mailer uses this preference for Judas to inform Jesus' genuine yet ineffectual sympathy for the poor.

The Father

The central relationship at the heart of this novel is the one between Jesus and the Father. It is acknowledged in the title; it is the point of Joseph's contribution; it is the focus of the encounter with Satan; it is the issue in the miracle accounts. Although Mailer does formally respect traditional orthodox beliefs in the equal relationship of the Father and Son, he explores this relationship exclusively from the psychological experience of his subject-narrator. His Jesus attempts to discover the meaning of his status as son or

Son of the Father. Mailer's method is to depict the painful impact of the process of discovery Ultimately, the Father in Mailer's version is enigmatic at best, cruel and uncaring at worse. The chilling cruelty of the Father's laugh in the miracle account becomes tragic in Mailer's version of the death on the cross.

Death and Resurrection

As we have seen in regard to miracles, the enigmatic role of the Divine becomes more apparent in Mailer's treatment of the crucifixion and the resurrection. In the one case a request for a miracle is rebuffed; in the second case the greatest miracle is trivialized. On the cross Jesus asks his Father for one more miracle, only to be met with refusal. God's stern response is presented like the voice in the whirlwind from Job 38–41. In Mailer it sounds more sinister: "Would you annul my judgement?" Jesus says no, but he soon repeats his request, which is greeted only by silence. At that moment Mailer's Jesus concludes that "if the Father does not hear him, he is no longer the Son of God. How awful to be no more than a man" (231).

At this tragic moment Mailer's Jesus quotes the same Psalm 22:1 as in Mark (15:34) and Matthew (27:47): "My Lord, why hast Thou forsaken me?" But Mailer has Jesus continue his reflections over the value of his relation to the Father. The immediate observation is haunting and pathetic: "There was no answer, only the echo of my cry." But he goes on a reverie filled with flashes from Genesis and the quest for knowledge of good and evil. His concluding response, in fact, returns to the judgment of Satan during the original encounter in the desert:

> Even as I asked if the Lord was all-powerful, I heard my own answer: God, my father, was one god. But there were others. If I had failed Him so He had failed me. Such was my knowledge of good and evil. Was it for that reason I was on the cross? (232)

There is nothing in the passage or in its context to suggest soteriological value in this scene. There is no appeal to the Suffering Servant passages in Isaiah to indicate vicarious and redemptive death. Mailer simply presents Jesus as a painful example of the human faced with the apparent meaninglessness of death.

This episode constitutes the climax of Mailer's novel. Jesus goes to his death in uncertainty and confusion. Absent is any confidence in his relationship to his Father; absent is any sense of mission. There is no hint of sacrifice and redemption. There is only the frustrated sense of the human quest for understanding of life and death at the hands of a peculiar kind of God. Mailer's God is a weak figure. He has only limited power. He is neither emotionally nor personally present. He can be capriciously malicious. In many ways Mailer's God provides a paradigm for the modern absent father.

In his account of the resurrection, Mailer remains in contact with his scriptural sources. He describes the resurrection and speaks of the position of Jesus "at the right hand of the Father" in heaven. But these episodes lack the tension and impact of the crucifixion. Jesus says that he "rose on the third day. But the disciples added fables" (236). Mailer's Jesus is very matter-of-fact about this event: "I left the sepulchre to wander through the city and the countryside" (238). We may assume that Mailer includes the resurrection simply to provide the source for this posthumous autobiography.

In the last chapter, Mailer's Jesus offers his final reflections on his relationship with his mother. Before returning to his relations with the other Gospels and his interest in the poor, he also offers his final reflections on his very distant relationship with the Father: "My Father, however, does not often speak to me. Nonetheless I honor Him" (240). Jesus then revisits the initial analysis of the Father offered by Satan. The Father remains limited, but his intentions are now considered in a more positive light. The Father loves as much as he can, "but His Love is not without limit" (240). Mailer's Jesus then rehearses episodes in the ongoing struggle God has with the Devil in the continuing history of the human race. Events from the destruction of Jerusalem in 70 to the Holocaust of the twentieth century are recalled as signs of this ongoing struggle. Mailer's Jesus expresses amazement that God has been able to promote the belief that a victory has been won by his death on the cross. If this is true then he, the son of the Father, is happy to be associated with a compassionate love for the poor. He concludes with an expression of hope still conditioned by a degree of uncertainty: "The Lord sends what love He can muster down to that creature who is man and that other creature who is woman, and I try to remain the source of love that is tender" (241).

Conclusion

Throughout his novel, Mailer remains in close contact with episodes in the four Gospels and their methods of employing the Hebrew Scriptures to interpret persons and events. Yet he provides a portrait so different from the original Gospels. His Jesus is sympathetic, well intentioned, and generous, but basically uncertain and tentative throughout. This is a far cry from the striking figure of the canonical Gospels. I suggest two reasons for this difference. One is based on the distinctions between the genres of Gospel and novel. The other is based on Mailer's construction of the divine. The canonical Gospels are the product of writers who believed in the mysterious uniqueness of Jesus, whose divinely sanctioned mission on behalf of humans culminated in the resurrection. Although Mailer retains most of the episodes in these Gospels, he changes his whole interpretation by making Jesus the confused and uncertain narrator of the events. Mailer constructs a God quite different from the various biblical treatments. His God is one of many and is limited in power and in goodness. Consequently, Mailer's God is a capricious and even cruel figure. Within this relationship, Mailer presents a Jesus who calls on the reader's sympathy and even pity. But the relation of this son and this father would be singularly ineffectual as a savior of anyone in the violent and cruel world that is the context of Mailer's prodigious literary oeuvre.

NOTES

1. See N. Mailer, *Why Are We in Vietnam?* (New York: G. Putnam's Sons, 1967); and Mailer, *The Armies of the Night: History as a Novel and the Novel as History* (New York: New American Library, 1968).

2. See N. Mailer, *St. George and the Godfather* (New York: New American Library, 1972); and Mailer, *Some Honorable Men: Political Conventions 1960–1972* (Boston: Little, Brown, 1976).

3. See N. Mailer, *Marilyn: A Biography* (New York: Grosset & Dunlop, 1973); and Mailer, *The Executioner's Song* (Boston: Little, Brown, 1979).

4. N. Mailer, *The Gospel according to the Son* (New York: Random House, 1997). References to this work appear in parentheses in the text.

5. See C. Rollyson, *The Lives of Norman Mailer: A Biography* (New York: Paragon Press, 1991); and M. V. Dearborn, *Mailer: A Biography* (Boston: Houghton Mifflin, 1999).

6. For an important discussion of Mailer's conceptions of the character of the Godhead and relation to the world, consult J. M. Lennon, "Mailer's Cosmology," in *Critical Essays on Norman Mailer*, ed. J. M. Lennon (Boston: G. K. Hall, 1986), 145–56. Within the context of themes in the American fiction of Melville and Hemingway, Lennon presents Mailer's notions of multiple gods each with serious moral limitations. Lennon summarizes Mailer's views on God in three phrases: "But . . . Mailer believes that God 'exists like us,' that He is imperfect in the way we are imperfect," that "He too can suffer from a moral corruption." The first two quotations are taken from P. J. Carrol, "*Playboy* Interview with Norman Mailer," *Playboy,* January 1968, 74, and the third from N. Mailer, *Advertisements for Myself* (New York: Putnam's, 1959), 351. See also J. M. Lennon, *Conversations with Norman Mailer* (Jackson, MS: University Press of Mississippi, 1988), especially the interview with Richard Stern at the University of Chicago.

7. See J. Miles, "Mailer's Gospel," *Commonweal,* July 18, 1997, 124; P.-L. Adams, "The Gospel according to the Son," *Atlantic,* June 1997, 279; and P. Gray, "Using the Lord's Name," *Time,* April 28, 1997, 17.

8. See M. Gordon's caustic review, "Jesus Christ, Superstar," *Nation*, June 23, 1997, 27. See also M. Kakutani's review, "Gospel according to the Son: Mailer's Perception of Jesus," *New York Times*, April 14, 1997, 146.

9. See F. Kermode, "Advertisements for Himself," *New York Review of Books*, May 15, 1997, 4–8. Kermode provides some of the explanations Mailer offered for this project. Apparently prompted by papal concerns about the plight of the poor in the Third World, Mailer revisited the Gospel narratives and grew to admire the figure of Jesus. Kermode summarizes Mailer's own observations, which he gave in an interview. Mailer felt it an advantage to be a Jew, who could sympathize with Jesus. This Jesus was no longer, as he had been to earlier generations of American Jews, an enemy or a renegade, but simply a good man.

10. In the history of biblical criticism, many productive intersections have occurred between biblical studies and the studies of other literatures. This has been true from the use of allegory in Greek literature and biblical texts explored in ancient Alexandria to the development of historical-critical methods for classical and biblical texts in the secular universities of nineteenth-century Europe. Biblical studies have tended to become increasingly specialized in the course of this century, but once again critical theories developed for other literatures are being selectively applied to biblical texts. For examples, consult F. Kermode, *The Genesis of Secrecy: On the Interpretation of Narrative* (Cambridge: Cambridge University Press, 1979); N. Frye, *The Great Code: The Bible and Literature* (New York: Harcourt Brace Jovanovich, 1982); R. Alter and F. Kermode, *The Literary Guide to the Bible* (Cambridge, MA: Harvard University Press, 1987); W. R. Telford, "The New Testament in Fiction and Film: A Biblical Scholar's Perspective," in *Words Remembered, Texts Renewed: Essays in Honour of John F. A. Sawyer*, ed. J. Davies, G. Harvey, and W. G. E. Watson (Sheffield: Sheffield Academic Press, 1995), 360–94. For a general overview, consult L. Ryken, "The Bible as Literature," in *Oxford Companion to the Bible*, edd. Metzger, B.M., and Coogan, M.D. (New York/Oxford: Oxford University Press, 1993), 460–63; and J. Barr, "History of Interpretation: Modern Biblical Criticism," *Oxford Companion to the Bible*, op. cit., 318–24.

11. See N. Ricci, *Testament* (Toronto: Anchor Canada, 2003).

12. In *The Gospel according to Jesus Christ*, trans. G. Pontiero (New York: Harcourt Brace, 1994), Saramago begins his own version by describing figures in a painting of the crucifixion. He gives details of all the figures in the Gospel account except for the key figure, Jesus. Then he returns to the beginning of the story but continues to retell the narrative from the perspective of an unidentified observer. That observer combines a deep empathy for the simple and the poor, perceptive psychological insight, and a compassion for the inevitability of death. This narrator lacks any sense of an all-knowing, benevolent God to give meaning to human suffering and death. This combination of perspectives gives this particular account genuine power.

13. Certainly in the biblical sources there are many references to wood, such as cedar and olive, but some of the other examples might be prompted by Mailer's New England background.

14. Matthew, for example, translates the Hebrew *Emmanuel* as "God-is-with-us" at 1:23, verse 1 of Psalm 22 at 27:47, and the Aramaic *Golgotha* as the "Place of the Skull" at 27:33. John translates the Hebrew *Rabbuni* as "Master" at 20:17.

15. In the Gospel of Matthew, for example, there are forty-one citations from the Hebrew Scriptures, with thirty-seven prefaced by the phrase "in fulfilment of the Scriptures" or some variant of it. Then there are echoes of earlier texts. From the Pentateuch come one from Genesis, five from Exodus, one from Leviticus, and seven from Deuteronomy. From the Major Prophets come nine from Isaiah, one from Daniel, and one from

Jeremiah. From the Minor Prophets come two from Hosea (with 6:6 repeated a second time), three from Micah, two from Zechariah, and one from Jonah. There are eight from the Psalms.

16. See D. F. Strauss, *Das Leben Jesu* (Tübingen, Germany: C.F. Osiander, 1836), and E. Renan, *La vie de Jésus* (Paris: Culman-Lévy, 1863). Strauss removes the miraculous and supernatural dimension and attributes them to the mythical character of the Gospel genre. Renan goes further and blunts the moral imperative and the apocalyptic urgency of the canonical Gospels.

3 | José Saramago's *Kakaggelion*

The "Badspel" according to Jesus Christ

J. ROBERT C. COUSLAND

I find the Gospels most unpleasant reading for the most part.

Northrop Frye

In the following essay I undertake to offer an exploration of José Saramago's *The Gospel according to Jesus Christ*. After a brief synopsis of Saramago's career and a short summary of the book, I move to a discussion of the work's style and influences. Thereafter, I propose to argue that the work is a satire that deliberately recasts the good news about Jesus—the gospel—as bad news.[1] Saramago inverts the traditional moral polarities of the Bible, namely, that God is good and the devil is bad, to expose the oppressive systems he sees as lying at the heart of the Christian evangel. These systems devour Jesus, who emerges in the novel not as the divine Son of God but as an unfortunate and deluded victim of a faulty religious impulse.[2]

Saramago

The Portuguese author and poet José Saramago has been acclaimed by Harold Bloom as one of the world's living geniuses.[3] Born of peasant stock in 1922 in Azinhaga, Portugal, Saramago gave up formal schooling in 1934 in order to learn a trade so that he could support his family. Although he was eventually able to secure a position in the shop of Lisbon's Civil

55

Hospital, his family nevertheless experienced considerable poverty and destitution.[4] This impoverished upbringing may have influenced Saramago's eventual decision to join the Communist Party in 1969, to which he still belongs.[5] His first novel appeared in 1947, and since that time he has produced an extensive oeuvre that includes a wide array of poems, plays, diaries, and novels.[6] Over the last two-and-a-half decades, he has been the recipient of many prestigious literary prizes, including the 1998 Nobel Prize for Literature.[7]

There is little doubt that one of the volumes influencing the decision of the Nobel Committee was 1991's *O Evangelho Segundo Jesus Cristo*, translated into English as *The Gospel according to Jesus Christ* in 1994. As with many works that reinterpret the figure of Jesus, this novel has garnered its fair share of controversy.[8] At one end of the critical spectrum, Harold Bloom proclaims that "it is an awesome work, imaginatively superior to any other life of Jesus, including the four canonical Gospels."[9] Other responses have been notably less fulsome, though all too often the criticisms leveled at the novel appear to arise from dogmatic rather than artistic considerations. A case in point is when the Portuguese government notoriously sought to prevent the work from being considered for the European Literary Prize because it deemed the work offensive to Catholics.[10] Nor has Saramago himself appeared averse to fueling controversy. A self-professed atheist,[11] he archly terms his novel a "heretical Gospel."[12] Certainly, as will become clear, he has deliberately chosen his own style of Gospel,[13] and it is fully as interesting and idiosyncratic as comparable works, such as Robert Graves's *King Jesus* or D. H. Lawrence's *The Man Who Died*.[14]

The Narrative

The work opens with a visitation to Mary in Nazareth. At this point she has married Joseph, an ineffectual carpenter. The visitation consists of an "angelic" annunciation, where a mysterious visitor bestows a jar of glowing earth upon Mary. Mary is pregnant with both Joseph's and God's child, and just at this time Joseph and Mary are required to participate in the Roman census and to return to their ancestral town of Bethlehem. They cannot find lodging and are forced to take refuge in a nearby cave, where Jesus is born. Joseph learns of Herod's plot to assassinate all the children age two and under in the region, but in his haste to save Jesus, he fails to notify all the other parents with newborns. Herod's troops slaughter them all, and Joseph's lapse haunts him in nightmares for the rest of his life. This is not destined to last long; shortly after the holy family returns to Nazareth, Joseph becomes unintentionally embroiled in the revolutionary struggle against Rome and, at age thirty-three, is crucified, though an innocent, in Sepphoris. Shortly thereafter, Jesus leaves Nazareth, visits Jerusalem, and ends up working for a number of years as a shepherd with Pastor (who, it transpires, is none other than the mysterious visitor who made the annunciation to Mary, and who, we later learn, is Satan).[15]

The end of his sojourn with Pastor comes about when he has an encounter with God, who reveals himself to Jesus as a pillar of fire and constrains him to sacrifice a lamb in his honor. After this sacrifice, Pastor refuses to allow Jesus to rejoin the flock. Jesus then wanders to Magdala, where he meets up with the prostitute Mary Magdalene and then revisits Nazareth, only to be largely reviled by his family. Returning to Mary, he embarks with her on a series of peregrinations around the Galilee. It is only now that Jesus' miraculous abilities come to the fore, notably in a profound capacity to catch fish. He then stills a local storm and turns water into wine at Cana. Yet after killing two thousand pigs in the exorcism of the Gadarene demoniac, Jesus begins to have qualms about his God-given abilities, all the more so when he finds he has withered a fig tree out of season because it has not produced fruit. These doubts surface in a primal encounter with God and Satan that takes place in a fog-shrouded boat in the middle of the Sea of Galilee and lasts for forty days and forty nights. Jesus for the first time sees God face to face and finds him to be "a big man, elderly, a great flowing beard over His chest, head uncovered, hair hanging loose, [with] a broad and powerful face" (306). More remarkable yet, he discovers that, except for the beard, God and Satan look exactly the same. Then, in a scene reminiscent of Aeneas's vision in book 6 of the *Aeneid*, Jesus is granted a preview of the coming "glories" of Christendom, including the Crusades, the Inquisition, and rivers upon rivers of blood. This revelation sparks in him the realization that God intends to use him to start a worldwide religion that will satisfy God's megalomaniacal desire for adherents. Once Jesus returns to shore, he performs many of the stories told about him in the Gospels, but his chief design is to thwart God's plan. To this end he engineers his own death, only to find out too late that this was precisely what God had intended:

> Jesus realized then that he had been tricked ... and that his life had been planned for death from the very beginning. Remembering the river of blood and suffering that would flow from his side and flood the globe, he called out to the open sky, where God could be seen smiling, Men, forgive Him, for He knows not what he has done. (376–77)

Sources and Style

The depth and detail present in Saramago's *Gospel* attest to his thorough acquaintance with early Christian sources. Apart from a clever and imaginative redeployment of episodes from the four Gospels, he draws on an array of supracanonical sources. He makes considerable use, for instance, of the *Protevangelium of James*, which situates the events of Jesus' birth in a cave and portrays Salome as midwife to Mary.[16] Other echoes of supracanonical materials include the *Infancy Gospel of Thomas* and the hagiographical traditions that grew up around the twelve disciples[17] and Mary Magdalene.[18] Saramago's motif of an earthenware bowl, an image that recurs throughout the novel, also suggests a familiarity with Gnostic sources,[19] as the image of glowing earth in the bowl furnishes an instance of the divine light imprisoned in the medium of earth—human clay.[20] It also serves as an effective image for the annunciation—a divine child sired in the earth of Mary's jar-like womb.

In addition to these ancient sources, Saramago's narrative style also seems to suggest points of contact with Ernest Renan's immensely influential *La Vie de Jésus* (1863).[21] Albert Schweitzer has suggested that Renan's work proved to be so successful because he "offered his readers a Jesus who was alive, whom he, with his artistic imagination, had met under the blue heaven of Galilee."[22] Much of this impression is a consequence of Renan's authorial stance where, instead of citing his sources, he simply imparts them to his readers. As the guide of all that they need to know, he pronounces with authority on Jesus' life. A case in point is his romanticized evaluation of Jesus' peasant existence in Galilee: Jesus' life

> was not like the gross materialism of our peasantry, the coarse pleasures of agricultural Normandy, or the heavy mirth of the Flemish. It spiritualized itself in ethereal dreams—in a kind of poetic mysticism blending heaven and earth. . . . The whole history of infant Christianity has become in this manner a delightful pastoral.[23]

In this manner, Renan becomes the arbiter of how his readers should feel or think, and acts as their exclusive—if not necessarily reliable—cicerone to the New Testament world.

Much the same can be said for Saramago's manner, except that he takes this whole process of mediation even further. In his novel there is minimal punctuation and no quotation marks—all speech is mediated through the one authorial voice. This technique seems to be one of the characteristic features of Saramago's mature style. In a recent interview, he situated *Gospel* in the first cycle of his works, which "articulated for the first time the distinct 'narrative voice' that from then on became the hallmark of my work."[24] And while the literary technique underlying this "narrative voice" appears to be straightforward, even pedestrian, such an impression is misleading. As Joaquina Pires-O'Brien observes, "The apparent simplicity of the text is achieved through a highly skilled use of syntax, where troublesome reflexive verbs and oblique pronouns are frequently flexed, although this aspect can only be fully appreciated in the original Portuguese vernacular."[25]

The dominant component of this style is its orality. Saramago explains that it came to him while he was writing his 1980 book *Levantado de Chao*: "I was 20 pages into writing the novel in what we might call the orthodox manner . . . when suddenly—and this was one of the most beautiful moments of my writing life—I dropped the usual style without thinking. The story forced me to do it. Their world of strictly oral communication gave birth to my style."[26] Naturally, given the oral roots of the canonical Gospels, Saramago's style is especially well adapted to produce a Gospel of his own.[27] This style also fits well with the stance assumed by the narrator. While this stance resists easy categorization, being a protean blend of various personae, its dominant tone is that of a naive but canny peasant, given to generalizing bromides about the human condition.[28] For instance, on one occasion where Jesus is reluctant to ask a question, the narrator observes:

> This often happens, we refrain from asking a question because we are unprepared or simply too afraid to hear the answer. And when we finally summon the courage to ask, no answer is forthcoming, just as Jesus one day will refuse to answer when asked, What is truth. A question that remains unanswered to this day. (191)

As this passage demonstrates, the narrator frequently employs the first-person plural to include the readers in his observations. On occasion, however, the tone varies, as when Saramago makes the narrator approach what one assumes would be Saramago's own voice.[29] Commenting on Jesus' circumcision, the narrator adds an ironic directive: "Anyone wishing to see that foreskin today need only visit the parish church of Calcata near Viterbo in Italy, where it is preserved in a reliquary for the spiritual benefit of the faithful and the amusement of curious atheists" (63). Saramago's readers only learn later, on the authority of Pastor, that Jesus' foreskin had, in actuality, been burned up in a fire (217).

As this sly episode makes evident, humor is also an essential stylistic feature of the novel—an unusual feature in the corpus of literary Lives of Jesus.[30] To this end, Saramago employs a variety of gambits, with a heavy-handed irony being one of the most prevalent. He is equally adept at introducing instances of paradox at various points, as in the following exchange between Jesus and God (which also hints at the liar's paradox): "Can gods lie. They can. And You are the one and only true god among them. Yes, the one and only true god" (320).[31] The work is further charged with the ridiculous, as when an angel discusses with Mary the difficulties involved in giving God a paternity test (263).[32]

The humor extends to the generic forms informing the novel. Its very title suggests not merely that it is calculated to replicate the Gospel genre, but also, given that it is implied to be Jesus' *own* Gospel, that Saramago intends to parody the genre.[33] He calls to mind the time-frame of *The Gospel according to Jesus Christ*, which corresponds to that found in the gospels of Matthew and Luke, and shares with them both characters and setting. In a technique of parody at least as old as Euripides' *Orestes*, the novel takes delight in stretching established and familiar characters out of all recognition.

Most of all, however, the entire *Gospel* is to be taken as an extended and bitter satire on the Bible, the Gospel genre, and the message contained in the Gospels.[34] As will become clear, despite his having entitled the work a Gospel, Saramago's *Gospel* contains no good news; it is unabashedly tragic.[35] Jesus dies horribly to slake the bloodlust of a tyrannical and megalomaniacal god, and there is no resurrection. When taken seriously, therefore, Saramago's *Gospel* reveals itself to be, instead, a *Kakaggelion—The Bad News according to Jesus Christ*.[36]

Saramago's *Kakaggelion*

The most distinctive and compelling feature of this *Kakaggelion* is Saramago's parodic inversion of the message and import of the canonical Gospels.[37] He retains many of the traditional and familiar features of the Gospel story, which creates an illusion of the familiar, but this impression is misleading since he fundamentally inverts and subverts the metaphysical framework of the Gospels.[38] The effect of this *bouleversement* is to make the title of his work ironic; instead of being good news (good *spel*), it becomes bad news—bad *spel*.[39] Saramago accomplishes this transformation by reversing the moral characters of God and Satan and, thereby, the moral polarities of the universe. Jesus is profoundly affected by this overturning of established categories, so much so that the story of his life can only be described as bad news.

Central to this reconstruction is the figure of Satan. Saramago prepares the reader for this transition: "If we met the devil and he allowed us to open him up, we might be surprised to find God jumping out" (201). The name Satan assumes in the work—Pastor—shows how radical this reconstruction is meant to be, since the designation "shepherd" is frequently attributed to Yahweh in the Hebrew Bible.[40] Nor is it lost on Saramago that it is also one of Jesus' self-designations (John 10:11).[41] Yet Satan does not simply assume the name Pastor but also the role associated with it. He tends his flock patiently and with care. Most importantly, he does not exploit the flock and its products for his own advantage. Unlike God, who demands blood from the sacrifice of innocent lambs, Pastor tends them selflessly: "The flock was here and somebody had to look after the animals and protect them from thieves, and that person happened to be me" (190). His ministrations are, in fact, so successful that the flock is described as one of the largest ever seen (246).

Pastor also becomes a shepherd in its metaphorical aspect, most notably in his continual oversight of Jesus. Instead of the archangel Gabriel making the annunciation to Mary, it is Pastor who provides his own sort of annunciation (13; cf. 225, 262–63). Pastor watches over Jesus at the various stages of his development and actually appears to care for him.[42]

God is the obverse of Pastor. Though his character remains elusive until the second half of the novel, its unsavory aspects gradually emerge. Pastor intimates that "on opening up God one might find the devil inside" (201–2), and his intimation proves to be correct. God's own unfallen angels confirm that human beings are fundamentally mistaken about God: "The Lord's way of doing things is invariably the opposite of what humans imagine" (263). His methods are, in fact, the antithesis of Pastor's. Instead of tending and caring for the flock, God relentlessly consumes it. Hosea 6:6 notwithstanding, he desires sacrifice not mercy, and he "inhales the odors of all this carnage with satisfaction" (208).[43] In a turning point in the narrative, God gives Jesus a lamb, solely that he might sacrifice it to him.[44] At first Jesus resists, out of repugnance at slaughtering such an innocent creature:

> In his mind's eye, he saw a horrifying vision, a vast sea of blood, the blood of the countless lambs and other animals sacrificed since the creation of mankind, for that is why men have been put on this earth, to adore and to offer sacrifice. And he saw the steps of the Temple awash with red, as blood came streaming down them, and he saw himself standing in a pool of blood and raising the lifeless body of his beheaded lamb to heaven. (209)

In the end, however, Jesus accedes to God's demand.

Jesus' acquiescence has serious consequences, since the lamb's sacrifice portends his own destruction.[45] Over the course of the novel, Jesus has a recurring dream that his father is coming to kill him; he is right, though it is not Joseph who seeks to destroy him but his divine father.[46] In contrast to the biblical Akedah episode (the sacrifice of Isaac) to which Saramago intermittently refers, where Isaac is saved and a ram is sacrificed in his stead, God compels Jesus to be a human sacrifice.[47] As he says explicitly to Jesus: "Don't play the lamb taken to be sacrificed, who struggles and bleats pitifully, for your fate is sealed, the sword awaits" (315). Jesus' death is inevitable. In contrast to Pastor, who cares for the flocks that are not even his own, God could not care less about his own son. Saramago's God emerges as an abomination—another Moloch.[48]

The satire in *Gospel* is largely a consequence of this inversion. The characters gamely repose their trust in God and revile Satan. Even the narrator is made to expatiate on the goodness of God (108) or the benefits of trusting God (205) in contexts that demonstrate that God is far from good or trustworthy. As with Pangloss in Voltaire's *Candide*, it does not take long for readers to recognize that the situation described is far from what it is purported to be. *Gospel*'s God is not the "best of all possible Gods"— indeed, one would be hard pressed to imagine how he could be worse or, for that matter, how Satan could be better.

This "reversed-polarity" presentation of God and Satan is a time-honored one, and Saramago is likely well aware that such portrayals are characteristic of Marcion and also the various Gnostic systems of the second century CE, where the God of the Hebrew Scriptures is characterized as a despotic and deluded demiurge who is to be distinguished from the true, heavenly God.[49] Yet Saramago probably has a more modern referent in mind, one with a political application. In a recent interview, he cited the following dictum of Marx and Engels with approval: "If the human being is shaped by his circumstances, then it is necessary to shape those circumstances humanely." He then added: "This contains all the wisdom I needed in order to become what it seems I am considered to be: a 'political moralist.'"[50] If one accepts this self-designation as descriptive of Saramago's endeavor, then it casts considerable light on the characters of God and Satan in his *Gospel*. They can be taken to symbolize the capitalist and communist systems. Such an identification would help to explain the multiplicity of deities mentioned in *Gospel*; they do not represent different deities so much as different ideologies, which may or may not be religious.[51] Capitalism and communism are well cast as siblings because they are both ideological progeny of the Jewish-Christian tradition.

Communism, which is often held in the West to be demonic because of its disdain for religion, reveals itself instead to contain a deeply humanistic concern for the well-being of people and animals.[52] In *Gospel*, the natural world belongs to all. Pastor is made to protest, "No, I'm not the owner, nothing in this world belongs to me" (190). Nevertheless, he still acts responsibly as its steward, just as he consistently watches over Jesus, even though Jesus is not his son. Pastor's "gospel" is not about accruing wealth or power, but precisely about shaping humane circumstances for humans and their fellow creatures. It is not calculated to pander to the interests of a small powerful elite, but to the needs of the whole.

Such, for instance, is the policy pursued by Pastor in his treatment of his flock. He shears the sheep to stop them from suffocating in the heat, not to sell their wool, and he does not sell their milk or cheese but only takes enough to satisfy his requirements. He never sells off the young animals to be sacrificial victims, even when they would fetch high prices. Every animal is considered valuable for its own sake, and Pastor takes care not to lose a single one or to leave the flock untended.[53] The only animals he does kill are the old and sick, when their debility endangers the well-being of the other, healthy animals. Under his nurturing hand the flock flourishes and becomes immense, but he does not profit from it. He does not own the flock, nor was he appointed its shepherd; he simply assumed the role because the animals needed to be protected from thieves. In effect, he does just what a servant or slave would do, except that he remains accountable only to himself (189–90, 246).

If these features are translated into political policy, then Pastor and his microcosm represent a system that is entirely structured around the well-being of the people as a whole. No members of the citizen body are exploited for the benefit of the few, even if these few are in positions of leadership. Rather, those in leadership roles are entirely beholden to those whom they protect, and they embody the Marxist ideal: "From each according to his ability, to each according to his needs."[54]

Gospel offers a further glimpse into a "Pastor-al" system, in its description of an alternative world, a demonic replication of God's creation that is "a perfect image and likeness of the one we live in" (195), the only difference being that when the devil created his man and woman he forbade them nothing.[55] Because nothing was forbidden, there was no original sin, and "because there was no original sin, there was no other kind of sin either" (195).[56] No sin would mean a world devoid of inherited guilt and responsibility, the very scourges that ceaselessly afflict Saramago's Jesus. In his Nobel lecture, Saramago remarked that Jesus, who inherits "the dusty sandals with which his father had walked so many country roads, will also inherit his tragic sense of responsibility and guilt that will never abandon him."[57] Saramago concludes this observation by quoting directly from his own temple dialogue between Jesus and a scribe: "Guilt is a wolf that eats its cub after having devoured its father, The wolf of which you speak has already devoured my father, Then it will be soon your turn, And what about you, have you ever been devoured, Not only devoured, but also spewed up."[58] Pastor's world, however, contains none of this ideological cannibalism. It is frankly utopian—a return to Eden, but to an Eden without God or serpent and the destructive ideologies they represent.

God, by contrast, is the classic exponent of a destructive ideology, one representing exploitation in its most virulent form—that of a rapacious capitalism. For Saramago, the roots of capitalism reach deep into the heart of the Christian religion, since the dominant ethos of Christianity is constructed, like that of many ancient religions, on notions of payment and exchange.[59] God's covenant is predicated, as he tells Jesus, on sacrificial payment, which is why he is so keen to have Jesus accede to his will. Once Jesus has entered into the agreement, God can demand payment: "The lamb was Mine and you took it from Me, now you will *recompense* Me with the sheep . . . or there will be no covenant" (221; my italics). As Saramago well knows, the notion of redemption—the "buying back" of the believer—that in traditional Christian theology is supposed to ensue from Jesus' saving death, is largely derived from the terminology of the slave trade.[60] Humans are commodities that can be bought and sold, not only at the slave market but in the religious sphere as well. Once they are commodified, they become dispensable; their death becomes meaningful only in terms of the debit column—their red blood transmuted to the red ink of the balance sheet.

And why does Saramago's God want to create the Christian religion? Simply because he is after market share; he is in competition with other gods for the allegiance of consumers. His Jewish adherents were incapable of satisfying his desires because, as Jesus rightly recognizes, they were too small a group: "He wants the entire world for Himself" (368). To accomplish this end he needs to oust all other gods and compel Jesus to die a martyr's death, one that will serve as an advertisement for his new religion. He says as much to Jesus:

> My son, man is a piece of wood that can be used for anything. . . . You will be the spoon I dip into humanity and bring out filled with people who believe in the new God I intend to become. Filled with people you will eat. There's no need for Me to eat those who eat themselves. (313)

Jesus, therefore, like all humans in God's perspective, is simply a tool—a means to an end to be exploited to the full. And, as becomes clear from Saramago's abecedary of saints and Jesus' vision of the future of Christianity, this type of exploitation does not come to an end with Jesus' death; rather, it endures to this day. God's adherents have continued to devour each other in the name of orthodoxy, in the name of conquest on behalf of the one true religion, and in the name of the strictures God has ostensibly imposed upon his people. The absolute claims of Christianity are used both wittingly and unwittingly by its adherents to oppress, exploit, and narcotize the people who believe them. At bottom, these claims are no different from conventional political propaganda. As Saramago's narrator ruefully observes, "Under this symbol [i.e., "SPQR"] and that flag, men go forth to kill one another, and the same can be said of those other well-known initials, INRI" (118–19).

It is evident, therefore, that it is not simply the latent commodification of human beings that perturbs Saramago, but also the implicit disregard for human life that he sees as being intrinsic to Christianity and the Scriptures. Here the sacrifice of the innocents, in particular, assumes paradigmatic importance for him.[61] Matthew's Gospel relates that God warns Joseph in a dream to take Jesus to Egypt to save him from the wrath of Herod (Matt 2:13–18). Why does God not protect the other innocent children as well, instead of allowing them to be slaughtered? By the Gospel's own account, it is Jesus' very advent that precipitates the massacre of all the innocent children of Bethlehem. Almost immediately, the good news devolves into virulently bad news. For Saramago this episode is far from unique; in fact, he regards such a juxtaposition as entirely characteristic of the doctrines of Christianity: "Millions of people have been sacrificed for a doctrine which is its opposite, a doctrine that promised and still continues to promise forgiveness, love and compassion."[62] Clearly, despite its claims otherwise, he believes Christianity fails to deliver what it promises. Here Saramago surpasses Nietzsche's charge that "the church participates in the triumph of the antichrist no less than the modern state and modern nationalism. . . . The church is the barbarizing of Christendom."[63]

Thus, for Saramago the choice between the above two figures and systems is obvious: he advocates an informed humanism that consciously rejects the destructive ideologies that have become entrenched in the modern world and that are supported by self-serving, capitalistic, and religious elites. As Lyris Wiedemann rightly and tellingly observes, Saramago "is merciless in his criticism of institutions that have based their power on the manipulation of man through the idea of sin, guilt, and the negation, or deformation, of man's true nature."[64]

Jesus and Saramago's *Vita Jesu*

The foregoing interpretation helps to elucidate how Jesus is characterized in the novel. The ways in which Saramago recasts the traditional plot(s) of the Gospels become determinative for his construction of Jesus' character. Jesus is represented as being poised between two competing ideologies, one that has been societally sanctioned and to which he unthinkingly conforms, and another that has been proscribed by society but that commends itself for its humanity. Compelled to choose between the two, he is led by his conditioning to make the wrong choice—with tragic and irreversible consequences for him. That Jesus makes the wrong choice stresses his fallibility and humanity.

As with many fictional portrayals of Jesus, Saramago is concerned with the humanizing of Jesus.[65] In making this construction, he especially emphasizes Jesus' affinities with Adam.[66] Of course, Jesus' association with Adam is at least as old as Paul (cf. Rom 5:12–21), but instead of making him a sinless second Adam as Paul does, Saramago shows him to be fallible, ignorant, and sinful. To develop these traits he conflates aspects of the Eden narrative (Gen. 3:1–24) with the traditions of Jesus' temptation in the wilderness (cf. Matt. 4:1–11; Mark 1:12–13; Luke 4:1–13). Jesus leaves Pastor and recapitulates the experience of Adam:

> He confronted the desert in his bare feet, like Adam expelled from Eden, and like Adam he hesitated before taking his first painful step across the tortured earth that beckoned him. But then, without asking himself why he did it, perhaps in memory of Adam, he dropped his pack and crook, and lifting his tunic by the hem pulled it over his head to stand as naked as Adam himself. (219)

Jesus then encounters God in the desert, who demands the sacrifice of the lost sheep for which Jesus had been searching.[67] Saramago constructs this episode as a temptation narrative.[68] Instead of Jesus being tempted in the wilderness by Satan, as happens in the canonical Gospels, he is tempted here by God, who makes him the standard diabolical offer: "I will give you power and glory" (220–21; 312).[69] Like Adam, and unlike the Jesus of the Gospels, Saramago's Jesus yields to the temptation. When he tries to return to Pastor, he is cast out from his presence: "Pastor drew a line on the ground, a furrow deep as a pit, insurmountable as a wall of fire, then told him, You've learned nothing, begone with you" (222).[70] This expulsion from Pastor's symbolic Eden is followed, as Adam's is often represented to be, by a profound sense of loss and grief (225).[71] And just as Adam's expulsion meant that he was now fated to die, the same holds true for Saramago's Jesus. By bowing to the authority of God and agreeing to sacrifice the lost sheep, he guarantees his own upcoming role as a sacrificial victim. Jesus' disregard for the creation has ensured that it will continue to be "subjected to futility" and remain in "bondage to decay" (Rom 8:20–21). His bleeding feet with their Fisher King-like trail of blood anticipate the rivers of blood yet to flow (223, 225). Jesus' failure, therefore, demonstrates his solidarity with the first Adam and his lack of resemblance to the Christ of the Gospels.

The association with Adam is also calculated to make Jesus into an archetypal human, a cipher for everyman. Jesus' ultimate victimization and enslavement to the social forces that God represents make him a symbol of the proletariat, the oppressed masses, who are unable to extricate themselves from the ideological coils of Christian capitalism. Yet, just as surely, Jesus' own victimization is calculated to point to a solution. By making his readers identify with Jesus' plight, Saramago brings them to consider what Jesus' mistakes were and how they could have been avoided. If Jesus had only acknowledged Pastor and his ideology, millennia of suffering could have been avoided. It remains open for *Gospel*'s readers to make the decision that Jesus did not make and to reject the tyranny of Christian dogma. In its way, therefore, the novel serves as an evangel for the humanistic communism Saramago espouses.

The consequence of making Jesus a cipher for everyman, however, is that Jesus loses many of the qualities that make him such a distinctive figure. Harold Bloom maintains that "the glory of Saramago's *Gospel* is Saramago's Jesus, who seems to me humanly and aesthetically more admirable than any other version of Jesus in the literature of the century now ending. . . . Saramago's Jesus paradoxically is the novelist's warmest and most memorable character of any of his books."[72] This may be so, but perhaps one of the reasons Bloom finds Jesus' character so attractive is because it bears such scant similarities with the character depicted in the canonical Gospels.[73] Despite its retention of many of the episodes derived from the canonical Gospels, Saramago's *Gospel* leaches out many of the recognizable features from the figure of Jesus. Saramago's Jesus is in a variety of respects not merely a pale Galilean but a positively anemic one whose character is highly unfamiliar. When one compares the traits of Jesus as depicted in the canonical—and even many of the noncanonical—Gospels with those in Saramago's *Gospel*, they emerge as virtual antinomies.[74]

While it is beyond the scope of this essay to consider the characterization of Jesus in its entirety, a representative example should suffice. If one examines Jesus' role as teacher in the Gospels, for instance, Jesus is portrayed as the teacher par excellence.[75] He teaches with authority (Matt 7:29), and such is his *exousia* and understanding of God's purposes that he is able to pronounce definitively on the law (Matt 5:17–48). Yet in Saramago's *Gospel* he is continually at a loss and is constrained to quiz Pastor, God, and Mary Magdalene to try to make sense of the world around him. In fact, *Gospel* does not even characterize Jesus as a teacher; instead, Pastor and Mary Magdalene are Jesus' teachers. Pastor tries to teach Jesus, but fails, and after training Jesus for four years, he sends him on his way with the reproach "You've learned nothing" (222). As for Mary Magdalene, Jesus says to her, "There is nothing I can teach you, only what I learned from you. Teach me, so that I may know what it is like to learn from you" (238). When in the closing pages of the novel Jesus turns to John the Baptist in an attempt to find out just what is expected of the Messiah, he is bluntly told to find out for himself (356).

The foregoing examples suggest that Saramago's Jesus is profoundly deficient in understanding, both of his own identity and the dynamics of the world around him. This state of affairs is in stark contrast to the four Gospels, particularly the Gospel of John, which uniformly portray a Jesus who is fully aware of who he is and who is secure in his relationship with God: "I know where I have come from and where I am going, but you do not know. . . . I testify on my own behalf, and the Father who sent me testifies on my behalf" (John 8:14–18). As this passage demonstrates, the problem that Jesus has to face is a profound ignorance on the part of those around him, be it the Jewish people, their leaders, or even his own disciples. Saramago's Jesus, by contrast, appears to be immured in a world where he is the naïf and where everyone is much better informed than he. Indeed, as with the victims tortured on "the device" in Franz Kafka's "In the Penal Colony," he only obtains illumination moments before he dies.[76] Bloom rightly observes that "Jesus' education as to God's nature will be completed only on the cross."[77] But as the quintessential victim, this Jesus has no control over the events unfolding around him. Instead of constraining the wheel of world history to move forward, as Schweitzer has famously described Jesus' endeavor, Saramago's Jesus simply becomes enmeshed in the cogs, his understanding being insufficient to change his destiny or to outwit God.[78]

The consequence of this type of characterization is that Saramago's Jesus is ultimately unconvincing in the guise of Jesus. He is certainly engaging and likeable, but hardly the inspiration for the emergence of a major world religion. None of the mystery or *auctoritas* of the dominical Jesus is apparent. On the very rare occasions, for instance, when Saramago does attempt to introduce an element of authority in Jesus' demeanor, it appears startlingly incongruous. The narrative of the cleansing of the temple is a case in point. In recounting the episode, Saramago is compelled to acknowledge that his Jesus' behavior is simply inexplicable:

> The disciples were not accustomed to being spoken to in this way or to seeing his face so severe, he was no longer the gentle, tranquil Jesus they knew, who went wherever God wished without a murmur of complaint. This change had been brought about by circumstances unknown. (357)

The disciples are not accustomed to this type of behavior and nor, may it be added, are Saramago's readers. Here he resorts to the time-honored contrivance of the *deus ex machina*—namely, "circumstances unknown"—to explain the anomalous behavior of his Jesus. The episode—one of the few that is specifically recounted by all four canonical Gospels (Matt. 12:12–13; Mark 11:15–19; Luke 19:45–46; John 2:13–17)—is then quickly passed over.[79]

One of the defining features of Saramago's Jesus, therefore, is his scant resemblance to the presentations of Jesus in the Gospels. Although the process is less dramatic, his Jesus undergoes the same type of distortion that characterizes the novel's portrayals of God and Satan. The consequence of this portrayal, however, is that as a kind of serious *Vita Jesu*, Saramago's *Gospel* is largely unsuccessful.

The reason for its want of success is quite simple. It is, arguably, not Saramago's intention to construct a standard Life of Jesus, and those who would wish to interpret his novel in that light actually misrepresent the work. Rather, the events and settings of the Gospels are used to provide a convincing costume for the very different figure that lies beneath them, and the lineaments of this passive and victimized everyman function as a foil to highlight the characters of God and Satan and the systems they enshrine. Ultimately, for Saramago, the historical figure of Jesus is irrelevant to the larger ideological conflicts that these two characters represent.

NOTES

1. The English word "gospel" is derived from the Old English *gÿd*, "good," and *spel*, "news." Similarly, our word "evangel" is derived the Greek *eu*, "good," and *aggelion*, "message," and also means "good news." *Badspel* (my neologism) and *Kakaggelion*, by contrast, mean "evil tidings" or "bad news."

2. For images of Saramago's God devouring his followers, see J. Saramago, *The Gospel according to Jesus Christ*, trans. G. Pontiero (New York: Harcourt Brace, 1994), 313. Hereafter, I will refer to this work as *Gospel* and will cite passages from the English translation in parentheses. Because I am unable to read Portuguese, I have been constrained to base my analysis on Pontiero's translation.

3. H. Bloom, *Genius: A Mosaic of One Hundred Exemplary Creative Minds* (New York: Warner, 2002), 11.

4. See *International Who's Who 2005: Authors and Writers* (20th ed.; London: Europa Publications, 2005), 527; C. C. Tesser, ed., "A Tribute to José Saramago, 1998 Nobel Literature Laureate," *Hispania* 82 (1999): 1–2. His Nobel lecture contains an engaging account of his impoverished upbringing: J. Saramago, T. Crosfield, and F. Rodrigues, "The 1998 Nobel Lecture," *World Literature Today*, vol. 73 (1999): 5–10.

5. Tesser, "Tribute to José Saramago," 1.

6. See the bibliography in Tesser, "Tribute to José Saramago," 2, as well as the surveys of his major works offered by a series of scholars in the same article.

7. For a detailed listing of his prizes, see *Who's Who 2005*, 527.

8. For a discussion of some of the early responses to the work, see D. G. Frier, "José Saramago's *O Evangelho Segundo Jesus Cristo*: Outline of a Newer Testament," *Modern Language Review* 100 (2005): 368.

9. H. Bloom, "The One with the Beard Is God, the Other Is the Devil," *Portuguese Literary and Cultural Studies* 6 (2001): 155.

10. See Frier, "José Saramago's *O Evangelho Segundo Jesus Cristo*," 368.

11. Saramago says in one interview, "I'm an atheist but I've got a Christian mentality. My values, my morality and customs are all impregnated with Catholicism" (B. Halton, "Listen Carefully," *SouthCoast Today*, January 3, 1999, http://www.s-t.com/daily/01-99/01-03-99/e05ae172.htm (accessed March 7, 2005).

12. Saramago et al., "1998 Nobel Lecture."

13. The word "heretical" is derived from the Greek word *hairey̆*, meaning "I choose." Saramago may simply mean that he has availed himself of this possibility.

14. Z. Ben-Porat ("Saramago's *Gospel* and the poetics of prototypical rewriting," *Journal of Romance Studies* 3 [2003]: 104#7) rightly points out that the "direct appeal to the Gospels distinguishes Saramago's rewrite from most other fictional biographies of Christ."

15. Some critics maintain that it is not Pastor but God who visits Mary; see, for instance, Bloom, "One with the Beard," 163.

16. *Protevangelium of James*, 17–21.

17. Jesus' fashioning birds out of mud for Thomas (*Gospel* 336–37) has obvious parallels with the *Infancy Gospel of Thomas* 2:1–5. Saramago is also familiar with the standard martyrologies of the twelve disciples (*Gospel*, 320–21, 337), and his puckish, four-page, abecedary of martyred saints from Adalbert of Prague to Wilgefortis, "the bearded virgin crucified" (*Gospel*, 321–25), displays more than a little acquaintance with various versions of the lives of the saints.

18. The depiction of Mary as Jesus' confidante and lover seems to owe much to the *Gnostic Gospel of Philip* 28, 48. Cf. *Gospel of Thomas* 21, and E. de Boer, *Mary Magdalene: Beyond the Myth* (Harrisburg, PA: Trinity Press International, 1997), 58–73.

19. The bowl motif serves as a symbol for Jesus himself. At the time of the annunciation, the bowl contains glowing earth, while at Jesus' death the same bowl is used to collect his blood as he dies on the cross. It effectively illustrates how the original religious impulse is ultimately distilled into violence.

20. The metaphor of God as the potter and humans as his pottery underlies Isa 29:16; 45:9; Jer 18:1–11; Sir 33:10–13; and Rom 9:19–24. On Gnostic understandings of divine light,

see, inter alia, *Book of Thomas the Contender* 138:20–30; *Apocryphon of John* 3:17; 4:1, and especially 6:13, where Jesus is described as "a luminous spark consisting of light in an image that was blessed." The *Gnostic Gospel of Philip* 44 distinguishes ceramics (pottery) from glass on the following basis: "Glass and ceramic vessels are produced with fire, but if glass vessels break they are remade, since they have been produced by means of blown air [spirit] while if ceramic vessels break they perish, since they have been produced without blowing." Both translations are from B. Layton, *The Gnostic Scriptures: A New Translation with Annotations and Introductions* (New York: Doubleday, 1987), 338.

21. For an assessment of Renan's influence, see W. Baird, *History of New Testament Research*, vol. 1, *From Deism to Tübingen* (Minneapolis: Fortress, 1992), 375–84. H. Kaufman ("Evangelical Truths: José Saramago on the Life of Christ," *Revista Hispánica Moderna* 47 [1994]: 450–52) makes a similar point about Renan and also hints at the influence of D. F. Strauss's *Das Leben Jesu.*

22. A. Schweitzer, *The Quest for the Historical Jesus*, trans. W. Montgomery (New York: Macmillan, 1968), 181.

23. ET, E. Renan, *The Life of Jesus* (London: Trübner & Co., 1865), 76; cf. Renan, *Vie de Jésus* (Paris: Calmann-Lévy, 1863), 125.

24. A. Klobucka, "An Interview with Nobel Prize-Winning Portuguese Novelist José Saramago," *Mass Humanities* (Spring 2002), http://www.mfh.org/newsandevents/newsletter/Mass Humanities/Spring2002/interview.html (accessed May 30, 2005).

25. J. Pires-O'Brien, "A Novel View of the Gospels," *Contemporary Review*, 274, no. 1599 (1999): 187–91.

26. Halton, "Listen Carefully."

27. See, in particular, W. H. Kelber, *The Oral and the Written Gospel* (Philadelphia: Fortress, 1983); and cf. L. Weidemann, "Saramago, José: *O Evangelho Segundo Jesus Cristo*" in Tesser, "Tribute to José Saramago," 24.

28. O. Grossegesse ("José Saramago: *O Evangelho Segundo Jesus Cristo* [1991]," in *Portugiesische Romane der Gegenwart: neue Interpretationen*, ed. R. Hess [ed.] [Frankfurt am Main: TMF/Domus Editoria Europaea, 1993], 126) rightly observes that this "entseht der Eindruck einer geradezu naiven *re-écriture.*"

29. Saramago regularly acknowledges his close connection with his work and the characters therein: "The author is in the book, the author is the book"; see J. Saramago, "Is It Time to Return to the Author? Between Omniscient Narrator and Interior Monologue," trans. R. Deltcheva, *CLCWeb: Comparative Literature and Culture: A WWWeb Journal*, September 2000, http://clcwebjournal.lib.purdue.edu/clcweb00-3/saramago00.html (accessed June 30, 2005).

30. The same could be said for films about Jesus, with Monty Python's *Life of Brian* being a notable exception.

31. On the liar's paradox, cf. T. Honderich, ed., *The Oxford Companion to Philosophy* (Oxford: Oxford University Press, 1995), 483.

32. Anachronisms further contribute to the ridiculous tone. The narrator remarks, "Tomorrow is another day is a well-known saying," and it is, at least to someone who has seen *Gone with the Wind.* Cf. Grossegesse, "José Saramago," 125.

33. On Saramago's use of parody, see H. Costa, "The Fundamental Re-Writing: Religious Texts and Contemporary Narrative (Gore Vidal's *Live from Golgotha*; Salman Rushdie's *The Satanic Verses*, José Saramago's *O Evangelho Segundo Jesus Cristo*)," *Daedalus* 6 (1996): 250. For recent discussions of the meaning and genre of gospels, see R. A. Burridge, *What Are the Gospels? A Comparison with Graeco-Roman Biography*, 2nd ed. (Grand Rapids: Eerdmans, 2004); and H. Koester, *Ancient Christian Gospels: Their History and Development* (London: SCM Press; Philadelphia: Trinity Press International, 1990).

34. By satire I mean "a mode of discourse or vision that asserts a polemical or critical out-look" (A. Preminger and T. V. F. Brogan, eds., *The New Princeton Encyclopedia of Poetry and Poetics* [Princeton, NJ: Princeton University Press, 1993], s.v. "Satire," 1114). As I hope to show, Saramago's satire employs a critical humanism informed by communism to skewer the foibles and excesses of Christianity. On the close relation of satire to irony, see W. C. Booth, *A Rhetoric of Irony* (Chicago: University of Chicago Press, 1974), 27–31.

35. The canonical Gospels cannot properly be said to be tragic; while they undeniably recount Jesus' passion, their inclusion of his resurrection ultimately makes them comic. Cf. N. Frye, *The Great Code: The Bible and Literature* (London: Routledge & Kegan Paul, 1982), 169–76.

36. Contemporary critical discussion has focused on the process of "rewriting" involved in crafting a Gospel; see, for instance, Ben-Porat, "Saramago's *Gospel* and the Poetics," 93–105; Costa, "Fundamental Re-Writing," 245–53; J. F. Duarte, "What Is It That Saramago Is Doing in *The Gospel according to Jesus Christ*? Rewriting the Gospels into Genre," in *Proceedings of the 17th Triennial Congress of the International Comparative Literature Association, August 8–15, 2004, in Hong Kong,* http://jupiter.ln.edu.hk/eng/staff/eoyang/icla/icla_menu.html (accessed February 7, 2005).

37. Frier ("José Saramago's *O Evangelho Segundo Jesus Cristo*," 375) comes close to this realization: "This depiction of the traditional representations of Good and Evil thus rejects—if it does not actually invert—the Manichaean polar opposites of Christian tradition."

38. I understand *subversion* to denote "the articulation or 'becoming visible' of any repressed, forbidden or oppositional interpretations of the social order" (I. R. Makaryk, ed., *Encyclopedia of Contemporary Literary Theory: Approaches, Scholars, Terms* [Toronto: University of Toronto Press, 1993], 636). Here, as I hope to demonstrate, Saramago offers an "oppositional interpretation" to Christian capitalism.

39. Grossegesse ("José Saramago," 124) also comments on the subversive nature of Saramago's enterprise. Drawing on Bakhtin's observations about *parodia sacra,* he notes that its central feature is chiasmus, involving the deliberate juxtaposition of categories such as truth and lies, body and soul, and God and the Devil (127).

40. Satan remarks, "If you insist on giving me a name, call me Pastor" (*Gospel,* 187). For a detailed discussion of the pastoral motif in the Bible, see J. R. C Cousland, *The Crowds in the Gospel of Matthew,* (Novum Testamentum Supplements 102 (Leiden: Brill, 2002), 86–93, 120–22, 169–71; B. Willmes, *Die sogenannte Hirtenallegorie Ez 34: Studien zum Bild des Hirten im Alten Testament* (Frankfurt: Peter Lang, 1984).

41. Compare Pastor's lament "I have nowhere to rest my head" (*Gospel,* 17) with Matt 8:20 // Luke 9:58.

42. Pastor is present at Jesus' birth as one of the shepherds (*Gospel,* 59).

43. Cf. Hos 6:6: "For I desire steadfast love and not sacrifice, the knowledge of God rather than burnt offerings."

44. The text actually says that it is "an elderly man with a long white beard" who gives Jesus the lamb, and adds that before Jesus could thank him, "he was gone, then suddenly the road was mysteriously empty" (*Gospel,* 207). This description makes it highly likely that God is in view. God later says to Jesus about this lamb, "The lamb was Mine and you took it from Me" (*Gospel,* 221).

45. This equation is made explicit when Jesus remarks, "If I save this lamb, it's so that someone may save me" (*Gospel,* 211).

46. Joseph himself dreams of killing Jesus in the guise of one of Herod's soldiers sent out to sacrifice the innocents (*Gospel,* 112), but this is likely a manifestation of his guilt for allowing the deaths of the other children.

47. On the Akedah, see *Gospel*, 213, 266. On the Akedah's place in Judaism and Christianity, see J. D. Levenson, *The Death and Resurrection of the Beloved Son: The Transformation of Child Sacrifice in Judaism and Christianity* (New Haven, CT: Yale University Press, 1993).

48. Whether Saramago intends the reader to think of passages such as Deut 18:10 is unclear.

49. On Marcion, see, most recently, P. Lampe, *From Paul to Valentinus: Christians at Rome in the First Two Centuries*, trans. M. Steinhauser (Minneapolis: Fortress, 2003), 241–56; for the Gnostics, cf. Layton, *Gnostic Scriptures*, 12–18.

50. Klobucka, "Interview." The Marx and Engels quotation is from *The Holy Family*.

51. On the plurality of gods, see *Gospel*, 312–13. The mysterious god who speaks while God, Pastor, and Jesus are in the boat has been identified by Frier as a Spinozan deity ("Newer Testament," 372#19). While his suggestion is intriguing, it may simply be that Saramago wants to emphasize the plurality of belief systems available to humans.

52. Saramago is hardly unaware of the barbarities committed by proponents of Communism, but would seemingly impute them to the human condition: "There is probably no difference between the negative things done in the name of communism and everything that the human being has done throughout history in the name of best intentions" (quoted in L. Calder, "The Militant Magician," *Guardian*, December 28, 2002, http://books.guardian.co.uk/departments/generalfiction/story/0,6000,865566,00.html [accessed June 30, 2005]).

53. See *Gospel*, 187. Cf. *Gospel*, 213: If the devil's "power saved this lamb, then something has been gained in the world today."

54. K. Marx, "Critique of the Gotha Programme," in *Selected Works in Two Volumes*, by K. Marx and F. Engels (Moscow: Foreign Languages Publishing House, 1955), 2:24.

55. Presumably this would include the sexual commerce with sheep that Pastor proposes to a shocked Jesus (*Gospel*, 197–98). But it is likely that Saramago is being deliberately provocative here and that he is more concerned to critique the failure of the conservative Catholic Church in Portugal to come to terms with human sexuality. See Frier, "Newer Testament," 376#31.

56. Pastor asserts, "I don't recall having invented sin and punishment or the terror they inspire" (*Gospel*, 325–26). On sin and the law, see Paul's observations at Rom 5:18–21.

57. Saramago et al., "1998 Nobel Lecture."

58. Ibid.; cf. *Gospel*, 175.

59. W. Burkert (*The Creation of the Sacred: Tracks of Biology in Early Religions* [Cambridge, MA: Harvard University Press, 1996], 136–37) relates that "the religious attitude so openly expressed over and over again has been characterized as . . . the principle of *do ut des:* 'I give in order that you shall give' . . . We even find the explicit term of 'loan' or 'investment.'"

60. F. Büchsel, "*lutron*, etc." in *Theological Dictionary of the New Testament*, ed. G. Kittel (Grand Rapids: Eerdmans, 1967), 4:340–72. For a seminal discussion of various interpretations of the atonement, see G. Aulén, *Christus Victor: An Historical Study of the Three Main Types of the Idea of the Atonement* (London: SPCK, 1931).

61. See the fuller discussion in Saramago et al., "1998 Nobel Lecture."

62. Cited in Calder, "Militant Magician."

63. F. Nietzsche, *Nietzsches Werke in zwei Banden* (Salzburg: Das Bergland-Buch, 1952), 1:763. Translation mine.

64. Weidemann, "Saramago, José: *O Evangelho Segundo Jesus Cristo*," 25.

65. On Saramago's Christology, see M. Boero, "La cristología de José Saramago," *Cuadernos Hispanoamericanos* 528 (1994): 134–37. Boero detects Nestorian and adoptionistic tendencies within the novel.

66. For references to Adam, see *Gospel*, 6, 20.

67. This passage displays an intriguing echo of Renan's description of Jesus' temptation: "But the God he found in the desert was not his God. It was rather the God of Job, severe and terrible, accountable to no one" (Life of *Jesus*, 78).

68. Ben-Porat ("Saramago's *Gospel* and the Poetics," 100) would include Jesus' sojourn with Pastor as part of the rewritten temptation narrative, but her inference is probably mistaken. Pastor does not seek Jesus' adoration, nor does he tempt Jesus with "power and glory."

69. Earthly power and glory are Satan's perquisites in the Gospels. The remarks of S. Garrett (*The Demise of the Devil: Magic and the Demonic in Luke's Writings* [Minneapolis: Fortress, 1989], 41), for instance, are representative: "In the narrative world of Luke's Gospel, Satan genuinely does possess the authority and glory of the kingdoms of the world."

70. Cf. *Gospel*, 224–25. The "wall of fire" is meant to advert to the cherub with a flaming sword preventing Adam and Eve from returning to Eden (Gen 3:24).

71. While Genesis does not itself mention Adam's grief, it becomes a common feature of later traditions and is at least as early as the *Life* of Adam and Eve (cf. 1:1 and *Apocalypse of Moses* 29:7).

72. Bloom, "One with the Beard," 162.

73. One is reminded, *mutatis mutandis*, of Caroline's remarks about balls in *Pride and Prejudice*: "I should like balls infinitely better . . . if they were carried on in a different manner; but there is something insufferably tedious in the usual process of such a meeting. It would surely be much more rational if conversation instead of dancing were made the order of the day." Bingley replies, "Much more rational, my dear Caroline, I dare say, but it would not be near so much like a ball."

74. For a very instructive comparison of Jesus' traits according to orthodox Christianity and those posited by Saramago, see O. J. Esqueda, "El Jesús de Endo y Saramago: La cristología de *Jesús* y *El evangelio según Jesucristo*," *Kairos* 31 (2002): 95–97.

75. The point hardly needs belaboring. Among the profusion of works devoted to Jesus as teacher, see R. Riesner, *Jesus als Lehrer: Eine Untersuchung zum Ursprung der Evangelien-Überlieferung*, 3rd ed., Wissenschaftliche Untersuchungen zum Neuen Testament 2/7 (Tübingen: Mohr, 1988); J. Yueh-Han Yieh, *One Teacher: Jesus' Teaching Role in Matthew's Gospel Report*, Beihefte zur Zeitschrift für die neutestamentliche Wissenschaft 124 (Berlin: Walter de Gruyter, 2004).

76. See F. Kafka, "In the Penal Colony," in *Stories 1904–1924*, trans. J. A. Underwood (London: Abacus, 1995), 163–64: "Ah, and then came the sixth hour! . . . The way we all took in the look of enlightenment on the tortured face." Kafka's reference to the "sixth hour" intimates that the crucifixion narratives are part of his subtext.

77. Bloom, "One with the Beard," 158.

78. Schweitzer's Jesus "lays hold of the wheel of the world to set it moving on that last revolution which is to bring all ordinary history to a close. It refuses to turn, and He throws Himself upon it. Then it does turn; and crushes Him. Instead of bringing in the eschatological conditions, He has destroyed them. The wheel rolls onward, and the mangled body of the one immeasurably great Man, who was strong enough to think of Himself as the spiritual ruler of mankind and to bend history to His purpose, is hanging upon it still. That is His victory and His reign" (Schweitzer, *Quest of the Historical Jesus*, 370–71).

79. For the centrality of the cleansing of the temple episode to reconstructions of the historical Jesus, see E. P. Sanders, *Jesus and Judaism* (Philadelphia: Fortress, 1985), 61–76.

4 | *The Master and Margarita* and Bulgakov's Antiauthoritarian Jesus

KATHERINE SIRLUCK

Mikhail Bulgakov's novel *The Master and Margarita* is densely interwoven with other literary and nonliterary texts, from Dante's *Inferno* to Goethe's *Faust*. The characterizations of both Jesus and the devil, and the detailing of events surrounding both, are richly fleshed out by borrowings from other texts. Yet at the novel's heart is a representation of Jesus that is paradoxically antitextual and experiential. The dynamic between the "fictional" and the "real" is central to Bulgakov's thesis. Within his narrative the figure of Jesus (with one notable exception) is encountered directly only in dreams, in the pages of an unfinished novel,[1] and in an account delivered by the Father of Lies. While this may have something to do with Bulgakov's need to navigate the channels of Soviet censorship, its primary causes lie deeper.[2] It may seem contradictory that the reliability of the narrative representation of Jesus is repeatedly called into question (it is only a dream, or the devil is the speaker, or it is a work of fiction) when Bulgakov's purpose is not only to publish his faith but also to assert the historical reality of Jesus. Bulgakov simultaneously undermines the *authority* of representation itself while endowing his Jesus with a hyperreality that somehow supersedes all the limits of representation. In other words, the Jesus of Bulgakov's text both exceeds and differs from all authorized textual accounts—such as the Gospels—and exists as a real and vital person in spite of the dubious veracity of the narrative "sources." Bulgakov is playing a complicated game for high stakes.

In the orthodox versions of the life of Christ, Jesus had many disciples. In this novel, Yeshua's only disciple and frequent companion is Matthu the Levite, who, though passionately devoted to Yeshua, doesn't understand him. He follows Yeshua everywhere, scribbling down his words in order to preserve them, but as Yeshua tells Pilate, he gets it all wrong. The Gospels as we know them, Bulgakov insists, are a garbled and inaccurate version of Jesus' ideas. There is no authoritative text for Christianity. There is imagination and the yearning toward goodness that is innate in the human. Above all there is love. According to Bulgakov, Jesus' central idea is that all men and women are good. This means that one of the fundamental doctrines of the Christian church—the doctrine of original sin, leading to the doctrine of innate depravity—is contrary to Jesus' true meaning. Yeshua must be killed for the same reason that the Master's book must be suppressed: because both are opposed to authority and undermine authority's illusion of infallibility. According to Bulgakov's Yeshua, all human authority is first or finally coercive, violating human freedom.

In this Bulgakov follows the example of John Milton's *Paradise Lost*, which posits the prime importance of human moral freedom as the reason underlying the existence of evil in God's divinely ordered universe. Without the possibility of choosing either good or evil, humans are not free; not free, we are neither moral nor responsible beings. Quite simply, we are not fully human without liberty of moral choice. Thus, instead of being authoritative, all true representations of Jesus are imaginative. As in the radical theology of William Blake, for Bulgakov Jesus has a life of his own in any truly creative act of the human imagination, persisting as an idea even where he is declared to be a fiction. An example of this occurs at the outset of the novel, where we encounter two figures from Moscow's literary elite sitting on a bench beside Patriarch Ponds. One of them is the proletarian poet who calls himself "Homeless," who has written (on commission) a long antireligious poem for a Soviet literary journal. The other is the journal's aggressively atheistic editor, Berlioz, who is taking "Homeless" (Ivan Nicolayevich Bezdomny) to task for the "errors" in his work:

> It is difficult to say what had tripped up Ivan Nicolayevich—his imaginative powers or complete unfamiliarity with the subject. But his Jesus turned out, well . . . altogether alive—the Jesus who had existed once upon a time, although invested, it is true, with a full range of negative characteristics.
>
> Berlioz, on the other hand, wanted to prove to the poet that the main point was not whether Jesus had been good or bad, but that he had never existed as an individual, and that all the stories about him were mere inventions, simple myths. (5)[3]

Poor Ivan has discovered that it is not safe to write about Christ at all under state-legislated atheism, for no matter what the intentions of the writer or the publisher, something about the very idea of Jesus seizes upon the imagination and generates a vitality that gives credibility to his existence, even in the work of a bad poet, even against that poet's will. Thus, on the one hand it is difficult to entirely repudiate Jesus without giving him life; on the other hand it is impossible to authoritatively represent Jesus without distorting his meaning. The Gospels themselves, as Yeshua reveals to Pilate, are full of error and seriously misrepresent what Jesus actually said. But in addition to the matter of accuracy, there is something more. The moment Jesus' words were written down by Matthu, his meaning was corrupted, hardened into "authority," and thus rendered false even on those occasions when what was transcribed was accidentally accurate. The consequence for religious truth is stunning: what is written as "gospel truth" is unreliable and even anti-Christian, in the sense that it asserts itself as authoritative and Jesus is antiauthoritarian. Only what is autonomously imagined under inspiration has spiritual validity. Thus, contrary to tradition, it is the imagination that is the agent of divine truth, the surest link to eternal reality.

Following the lead of Ernest Renan, whose *Life of Jesus* was one of his most important sources for the Yershalayim material,[4] Bulgakov makes it clear that the writings of the disciples are inaccurate and reflect their inferiority to Christ himself. Indeed, Andrew Barratt shows how Bulgakov insistently alters crucial details both of the Gospel accounts of the life of Jesus and of other serious historical accounts, in order to produce a version that differs notably from all others.[5] Jesus' followers, try as they might, could not always understand his words and acts in such a way as to avoid distorting the truth. Jesus is not something about which we can be authoritative. Thus, it cannot make sense to go to war in his name, or to condemn others for their deviation from his word.

However, this does not discredit the Gospels, any more than the fictive depiction of Jesus in the Master's novel is discredited by Yeshua's insistence that the work is unfinished. Rather, we are led to understand that all great imaginative mediations of Jesus are linked to the same luminous reality, to humankind's pursuit of goodness and truth in his image. While Matthu Levi inadvertently misrepresents Yeshua's words, he is still his heavenly emissary at the novel's conclusion. Bulgakov, under Renan's guidance, sifts through the excesses of the Jesus legend in order to produce an account that is more to his purpose than the Gospel versions. It makes Jesus less charismatic, less powerful, less magical, and more frail and human. His sole attraction—and it is breathtaking—is his goodness and his belief in the goodness of human beings of whom others have despaired.

Bulgakov's account is full of details reflecting the daily lives of the Jews and their Roman colonizers, the particularities of architecture, landscape, weather, of the markets and the cooking, the flora and the fauna—the intricate fabric of life at the time of the crucifixion. As Krugovoy and many others have noted, Bulgakov also drew upon Frederic W. Farrar's *The Life of Christ*, D. F. Strauss's *Das Leben Jesu*, and the work of Josephus Flavius. His more standard sources were, of course, the apocryphal *Gospel of Nicodemus*, the Epistles of Peter, the Gospels of Matthew, Mark, Luke, and John, the Book of Revelation, and 1 Corinthians.[6]

For Bulgakov, the crucial passage from Paul is 1 Corinthians 15:24: "Then cometh the end, when he shall have delivered up the kingdom to God, even the Father, when he shall have put down all rule, and all authority and power" (KJV). But Bulgakov's interpretation of this passage is more radical than it is orthodox, as he seems to believe that God will not only "put down" earthly power, but, as Milton has it, "[Himself] his regal scepter shalt lay by."[7] Yeshua's insistence that all authority is coercion appears to apply even to the manifestation of the divine as authority.

The Jerusalem chapters that deal with Jesus' sentencing and execution—chapters 2 and 16—reveal both Bulgakov's interest in the "historical Jesus" and his need to rework the existing materials in order to produce a new, original imaginative construct. Chapter 2 deals with Pilate's confrontation with Yeshua and his reluctant sentencing of the prisoner. One departure from tradition is that throughout the events in the chapter Satan is ubiquitous, though he is never named. His influence is manifested in Pilate's physical anguish (headaches or sudden pain in the heart in this novel always indicate demonic interference), his inexplicable impulse to shout "Hang him!" and be rid of Yeshua (22), and in his extreme fear of Tiberius. This fear takes hallucinogenic form for Pilate when a ghastly vision of Caesar's bald, gold-crowned head displaces Yeshua's own features for a moment (28). The image also suggests the degree to which the "Christ" worshipped on earth is often only Caesar in disguise. All of these details indicate that Pilate/Hegemon is under assault by demonic forces seeking to counteract the effect of Yeshua on Pilate's thoughts, character, and feelings. "What is truth?" Pilate asks Yeshua (23), and he is instantly plagued by the impulse to take poison (the impulse to commit suicide, often with poison, is another unfailing indicator in this novel of Satan's attempts to sabotage Yeshua's influence). Yeshua's answer is that the "truth is" that Pilate's head aches terribly but will soon be better; the truth is, Pilate has "lost all faith in men" (24). These truths are simple and irrefutable. They do not partake of the kind of miraculous grandeur we might be expecting in response to Pilate's query.

Pilate's headache vanishes, but this could be the power of suggestion. As for Yeshua's mysterious knowledge that Pilate is contemplating suicide, it could be just a good guess (23). Yeshua explains how he knew that Pilate was waiting to be alone with his dog, in such a way as to entirely demystify the insight. Though not a physician, he diagnoses Pilate accurately, prescribing less solitude and more faith in his fellows. Yeshua is a philosopher, but not an abstruse or a demanding one. He appears to be simply a man who has strange ideas, a man without relatives and only one follower.

> "Yeshua Ha-Nozri, do you believe in any gods?"
> "There is one God," answered Yeshua. "And I believe in Him."
> "Pray to him, then! Pray harder! However . . ." Pilate's voice dropped, "it will not help." (31)

Pilate's terrible moment of choice is presented in great detail. His yearning toward what Yeshua seems to offer—peace, understanding, goodness, freedom from despair, even immortality—is countered by his sense of the fearful oppression of his own role as procurator. He is responsible for maintaining unquestioned the absolute power of Tiberius Caesar. He is tormented by a sense of *necessity*. Yeshua has said that all authority, including Caesar's, is coercion and ought to end. Pilate must silence any voices challenging Caesar's supremacy and benevolence, or die himself. Yeshua has said "that the Temple of the old faith would fall and a new Temple of truth would arise" (23). The High Priest of Jerusalem, Kaiyapha, sees Yeshua as a threat to the temple and refuses to be intimidated by the procurator into releasing him for the Passover celebration. Instead, he demands a pardon for the Sanhedrin's own agent, the revolutionary Bar-Rabban. Yeshua has been caught in a web, with the treachery of Judas and the inflexibility of Roman law sealing his fate.

Pilate's dilemma is a paradigm of human moral choice and of the difficulty of doing the right thing here on earth, where Satan's power is strong. Pilate makes the wrong choice and will suffer torments of remorse for 12,000 moons before being freed to resume his heavenly conversation with Yeshua, as they ascend the moonlit path together. Pilate's redemption, together with Yeshua's assertion that all men and women are good, suggests strongly that Bulgakov shares Origen's unorthodox Christian belief that all sinners will ultimately be saved and that no damnation is final. How could it be, if men and women are good?

Bulgakov's portrait of Yeshua resonates with Kierkegaard's concept of faith, as he outlines it in *Fear and Trembling*. Kierkegaard insists upon the primacy and particularity of the relationship to God. No intermediary—whether church or state, family or marketplace, or even the "universal"—may interpose itself between the individual and God, to prescribe the articles of faith: "Inwardness is higher than outwardness. . . . The paradox of faith is this, that the individual is higher than the universal."[8] The correlative point as Bulgakov presents it is that authority is antipathetic to faith, as is power. Linked to this idea is the understanding that all external ratification or compulsion of faith, all "miracle," all wish fulfillment, all earthly sway, are also antithetical to faith, and to Jesus' vision. Woland, the devil, is the one associated with earthly power and compulsion; he fulfills wishes, performs dazzling acts of magic and miracle, lends earthly aid to his worshippers, and gratifies their longings. He also frightens them with punishment or death if they do not submit. He is, in a sustained sense, a parody of the cruder notions of what God is and ought to be: a sugar daddy, who answers our prayers here in this world but who can be cruel and vindictive if not obeyed. He is an earthly, not a spiritual, redeemer.

Riitta H. Pittman observes that in this novel "reality is rendered transparent through dreaming."[9] As Pilate observes, Yeshua is a dreamer, and his dreaming is a way of transcending the limits of empirical reality, the realm of shadows that belongs to Woland. In practice, authority and indeed consensual reality destroy our belief that any ideal form of truth is realizable. In Bulgakov's view, Yeshua represents the truth of our radical liberty, and thus he is a threat to the assertion of necessity that is every tyrant's plea and every coward's excuse.

Woland exists because evil must be possible; Yeshua exists so that good remains believable. For Bulgakov, to despair of humanity, or to despair of the good, is to renounce freedom. Rome and Stalin's Russia are golden dragons whose scales shine with the accumulation of false values, false limits, and false gods. What Yeshua reveals is their emptiness, their fallaciousness, in the face of divine reality, on the one hand, and human spiritual freedom, on the other. In this respect, the idea in Augustine's *The City of God* that evil is the "privation of good" links up with Bulgakov's idea that Satan works to deprive humans of their belief that goodness exists, or is possible. If evil—or submission to it—is perceived as the only choice, freedom *as a state of mind* vanishes. Yeshua reaffirms the viability of good as a choice, in spite of the price.

The Master and Margarita involves a strange cross-genre dynamic. It pairs anti-Soviet satire with a profoundly serious, visionary reimagining

of Jesus' final day on earth, and of his crucifixion. In order to fully understand Bulgakov's Jesus, Yeshua Ha-Nozri, the "magician" who cures Pontius Pilate's migraine and then demystifies himself, the "rebel" and
"outlaw" who staggers under the whip of Pilate's Centurion, it is important to understand Bulgakov's Satan, the central figure in the satiric plot.
Bulgakov develops these two figures in antithetical relation to each other,
such that the actions and nature of each only become comprehensible by
contrast with the other. As Malcolm V. Jones notes, the Moscow material,
which we might expect to be realistic, is permeated by the supernatural,
and the Jerusalem material, which we might expect to be permeated by the
supernatural, is largely realistic.[10] There are some exceptions (such as
Yeshua's uncanny "prediction" of when Pilate's migraine will end, and the
various suggestions of demonic interference), but on the whole the inversion is maintained.

Woland, Bulgakov's Satan, is consistent with medieval and Renaissance representations of the devil in that he is both humanity's deceiver
and our accuser, an adversary of God. In this novel, moreover, he represents earthly power and authority, and his ability to predict the future
suggests that his powers here below are great indeed. He is the force that
spreads fear, despair, and the lie that we are compelled to do evil because
we are not free. By contrast, Yeshua stands for the absence of earthly
power and authority and for an almost limitless vulnerability that nevertheless, and absurdly, marks our freedom even in the face of tyrannical
force.

Despite Woland's dazzling powers and Yeshua's apparent weakness,
Woland's attempts to destroy Jesus and to capture the souls of twentieth-
century Muscovites tend to culminate in a reversal of his acts of malign
will. This is not, I would argue, because Bulgakov's Satan secretly serves
God, as some scholars have claimed, but because Yeshua is able to manifest
himself, through imagination and spiritual yearning, as something intrinsic to the human, however often it is alienated from us. He exists everywhere human beings exist; he cannot be extirpated, because he is an aspect
of the human—the divine aspect, the incommensurable and loving
aspect. In this novel, his presence can be recognized in the thoughts and
actions of numerous characters, in the sudden generous impulse, the
moment of compassion or repentance, the hunger to believe in goodness,
and even the thirst for justice.

Bulgakov's Yeshua is, ultimately, inseparable from the human. Both
before and after the crucifixion, he remains an earnest philosopher, without any absolute authority. His emissary Matthu Levi must "plead" with

Woland in order for Margarita to be allowed to accompany her lover the Master into their "eternal refuge."[11] Even after his ascension, Yeshua cannot merely issue commands concerning human fate any more than he can stop war or save himself from death, for in doing so he would become Caesar, his own antithesis, however benevolent, and human moral freedom would vanish. But because Yeshua is represented as so nearly powerless, so limited in his prerogatives, and because Woland/Satan seems to possess so much autonomous agency, many scholars have argued that Bulgakov's novel is Gnostic—either a Christian Gnosticism, or a Gnosticism altogether beyond the limits of doctrinal Christianity.[12] The former view implies that in the micro- and macrocosmic struggle between good and evil, in which the human soul is contested, the phenomenal world belongs to Satan and only the spiritual world to Yeshua. In the latter view, while many of the same elements remain, Woland and his agents are perceived as divine messengers, sent to convey an esoteric, mystical *gnosis* or truth to those persons capable of receiving it.

While the first interpretation is more persuasive, certain additions may be made to it. Bulgakov's Yeshua is more strictly human, and less authoritative, less a king, than we might consider compatible with traditional Christian theology. But he is entirely compatible with a Russian idea descended from Dostoyevsky's *Brothers Karamazov*: of Jesus as suffering rather than doing; as neither compelling nor punishing but attracting followers through the idea of goodness alone. Edward E. Ericson sees the novel as Bulgakov's testament to Eastern Orthodox Christianity, but Bulgakov is less orthodox than this allows for.[13]

Bulgakov's Jesus may be banished from the totalitarian state, but he will remain in odd corners of the human psyche, quite simply because he is *inherent* and because human spiritual freedom requires that the possibility of Jesus and his embodiment of the good continue to exist. Yeshua is crucified by Rome, and though he has already left an indelible mark on all those who encounter him, his death is experienced by them as utter defeat. Yet his very perversity, as his executioners see it, forces a split in their apprehension of the real. Caesar's reality is everywhere enforced. Evil and mundane, it is governed by the assertions of necessity that usher in the kingdom of despair.[14] Yeshua's vision of reality is maintained even in his death. He sees the goodness in everyone; he sees the real as it is at the level of the ideal. In his person the ideal becomes the real; thus, what is true through him becomes possible for all.

In chapter 2, Pilate asks Yeshua what he said to Judas that could have led to his arrest:

"I said, among other things," the prisoner answered, "that every form of authority means coercion over men, and that a time will come when there shall be neither Caesars, nor any other rulers. Man will come into the king-dom of truth and justice, where there will be no need of any authority." (30)

Brokenhearted as he hears in these words the "inevitability" of Yeshua's execution, Pilate utters the required formula:

"There was not, is not, and never shall be any rule in the world greater and more beneficent to men than the rule of the Emperor Tiberius!" Pilate's bro-ken, sick voice rose and spread around him. The procurator looked at his sec-retary and the convoy with hatred. (30)

As in the Soviet Union, truth in the colonies of the Roman Empire is dead, and power determines what must or must not be said. Liberty, hope, and integrity must be sacrificed to the hungry maw of authority. Pilate cannot bear it, yet he is bound to it. In a rage of cynical misery, he demands of Christ shortly before he sentences him to death:

"So Mark Rat-killer, a cold and confirmed hangman, the people," the procu-rator pointed to Yeshua's mutilated face, "who beat you for your sermons, the outlaws Dismas and Gestas, who with their henchman killed four soldiers, and finally, the filthy informer Yehudah—all these are good men?"
    "Yes," answered the prisoner.
    "And the kingdom of truth will come?"
    "It will come, Hegemon," Yeshua answered with conviction.
    "It will never come!" Pilate cried suddenly in such a dreadful voice that Yeshua started back. (30)

Pilate's ferocious and despairing assertion voices his rage at being unable to save Yeshua—at least, not without taking his place upon the cross. Pilate accepts that the cosmos is empty of all goodness and ruled by human tyranny; thus, he is dying inside. Neither he nor Yeshua's own dis-ciples can understand the vision that refuses to acknowledge the supremacy of "reality" as manifested in terms of earthly power and the consequences of resisting it. Roman and Soviet power are virtually identi-cal; both seek to maintain their prerogatives by revoking human moral and intellectual autonomy, and calling this enslavement "benevolence."

The execution itself is described in chapter 16, apparently as a drug-induced dream experienced by Ivan, a "holy fool" character who becomes the Master's "disciple" as he sleeps in Stravinsky's psychiatric clinic. However, we are not quite sure, since Woland's account, the Master's novel, and Ivan's dream seem to be all of a piece—a tonally unified, objective but inspired whole. In any case, this is one of the most powerful chapters in the novel. In its colorful, concrete details, it gives the effect of lucid historical reality: the thronging multitudes of people and animals, the soldiers, the arid landscape where every hill and bush stand out distinctly. Satan's numbers, 2 and 6, are everywhere: the double cordon, the Second Cohort, the two languages, Aramaic and Greek, the 2,000 onlookers, the six executioners, and so on.[15]

"Tormented by the heat, bored and exhausted," the soldiers "cursed the three outlaws" (183). The sun is so merciless that it alone is enough to kill the crucified men, but slowly. By the fourth hour of the execution, all the onlookers have gone. Only the military personnel and Matthu Levi, and presumably Woland, remain with the crucified men. Two panting dogs (demon familiars?) lie on the hillside. "No one had made any attempt to rescue the condemned" (184). Considering the importance of this event historically and—in Bulgakov's view—spiritually, the indifference of all but Pilate and Matthu is overwhelming. Roman discipline is preserved by Mark Rat-killer, Pilate's faithful, cruel officer, who kicks aside the bones of innumerable victims with his idle boot. The hill of the crucifixion is a monument to death and to the deadly inhumanity of human law, human politics, and human power, untempered by love.

By the "sickly fig tree" (standing for life blighted by death), on the "heaven-cursed waterless earth" (185), Matthu watches, inconsolable, half-maddened by horror and grief. Having tried and failed to approach the place of execution, he sees only the vultures in the sky, no rescuing angels or merciful God. Skulls, lizards, and death fill up the world. He curses himself for having let Yeshua go to the city alone. (Woland may be responsible for the strange fever that prevents Matthu from rejoining Yeshua in time to save him from Yehudah.) He rebels against God for allowing Yeshua to undergo such unending pain, partly in the hope that God will strike him dead. He has stolen a knife with the goal of cutting short Yeshua's suffering by stabbing him in the back and then killing himself (Woland's influence again). Other gods, he accuses, "would never have allowed a man like Yeshua to be consumed by the heat of the sun on a post" (191). Better gods, he implies, would manifest their divinity in useful demonstrations of earthly power so that justice is done here on earth. What Matthu fails to grasp, in Bulgakov's view, is that such a god would undermine human freedom and enforce belief through material coercion.

In the fifth hour the agent sent by Pilate arrives to end it. Gestas and Dismas, maddened by suffering, await death. Yeshua's face and body are covered with flies (evocative of Beelzebub). He has "suffered blackouts" repeatedly. Bulgakov departs from the usual emphasis on Christ's unremitting conscious agony. The victims are tied with ropes, not nailed to the posts as in most traditional depictions. His Yeshua drinks with joy from the sponge, as the thirsty Dismas glares at him in hatred. Then Yeshua begs that Dismas be given a drink, returning compassion for hatred. As the executioner pricks his heart, Yeshua's last word is "Hegemon," as if he were still engaged in a conversation with Pilate (194). He does not address God or comment on his mission. As darkness sweeps down upon Jerusalem with raging torrents of rain, like a second flood, all alone in the apocalyptic landscape Matthu cuts the bodies down from the posts and carries Yeshua away for burial. The solitude of these two figures and the wild destruction of the scene indicate the benightedness of this world. The distinct impression given the reader is of an exceptional man undergoing a fearful death, ending in obscurity, without any clear supernatural intervention. It ought to be an inducement to despair, but its meaning is quite the opposite. As Andrew Barratt and others have noted, Soviet critics of the novel upon its first publication in November of 1966 attacked Bulgakov for "advancing a philosophy of passivity" and "attempting to persuade us that all action is pointless."[16] This is not the implied significance of Yeshua's death, which is a triumph over passivity and a demonstration that it is possible to do and believe what is right, whatever the cost.

The drama of the Passion is drawn with no hint or shadow of irony. In the chapters on either side of it, and in juxtaposition with it, Bulgakov ironically depicts Woland's visit to Soviet Moscow. Woland has come in order to damn the unwary and celebrate the exaltation of atheism over faith, which is the consequence of the materialism and totalitarianism of the state. Instead, try as he might, he serves only to throw a bomb of subversive chaos into the pseudorationalist equilibrium of official orthodoxy. In other words, as Bulgakov indicates with an opening reference to the devil of Goethe's *Faust*, Satan is "that Power which eternally wills evil and eternally works good." Drawing on Goethe's Mephistopheles and also perhaps on Pushkin's *Eugene Onegin*, Bulgakov gives us a devil who is associated with defiance, spiritual ennui, indifference to suffering, and contempt for humankind. He is Bulgakov's primary voice for the satiric interrogation of the "spirit of the times." But he is also Yeshua's opposite.

More indirectly, Bulgakov draws on the Grand Inquisitor of Dostoyevsky's *Brothers Karamazov* for his depiction of a Satan whose malevolent power is identical to the force behind all institutionalized absolutism. The Inquisitor is the model for Bulgakov's invisible heads of state, Stalin and Tiberius, such that we recognize the identification of the two states, separated by almost two thousand years. While Woland himself initiates the evil that Yeshua transforms to good, the genuinely satanic energies of Bulgakov's novel are invested in the political and social order itself. This is a world ruled by abject materialism combined with manipulative rhetoric—truly the voice of Satan, who has his work done for him by the engines of state control, which have killed God in order to become God. In this sterile, blasted, spiritually insane realm, Yeshua's is the voice of the madman and the dreamer crying out in the marketplace, only to be disregarded. Yeshua is described by Pilate as a mad dreamer, and the Master—Pilate's biographer—is diagnosed as a schizophrenic. In both instances, this is like the divine madness of Plato's *Phaedrus*: the ability to see (a little) as God sees, where the real and the good are one. Yet it puts the dreamer in a situation of living paradox, where he fits neither reality entirely, and spans in his person an almost unbridgeable gap. The reality is that this world is full of evil and suffering; yet from the perspective of Bulgakov's Yeshua, all men and women are good, and evil is temporary, something to be transformed, and therefore not "real" in the final or absolute sense.

Bulgakov is very clear about the functional reality of evil in everyday life. Fear of God is displaced in the Rome of the Yershalayim chapters by fear of Caesar, and in the Moscow chapters by fear of arrest. In Moscow, love of one's neighbor has been remodeled into the false solidarity of regulated cooperatives, in which envy and greed predominate over love. Morality in Moscow is little else but outward conformity to prescribed ideology. This is hell, in Bulgakov's view: a universe where man is the measure of all things, where truth is the ratio of the five senses, and even this is subject to revision by authority. Thus, the presence of Woland and his crew—Koroviev, Azazello, and the black cat Behemoth—can, if we are incautious, appear to afford us with a carnivalesque entertainment that is infinitely seductive amid the arid deadliness and intellectual claustrophobia of Soviet Moscow. Woland's Trinity seems to represent magic, liberty, and dreams come true, but in actuality they stand for temptation, transgression, and punishment. This is a vicious circle that offers no way out. Yet *Yeshua* is the way out, suggested in this novel by the image of a path of moonlight.

Woland and his fiendish three expose the hypocrisy of a bureaucratic state that claims to serve the interests of the collective and yet operates entirely through appeals to self-interest at the expense of others. Woland derides the state's propagandistic use of art, law, medicine, and journalism to kill God and bury any reference to his existence. Woland and his minions run like wildfire through the state-run literary and theatrical institutions, where Bulgakov himself suffered something in the nature of a hellish torment. Woland's crew generates a storm of mischief and mayhem that inspires the "artistic" impostors and petty bureaucrats of Moscow with a devout fear of the devil and all his works. God is suddenly remembered as the only antidote for demonic persecution. Cynical opportunists whose only concern has been gorging themselves at the elite restaurant of Moscow's privileged literary organization, MASSOLIT, or wangling a holiday villa by the Black Sea, end up clutching religious icons to their breasts, muttering prayers, and waving crosses. People who would sell their mothers or any of their fellow citizens for a three-bedroom apartment find out what it means to deal with the devil.

Scientific materialism and state-imposed atheism dictate paradigms for reality which exclude all aspects of the metaphysical, including such things as immortality, supernatural beings (Satan, witches, vampires, talking cats, etc.), the black magic of Woland and the spirituality of Yeshua. The mechanical laws of cause and effect and the scientific laws of probability that have shaped the expectations of Soviet citizens constitute a "faith" in empiricism exclusive of all other possibilities. When Woland and his crew begin to generate "impossibilities" in the form of inexplicable events and magical phenomena, this empirical model of reality is exploded. Muscovites are stricken by terror and confusion. However, despite Woland's intentions, his efforts largely serve to bring God back into the hearts and lexicons of the Russian people. The institutions that have made it their business to denounce or destroy any artist of true genius or visionary potential are laid waste. Indeed, Margarita, who becomes a witch in order to rescue her lover, the nameless writer known only as the Master, goes on a rampage, destroying the apartment of the literary critic who ruined her beloved and blocked all chance of publication for his great work.

In this novel, Satan and his legions have spent all the centuries since the crucifixion trying to regain the ground they lost when Yeshua's ordeal redeemed humankind. Rather than having arrived at some kind of acceptance of their role as part of God's plan, as may at first appear, they obdurately continue in their efforts to corrupt and subdue the souls of men and women. They may seem like Pilate to be merely administrators, perhaps in some Gnostic bureaucracy, but this is merely another of their efforts to appear friendly. They serve darkness against the light. However, they are bound by Yeshua's spiritual triumph and are eclipsed in any direct confrontation with his influence. They work at the level of observable and tangible rewards and punishments, to arouse base appetites and to intimidate their prey. Yet as the little gods of this world, their attempts to pervert are so clearly demonic that they end by inadvertently teaching humanity about the limits of worldly power and worldly perspective. The demons, seeking to parody and subvert divine metaphysics, against their wishes prove the existence of God. Through a blatant display of vulgar miracle and vaudeville-style magic, they nevertheless demonstrate the possibility of the impossible and the disturbing immortality of the mortal, even if only in the grotesque form of vampires, revenants, and the resurrection of beheaded theatre employees. They make clothes appear and disappear, money change denomination, and pigs fly. They reveal that prudence is not a virtue and that security is a mortal's chief enemy. Seen through Woland's satiric monocle, Moscow is turned upside down. Soviet "virtues" are exposed in their true shape, as vices: respectability is tantamount to prostitution; good citizenship is spying and informing for personal gain; kindly psychiatrists are employed by the state to euthanize the soul and silence all dissent. Pleased as Woland is to see the demoralized and banal condition of Moscow in the twentieth century, he does not leave it quite as he found it. He has attempted to prove that a lack of faith in humans is only common sense, but he has not quite succeeded.

It is not socialism per se that is under attack in the Moscow chapters, but rather legislated materialism. The Soviet state appears at the outset in the person of one of its agents, the editor Berlioz, whose task it is to control what is thought, published, and even what may be spoken aloud. The state does this where possible through a system of gentle coercion, offering rewards and bribes for those willing to produce propaganda in service of the current regime. For those who resist, however, harsher methods of control are available, from the suppression of publication, to arrest, imprisonment, captivity in mental institutions, and utter ruin. Millions died under Stalin's government, but Bulgakov has no need to mention this; the knowledge hovers in the background, behind the comic slapstick of arrests for possession of foreign currency and the sudden disappearance of various characters to far-flung places like Yalta. Even their reappearance as corpses or vampires or wandering lunatics points toward a more sober reality outside the bounds of the novel's overt representation of magical events.

Woland's methods are similar to those of the state. Either he flaunts his own power in order to terrify humans into obeying him, or he uses his magic to indebt them through his appearance of benevolence. In this he stands in contrast to Yeshua, who rejects earthly dominion and instead undergoes the torment of crucifixion in order to redeem others. The distinction between these two means of influencing human choice is fundamental to Bulgakov's vision.

Berlioz, like everyone Woland meets in Moscow, is out of his depth. Woland predicts Berlioz's death to Ivan, and to Berlioz himself, as the seventh proof of God's existence. He predicts the death in precise detail because he can see beyond the limits of linear time, or because he has the power to ensure that death. In any case, through empirical demonstrations, and through sheer terror, he compels belief not in God but in himself.

Ivan, "with a chill in his heart," boldly confronts Woland about Berlioz's streetcar "accident"—"You are a murderer and a spy!"—and then tries to get Woland's henchman Koroviev to help him chase the absconding criminal (52). All in all, Ivan shows tenacious dedication to the principle of justice throughout the novel, in spite of the danger. He traverses the city trying to catch Woland in order to call him to account for his crime. Arming himself with a candle and a paper icon, which he pins to his chest like the shield of faith, Ivan is both the "holy fool" out of Russian legend and an outrage to all who meet him.

At Griboyedov's restaurant in MASSOLIT headquarters, privileged state-owned artists and intellectuals gorge themselves on the same kind of delicacies and luxurious wines that the merchants and aristocrats of prerevolutionary Moscow would have treated themselves to at the expense of the impoverished working classes. None of them sees any irregularity or contradiction in this favored existence, and no one offers to share the spoils with the less fortunate. It is not only a dog-eat-dog world; it is a world where the obedient dogs stuff themselves on quail, sturgeon, and thrushes, guzzle fine wines and vodka, and compete ruthlessly for any advantage they can grab. While the MASSOLIT executive waits impatiently for the arrival of the chairman, Berlioz, the reader is treated to a vision of his headless, mangled corpse set out on three zinc tables. Berlioz undergoes dissection by forensic scientists, who, of course, find nothing there but meat and bones in confirmation of their materialistic view of life.

The majordomo of the restaurant, the fearsome Archibald Archibaldovich, is clearly an initiate of Woland's secret ministry. He fattens up the sinners, and knows when to call the militia and when to bow to black cats. Most of all, he knows when to cut and run, escaping the fire in chapter 28 with two rolls of the finest sturgeon tucked under his coat. In chapter 5 he is compared to a buccaneer, in a curious passage that then protests that buccaneers never existed, that the Caribbean never existed, and, finally, that

> there is nothing and there never was. There is only a stunted linden tree out there, an iron fence, and the boulevard beyond it. . . . And ice melting in the bowl, and someone's bovine bloodshot eyes at the next table, and fear, fear. . . . Oh gods, gods, poison, give me poison. (67)

This passage is an excellent example of Bulgakov's poetic technique, where he turns a few small details into a key passage in the novel. These scant lines reveal the true nature of existential despair in Bulgakov's world. They begin with an assertion of nothingness, followed by a feeling of inexplicable fear, alienation, and meaninglessness, and then a demonic temptation to suicide. The latter results from the utter failure of the imagination, together with the collapse of human empathy. The dusty linden evokes the dying fig tree Matthu Levi notices during Yeshua's crucifixion, as well as Matthu's own reviling of God and temptation to kill Yeshua and then himself as a way of ending the suffering. The absence of anything beyond the iron fence (the limits of empirical reality) and the boulevard (perhaps social order?) suggests the absence of the spiritual. The red, bovine eyes evoke the way we see others in proximity to ourselves when we have lost all fellow-feeling and forgotten Yeshua's belief that there is goodness in everyone and that everyone can be redeemed. Woland has entered the narrator's brain.

But just when the narrator is indulging in this feeling of desolation, barefoot Ivan thrusts himself into the story in his ragged underwear, a momentary incarnation of Yeshua, babbling an impossible tale and urging his MASSOLIT companions to pursue the nefarious foreigner before he does untold damage. Ivan as the holy fool disrupts the all-encompassing *finitude* of the nauseated meditation on the stunted linden and the iron fence. He comes from an encounter with what is *beyond* it. As such, he is both an embarrassment and a threat at MASSOLIT headquarters. The poet Ryukhin escorts him forcibly and in tears to Stravinsky's mental health clinic. We receive a clear message: the only ones who can see the truth will be imprisoned as madmen.

In chapter 6, Bulgakov uses Stravinsky's clinic to show us that in a materialist world, mystical vision, faith, and imagination are diagnosed as mental disease. The doctor, who seems so well-meaning, and the kindly nurses, who are so thoughtful of their patients, persuade even the seriously enlightened that they are deranged and may be cured with medication, therapy, and above all, rest. Stravinsky is eminently reasonable, the very voice of calm, logical self-examination. After a few minutes' conversation with him, Ivan blushes at the icon he has pinned to his shirt, though he admits, "It was the icon that frightened them most of all. . . . He's in league with the evil ones" (77). Ivan, the doctor says, "must have seen someone who struck his disordered imagination" (79). An "ordered imagination" is one that does not function independently of what is licensed and sanctioned by the authorities.

Ryukhin's visit to the "house of sorrow," where he has committed Ivan, leaves a terrible impression on him. Ivan's accusation that he is a dreadful poet and a hypocrite reverberates within him, taking on the force of a compelling truth. Seeing Pushkin's statue, Ryukhin is convulsed with envy. Back at Griboyedov's he perceives Archibald Archibaldovich's total indifference to Ivan's fate, and envies it, in a moment of "cynical, self-demolishing hatred" (81). He downs glass after glass of vodka (a form of poison, indicating Woland's influence) and soon yields to Woland's suggestion: "Nothing in his life could be repaired any more . . . All he could do was forget." He feels that his life, like the night, is "lost beyond redemption" (82). These thoughts link him with Pilate, the Master, and Margarita, who all have similar thoughts under Woland's assaults. To doubt one's own capacity for goodness, and that of others, is to turn away from Yeshua and surrender to Woland.

In chapter 7, Styopa Likhodeyev, director of the Variety Theatre, wakens with a dreadful hangover (Satan and headaches again) and a muddled memory of amorous misdeeds. The apartment (no. 50) that he shared with Berlioz is about to be commandeered by Woland. He lives in a flat that once belonged to a jeweler's wife, a place redolent of avarice and hoarding, very appropriate for Satan's den. Woland materializes with offerings of vodka and caviar, insisting that Styopa has already signed a contract with him to host a black magic show at the Variety Theatre. Having convinced him that he is going mad, Kroviev and Behemoth spirit him away magically to Yalta.

As Likhodeyev faints in Yalta, Ivan wakes up from his hypodermic-induced sleep in Stravinsky's clinic. The frosted cylinder at the foot of his bed seems to offer him numerous choices, such as "Drink" and "Attendant," but as in the totalitarian state at large, these "choices" are preselected and strictly controlled. Ivan can have pajamas or a bathrobe, but not street clothes. He can write down his thoughts, or he can sleep, but he cannot leave. When Stravinsky visits him, it strikes Ivan that the doctor is "just like Pontius Pilate" (98); both wield the authority of the powers that be. Ivan tries to tell Stravinsky about Pontius Pilate, and the unknown woman, Annushka, who spilled the oil on the streetcar tracks, causing Berlioz to slip and die, all according to Woland's prediction. He struggles to describe this foreigner Woland and his retinue, who seem to be behind it all. The doctor answers, "There is only one *salvation* for you now—complete rest" (103; italics mine). This is the same conclusion that Woland drives the Master to accept at the end of the novel, but it is, in both instances, a lie.

Rimsky, the financial manager of the Variety Theatre, and Varenukha, the house manager, are irate at the failure of the magically abducted Styopa Likhodeyev to show up for work. Playbills appear announcing Professor Woland's "Black Magic Act Accompanied by a Full Exposé." Varenukha insists that the exposé is "the whole point," meaning that the act is being permitted because its purpose is to demystify magic and make the trickery behind all such performances plain to the audience. This, he thinks, will be a magic performed in order to deconstruct magic, to show its rational explanation—the weights, pulleys, trick swords, and false bottoms of illusion. This parallels Berlioz's wish to expose the "fraudulence" of Christian religious teachings and the "credulity" of the superstitious who trust in them. This performance will, he thinks, serve the propaganda interests of the state by showing the audience that there is nothing "beyond" the dusty linden tree and the iron fence. However, Woland's exposé is of the audience, not the performance. They are to be exposed in their greed, vanity, and concupiscence. The point he hopes to make is that human beings are nothing but the walking damned. They are all his.

In his office, Rimsky is determined to get to the bottom of Likhodeyev's disappearance. He examines the evidence, attempts to contact the authorities and to send them the telegrams, and is instantly warned off by Woland's accomplices. Like Ivan, he is seized "with an angry desire to expose the scoundrels" (126), but as the world darkens, storm clouds approach, and fear begins to build. Varenukha, "suddenly" needing to visit the toilet, is ambushed and brutally beaten there by Behemoth and Koroviev. He is then taken to Hella, the vampire, who preys upon him and makes him a vampire like herself. At this point, the entertaining qualities of Woland and his minions begin to appear in a less attractive light. Varenukha may not be a particularly good man, but does he deserve the horrors that befall him? Those critics who see Woland and his crew as the real heroes of the novel emphasize that only the guilty are punished, but this is not strictly true, and the guilty are punished in excess of their crimes. Some of the penalties are afterward revoked, but that is no indication of goodwill on Woland's part. He wants to persuade the Master and Margarita that he is benevolent so that they will accept his offered "solution" for them—"eternal rest." Furthermore, even his powers are limited.

Ivan, incarcerated in the mental hospital, weeps with frustration at his inability to compose a plausible report for the police. He finds himself writing instead about Pontius Pilate, indicating his future role as the Master's disciple. The clinic staff, alarmed by his prolonged weeping, give him another injection, which "calms him down": "Now everything would pass, change, and be forgotten" (130). This is evocative of the "eternal rest" offered to the Master and Margarita at the end of the novel. Like the "reward" of a refuge in limbo, the drugs detach Ivan and prevent him from striving. But in this novel, as in Goethe's *Faust,* the only path to enlightenment is *eternal striving.* The drugs, and the offer of refuge after terror and persecution, induce a state of willing passivity in which all urgency in the pursuit of truth and goodness fades to a dim memory.

As the "house of sorrow" falls asleep, the "frosted white bulbs in the quiet corridors went out; and in their place, according to established order, the faint blue nightlights were turned on" (131). This is a parody of God's naturally ordered cosmos, just as the "romantic refuge" in limbo Woland offers to the Master is a parody of completion. The state and, in the latter instance, Woland displace God and assert their absolute control, over day and night and consciousness itself. But Yeshua's side fights back. Just as Ivan is sinking into indolent, self-mocking indifference, the Master slips out of the moonlight and into Ivan's room through the balcony door.

While the fateful encounter between the novelist and the poet takes place in the madhouse, the black magic show is about to begin at the Variety Theatre, preceded by a display of acrobatics and vaudeville-style antics. This evokes the tawdry carnival "mystique" of the theatre, the atmosphere of confident trickery and chicanery that characterizes Woland's crew. In the theatre itself, Woland appears in a formal black frock coat and half-mask. George Bengalsky, the master of ceremonies, introduces Woland by assuring the audience, "You and I know that there is no such thing in the world [as magic], and that it is nothing but superstition" (136). Woland, he insists, is simply a master of the "technique of tricks." This is truer than Bengalsky knows, for while Woland's magic is real on the level of observable phenomena, on the level of higher truth it is indeed nothing but tricks and illusion.

Woland conjures an armchair onto the stage and sits in it while Koroviev and Behemoth perform the expected card tricks and "psychic" demonstration, but their mind reading is all too accurate, as they expose the more embarrassing secrets and sins of the audience members. When they conjure "real" money into people's pockets and then cause it to rain down from the ceiling, the theatre goes wild with greed as people scramble for the ruble notes. Woland has his hooks well sunk into the audience by the time Behemoth twists Bengalsky's head off in an attempt to add cruelty and bloodlust to the audience's sins of greed and mendacity. But, beginning with the women, the whole theatre demands that the poor man be forgiven (he has committed no real offense) and his head restored. Woland pretends to be philosophical, but he is clearly disappointed at the unexpected compassion of the frivolous people of Moscow. The head is grudgingly replaced, but Bengalsky remains permanently traumatized.

The vanity of the ladies is then tempted with forbidden and unobtainable fashions, stockings, and perfume, all reminders that people in the Soviet Union are so deprived through shortages of goods that they are easily intoxicated by luxuries. Hella, Behemoth, and Koroviev exchange the women's real clothing for illusory Paris gowns, which will soon vanish, leaving them naked. This reveals the larger theme: Satan's gifts are unreal and will leave us naked before the eye of eternity. The phenomenal is illusion; addicted to shadows, we miss the substance, grasping at nothing.

Yet the tone of the novel is not overtly moralistic; instead, it seems at first glance to encourage both tolerance and—somewhat inconsistently—our acceptance of all sorts of punishments administered by the demons to anyone considered guilty of anything, from lying to being dull or silly. This leads many readers to view all of Woland's actions as either pure fun, or as the justifiable punishment of sinners. What this tolerance for the devil, and intolerance for his victims, seems to overlook is the degree to which ordinary people are beaten, tortured, terrified, misled, and manipulated out of pursuing any higher path. It is hard to remember that Yeshua does not seem to believe in punishment, but only in persuading people toward goodness. In this respect, the devil operates much as the totalitarian state does. Though he seems to undermine the state with his disruption of business as usual, he nevertheless duplicates its effects.

It is perhaps surprising that the titular hero of the novel, the nameless "Master," does not appear until chapter 13, where we encounter him as a patient in Stravinsky's clinic. He is already some distance along the path of his "fate," and we hear about his past in flashbacks told to Ivan. When Ivan confesses that Pontius Pilate brought him to the clinic and tells the Master about Woland's eyewitness account, the novelist is entranced to hear his own vision verified—even if by the devil: "How well I guessed it!" The visionary intuition of truth links the Master's novel with all genuine art, and also with most of the dreams in Bulgakov's novel.

The Master is gratified to hear of the despised Berlioz's death, and laughs with delight at the antics of Behemoth. This shows he is already predisposed to be on the devil's side—so long as the devil seems to oppose his enemies. "The enemy of my enemies is my friend" is a dangerous principle to adopt in a world where the devil is always ready to offer assistance—at an unstated price. Like Margarita, the Master is not alarmed at first. He calmly tells Ivan that "it was Satan whom you met last night" (152).

By the light of the moon, "the nocturnal luminary," the Master asks Ivan to "face the truth": "both you and I are madmen" (153). Ivan has been maddened by Woland's crew, and the Master by both Woland and political persecution (which in this novel amount to almost the same thing). The Master tells his story, from the winning of the lottery to the meeting with Margarita, when love leaped at them "like a murderer . . . like lightning" (157). Each lover rescues the other from the adverse effects of spiritual solitude. Pilate was alone except for his dog; Yeshua had no family, and only one follower amid so many enemies. But the Master and Margarita have each other. Yielding to Woland's suggestion that her life is empty, Margarita was about to poison herself before the Master offered her something to dedicate herself to. In this respect, each carries Yeshua's message of love and goodness to the other. In their secret Eden, in the basement with the lilac trees outside the window, they seek to make up to each other for the desolation of the outside world. But the novel becomes their lives, and its rejection crushes them both. A critic by the name of Ariman (a Persian name for Satan) accuses the Master of attempting "to smuggle an apology for Jesus into print" (161). God is contraband in the USSR. The Master, absurdly, is indicted for "Pilatism" by the critic Latunsky, an agent of government censorship. The Master plunges into deep depression, becoming prey to irrational fears and incipient madness: "the devil knows what it was" (162).

Woland has begun to practice his rougher techniques on the Master, to prevent the completion of the novel, which is a threat to the supremacy of atheism in the state. The Master confides, "A cold and sinuous octopus was feeling with its tentacles directly for my heart" (162). Woland has struck, and the darkness floods in: "I was no longer in possession of myself" (163). The Master calls upon someone, anyone—but not God—to help him, "but no one came," and the Master burns his novel in a state of terror. It is significant that Gogol, under the belief that he was besieged by the devil, burned the manuscript of the second part of *Dead Souls*. Similarly, Bulgakov, subject to relentless persecution, burned manuscripts of his own work, including an early version of his novel about the devil.[17]

When a horror-stricken Margarita confronts him, he admits, "I've come to hate the novel, and I am afraid" (164). Like Pilate, when he envisions Tiberius Caesar's grotesque head on Yeshua's shoulders and cannot believe in any redemptive possibility that can outweigh his fear of Rome, the Master surrenders out of dread of persecution. "I will save you," Margarita promises. She sees the Master's illness as a punishment for her adultery and in particular for her deception of her innocent husband, but her remorseful rationalization, while assisting in her own regeneration, fails to account for Woland's interest in silencing the Master.

The Master flees to prevent her from sharing the impending doom he senses, and he contemplates throwing himself under a streetcar (an impulse sent by Woland). A compassionate truck driver, one of the novel's many momentary incarnations of Yeshua, rescues him from being frozen to death on the road. However, he is almost as effectively silenced when he ends up in Stravinsky's clinic, and soon enough his life will be over. "Cowardice," Yeshua says to Pilate in a dream, was "one of the most terrible vices" (334). What is it that the Master has been prevented from writing about? Why is Matthu Levi sent to instruct Woland to tell the Master that Yeshua has read his novel and that his only comment is that "unfortunately, it was not finished"? What comes after the burial? The resurrection comes, the rolling aside of the stone (standing for obduracy of the material realm), and the resumption of the endless conversation, for Yeshua's death was "sheer misunderstanding," and of course "he was alive." Yeshua's message to the Master points to the crucial truth that death is not the end. The "philosopher, who had invented the incredibly absurd idea that all men are good" (334), has not finished with us, nor we with him, in Bulgakov's view. *It is not finished*—thus, we remain responsible and alarmingly free.

In chapter 14, Rimsky is terrorized much as Varenukha and the Master have been. Attempting to impose damage control on the scandal spreading around Woland's performance, he plans to "lie . . . back out of responsibility, blame everything on Likhodeyev to save himself, and so on. The devil take it all!" (170). Here, in miniature, is precisely our temptation and Pilate's. Lie, back out, blame everything on our fellow men and women, and the devil takes all. Perhaps these thoughts summon the demons. A voice over the phone warns Rimsky not to call anyone; supernatural dread invades him; malarial dampness and spectral cold announce the arrival of the vampires, Varenukha with a "thievish, cowardly expression in his eyes," and Hella, clawing outside at the window. "He casts no shadow!" Rimsky realizes, and has just enough strength to whisper, "Help!" (176). Absurdly, he holds out his briefcase like a shield (or a cross), as if bureaucracy held the power to fend off demons. But what saves him is the "joyous cockcrow" that announces dawn, the rooster that stands for Christ and the resurrection, whose crow traditionally banishes the ghouls and demons of the night and in this novel terminates the festivities at the Ball of the Spring Equinox, where Satan plays host to the damned once a year. But Rimsky's hair has turned permanently white in the space of a single night. Woland has stolen his youth. He dashes to catch a train out of Moscow, like all the others who flee, or end up at police headquarters begging for a nice, safe cell, or at Stravinsky's, hiding from the devil.

Meanwhile, Nikanor Bosoy is interviewed by the police. The greedy and dishonest house chairman of 302b Sadovaya Street was set up by Koroviev, who "gifted" him with a bribe and then turned him in for possession of foreign currency. "God, the true and almighty," Bosoy tells the police interrogator, "sees everything, and it serves me right" (180). He confesses to taking bribes and sees the devil everywhere: "Spray the room with holy water!" (180). Raving and praying, he ends up at Stravinsky's clinic, in room 119, next to Bengalsky, who in room 120 is still searching for his head, and next to the restless Ivan in room 118. All of the "madmen" are sedated, and Ivan dreams of the execution of Yeshua. The divine is leaking into the carefully sealed vessel of the materialist-rationalist state.

At the beginning of book 2, the narrator finally turns to Margarita. In Goethe's *Faust*, the titular male protagonist is the primary agent and Margaret, the girl he has seduced, is a more passive figure. In Bulgakov's novel, it is the woman, Margarita, whom many critics see as the true protagonist. She blames herself, just as Matthu Levi does, and for the same error. "Why did I leave him that night?" she asks, referring to the night the Master burned his manuscript and fled. "I returned like the miserable Matthu Levi—too late" (237). It maddens her not to know where he is, and this makes her vulnerable to temptation. On Good Friday, she awakens with a premonition: "I believe!" Her urgent but vague faith is linked to the hope that though she is guilty of adultery and lies, even this "does not deserve such cruel punishment" (237). She has the same attitude toward the sins of Frieda and Pilate as she does toward herself: sin is not unforgivable, at least not forever.

Her instincts align her with Matthu and Yeshua, but Woland interferes. Margarita has a dream, which perhaps is a warning sent from Yeshua. In a deadened landscape, the Master appears at the door of a shack (evocative of Stalin's labor camps), "sick and troubled" (238). The dream reveals the Master's current—and perhaps future—state. It is such a grim scene that it motivates Margarita to do *anything* to save him. Sitting on a bench by the Kremlin wall, she asserts, "I would pawn my soul to the devil to find out whether he is alive or dead" (242). Instantly, the demon Azazello appears, with his single fang and his fiery hair. She takes him at first for a pimp, which is not far from wrong, but when he begins to quote the Master's (unpublished) novel, she agrees to his proposal to meet Woland, whom Azazello describes merely as "a foreigner." The demon is obviously uncomfortable around Margarita's intense love. Her qualms of conscience are troublesome, and to punish her he makes her beg for his help. The demons all have to be careful around Margarita, because people who are motivated by love are easy to tempt but liable to heroic acts of self-sacrifice that may redeem them at the last moment. It is easy to bring Margarita to agree to act as hostess at Satan's Ball in exchange for the Master's return; it is not so easy to damn her.

Azazello gives Margarita a magical cream that turns first Margarita and then her maid Natasha into witches: younger, wilder, and able to fly on a broomstick or a pig by the light of the moon. Since her meeting with Azazello, Margarita has had a "nagging pain in her temple" (249), signaling demonic influence. When she anoints herself with the cream, this pain vanishes and she becomes intoxicated with excitement. But she is risking her soul. In demonstration of this, she cuts free of all ordinary human responsibility by writing a farewell letter to her husband and giving away all her clothes and belongings to Natasha. It is clear she will never return. The magical pleasures of flight, speed, revenge, and power replace the already fading responsibilities of her former life. Foolishly, she now tells herself that the "foreigner is not dangerous," though she intuits who he is. As she has become a witch, Woland is now her patron. Her new freedom generates a feeling of detachment from the rest of humanity, and she becomes indifferent to the ordinary claims of morality. Her nakedness, her desertion of her husband, and her destruction of Latunsky's apartment make no impression on her. The reader is gripped by her exultation, and by the delicious fantasy of revenge against the whole of the Soviet literary and dramatic establishment—which persecuted and tormented Bulgakov, as it does the Master in Bulgakov's novel. Together with Margarita, and with the author himself, the reader lusts to see justice done, even if it is only a fictive justice. We are swept up in the wonderful delirium of her flight across Moscow. Satan seems to offer joyous anarchy, as antiauthoritarian as we could wish. But freedom from moral responsibility is not what Yeshua offers, and in any case it is an illusion, for we are responsible whether we want to be or not.

Margarita's witchness appears first as an intoxicated sense of liberty, and then as senseless rage. She beats a street sign to ruins because she flew into it. Her subversion of authority leads directly to her assault on Latunsky's apartment. Here, the reader is tempted to share in the excitement of Margarita's social dissidence and in the violent pleasures of vigilante justice. At Dramlit House, the elite residence of those pampered writers of Drama and Literature who prostitute themselves to the interests of the state, she causes a flood—like Noah's—meant to purge the Moscow dramatic and literary cabals in a wash of destruction. Generating fear in others, however, she has become an agent of the devil. But a little boy who is crying in terror alone in his room recalls her to her better nature. "Don't be afraid, little one," she rasps, "trying to soften her criminal voice" (259). Becoming the consoler of a frightened child restores her to her humanity. The little nightlight by the boy's bed suggests symbolically that the child is an instrument of Yeshua, set in Margarita's path to help her resist her worse instincts of rage and hatred, which Woland's cream and its powers have aroused.

Abandoning the city, Margarita "baptizes" herself in a moonlit river in what amounts to a witches' Sabbath. Served by mermaids and satyrs, bowed to as a queen by naked witches, Margarita is inflated with a sense of her own importance, like the frogs whose croaking provides the "natural" music for the wild bacchanal. She is taken in a limousine driven by a rook to perform her task as Satan's hostess. Margarita guesses she is going to meet Satan, "but it did not frighten her" (263). She has been desensitized both to moral dread and to her own spiritual danger. Suffering, loneliness, the yearning for happiness, and her determination to save the Master motivate her to risk all, but her experiences as a witch harden her.

Apartment 50 contains demonic space within its narrow Moscow dimensions. This parody of divine presence allows a vast multitude of the damned to celebrate Christ's death on a narrow square of upper earth. It also allows the denizens of hell to "get out of town" for the brief period when, according to Christian tradition, Christ is below, harrowing hell. This harrowing traditionally entails the rescue of all the virtuous and repentant who died before Christ's birth and were damned until such time as his sacrifice should redeem them posthumously. Christ liberates all these good people and leads them up to heaven when he ascends from death to eternal life. The orthodox view is that this harrowing took place only once, at the time of Christ's interment. But for Bulgakov, it seems, the harrowing never stops; Yeshua allows Frieda, Pilate, and presumably all those in hell to work out their redemption over time. The fifth dimension applies to time as well as space: infinity exists within finitude, eternity within temporal duration.

At the ball, Koroviev and Behemoth proudly introduce the damned, but call Frieda a "bore." She is boring, of course, because she is repentant. When Margarita wants to know why the employer who raped Frieda and impregnated her, thus driving her to murder the child, is not in hell, Behemoth nastily replies, "What has the owner to do with it? It was not he who smothered the infant in the woods" (283). However, it is very likely that the rapist *is* in hell; Behemoth's comment is meant to place Margarita off balance morally, in order to loosen her ties to any idea of an operative divine justice. It is meant, like all of Woland's interventions, to encourage despair. The reason that Frieda is in hell is her commission of infanticide; the café owner, unless he has repented, will be there too.

The reader's own sense of justice, like Margarita's, is baffled and dissatisfied by the devil's apparent arbitrariness. But Yeshua is not arbitrary. Frieda has a chambermaid "assigned to her" (we are not told by whom), who every day brings back to Frieda the handkerchief with which she suffocated her baby. This endless return of the token of her crime that so torments the infanticidal mother represents not her punishment, as the devils intend, but the means of her ultimate redemption. Yeshua's idea of the good informs Frieda's repentance; Yeshua is made manifest in Margarita's mercy. Because Frieda cannot forget, because like Pilate she continues to suffer for what she has done, she is saved—partly by Margarita, but also, through her, by Yeshua. And Margarita, in redeeming Frieda at the expense of her own hopes, unknowingly lays the foundation for her own redemption, which—though it may be deferred by her own choice of "rest" with the Master rather than continued pursuit of enlightenment— will not be postponed eternally. Just as Yeshua sends the kerchief in order to harrow Frieda out of Hell, so he has ensured that Margarita, confronted with Frieda's desperation, will have a chance to choose compassion over selfishness and thus avoid being genuinely corrupted by her transformation into a witch. Yeshua does not compel; he cannot forcibly redeem anyone. However, he offers the renewal of free choice when all freedom seems already forfeited. He provides inspiration where cynicism and despair are thickest. And he sends the means of rescue over and over again to those who appear beyond rescue. According to Bulgakov's novel, Yeshua didn't harrow hell once, in order to redeem those virtuous ones who died before his coming; rather, he never ceases harrowing it, and he saves not only the virtuous but also the deeply flawed. His mercy is infinite, but so is his respect for spiritual and moral freedom. Humans must earn their fates, even if they do so two thousand years after they have died.

Koroviev confides that the mortal hostess of Satan's Ball must always be named Margarita, which echoes the heroine of Goethe's *Faust*. The name means "pearl," a traditional symbol of the soul. Satan is showing off Margarita to boast of his triumph over the human soul. When she enters Woland's chamber, she finds Woland sprawled on the bed in a dirty nightshirt, as if he has abandoned all pretense, though this is not the case. His skin is forever scarred from the war in heaven (a detail taken from *Paradise Lost*), and his mismatched eyes stand for corruption (green) and nothingness (black), the twin horrors of a world without spirit. In the room is a game played with live chessmen, perfectly expressing the game Woland plays with human lives, seeking to win them away from hope into despair. His magic globe shows everything that is happening in the world—war, slaughter, and famine. He looks on with a proprietary air as Margarita beholds the tiny figure of a mother lying dead in a pool of blood beside her baby. Another of Woland's henchman, the angel of death, Abaddon, is credited with this achievement. Woland's brutal comment is that "he had had no time to sin. Abaddon's work is flawless" (274). Of course, this is no justification. The baby had no time to live, or love, or choose for himself.

The devil's pretended good intentions are obvious hypocrisy, but he is testing Margarita to see how far her acceptance of the situation will go. After all, she believes the Master's rescue depends upon her compliance with Woland. Unable to respond with compassion, and instead governed by her fear, Margarita answers, "I should not like to be on the side opposed by this Abaddon" (274). The opposing side is Yeshua's, and Margarita has just been bullied into renouncing goodness out of an instinct of self-preservation. Woland's response is a lie: "He is remarkably impartial and sympathizes equally with both contending sides" (275). Abaddon, like the other demons, is on the side that is dedicated to the destruction of humanity, against their salvation. He sympathizes with neither warring human group but rather stirs them both up to acts of violence. Terrified by the sight of the destroying angel, Margarita clings to Woland's knee, which is a perfect example of jumping from the frying pan into the fire. In this scene, Yeshua's presence is signified by the baby and its claim on human compassion. The infant also relates to the Master's unfinished novel, which Margarita, like Hedda Gabler before her, views as their "child." As Margarita abandons the infant here, so the Master abandoned their child when he burned the novel; both act out of immediate fear of an implicit demonic threat.

In preparation for the ball, Margarita is washed in blood (a parody of baptism again) and then in rose oil (which recalls the "detested" smell of rose oil that pursues Pilate on the morning of his encounter with Yeshua and which is connected to his migraine). Margarita is weighed down with a heavy pendant, namely, a black poodle, the devil's sign from *Faust*. She is commanded to meet all the damned with polite impartiality and to "force" herself to love each one. This imposes moral neutrality (or amorality) on her, rather than true charity, and it parodies divine love and forgiveness, substituting an artificial politeness. The gaudy magnificence of the ball—with its tulips and parrots, its fountains of champagne and pools of wine, its frenetic orchestras both human and animal—both offends against the solemnity of Easter and is a demonic version of heavenly pleasures. The glass floor with the infernal cooks below is a glimpse of hell reminiscent of Dante's *Inferno*. The guests who come down the chimney as rotted, skeletal corpses and are transformed into fancy-dressed revelers display in reverse order the process of corruption and deadliness that has led to their damnation. These celebrities of hell are murderers, traitors, assassins, and so on, whose stories remind us that hell is already here on earth. Margarita performs her function "mechanically" and "monotonously" (283) until she has to be revived with more blood bathing. "Of all this pandemonium, Margarita remembered only one woman's face . . . and one word, Frieda" (286). Her compassion for Frieda's suffering—against Koroviev's express command to show no favorites—allows Margarita to cling to a slender thread of humane feeling in the devilish mayhem of the ball.

At the climax of the ball, Woland conjures up the shade of Berlioz and tortures him by assuring him he has forfeited immortality as a consequence of his atheism. "There is even a theory which says that every man will be given according to his belief," says Woland (287). But Yeshua is committed to the idea that wrong beliefs can be changed. Azazello shoots the informer Baron Maigel, and his blood is poured into Berlioz's severed skull. Margarita is then made to drink the blood in a satanic parody of Communion, allowing herself to be persuaded (though she has seen Azazello kill the Baron) into thinking the blood "has long run down into the earth" and turned into grapes (289). Just as she drinks, in what seems an irrevocably damnable act, she hears "roosters crowing" deafeningly. Yeshua is calling, breaking up the ball, returning the damned to dust, banishing illusion, and sending in the salutary light of dawn.

After the ball, an exhausted Margarita awaits her offered reward, too proud and independent to ask for it, much to Woland's disappointment, though he pretends to admire her for it. Woland tests her spiritual state by offering to punish the critic Latunsky, but Margarita implores him not to interfere (292). Perhaps the taste of the Baron's blood has taught her to avoid revenge. He then cunningly offers her "one wish" but is disgusted when she gives up her single chance to be reunited with the Master—for which she has endured so much, putting her own soul in peril—so that she can save the hapless Frieda. Her unexpected act of mercy places her out of his reach. Frieda is "forgiven" (296). Woland is forced to assert that since he "hasn't done anything" (which is quite true), he will not "take advantage of an impractical person" and she may wish again (297). When Margarita is offered a second "wish," Woland wins, for she asks for the Master to be returned to her. A disturbed and ravaged Master instantly appears, exclaiming, "I am no one today" (298). Woland even restores the burned manuscripts of the novel, though the frightened Master now professes to hate it, thus renouncing Yeshua and his own visionary path. Woland returns the lovers to their lost apartment, destroys the Master's medical records, and even—since Margarita is watching—restores the reluctant vampire Varenukha to his human state. What a beneficent power he is! Who could refrain from worshipping him? Margarita's only fear is "that all of this was only witchcraft" and won't last. But no, the "omnipotent Woland was indeed omnipotent" (311). God, she thinks, has not helped her, but Woland has. Perhaps he is really just God's other "department," as he suggests. And as she thus surrenders herself to Woland, she reads in the Master's novel, "The darkness which had come from the Mediterranean shrouded the city hated by the Procurator," as it now shrouds her (311). We must not choose our own advantage and those who further it over the truth, or the good, Bulgakov insists. No matter how hard it is to endure the suffering that is placed in our path, to embrace the torturer as the redeemer just because he suddenly gives us what we want is self-delusion.

In the chapter that follows Woland's "salvation" of the Master and Margarita, Bulgakov offers a parallel scenario that exposes the hidden meaning of Woland's actions. Margarita reads the Master's ironic account of how Pilate "saves" Yehudah, much as Woland "saves" the Master by setting him up for destruction. Pilate is attempting to ease his conscience of the guilt and shame he feels at having pronounced Yeshua's death sentence. He sends his agent, the chief of the Roman secret police in Jerusalem, an assassin and a spy, to murder Yehudah. Aphranius is paid for the murder of Yehudah just as Yehudah was paid for the betrayal of Yeshua. It is little more than revenge, with an element of transferred blame. Yehudah may have entrapped Yeshua, but it was Pilate who condemned Yeshua to crucifixion. Yeshua would not have wanted Yehudah killed; he would have walked with him and tried to persuade him. Pilate is not doing Yeshua's will when he has the young man killed, but his own. Matthu also intends to murder Yehudah and is fiercely glad when he hears Pilate has already had Yeshua's betrayer killed. To show his approval of Pilate's action, Matthu accepts a fresh parchment from Pilate, a rather shocking concession. How can Pilate's violent revenge against Yehudah cancel out the fact that it was Pilate who gave the order for Yeshua's execution?

Both men love something they do not fully understand. The storm that rages through Yershalayim reveals the truth. The "great bulk of the Temple with its glittering scaly roof" rises and falls like an embattled dragon torn between the fire from heaven and the "dark abyss." The palace of Herod the Great (who tried to have the infant Jesus killed and who slaughtered the innocents in the process) is similarly beset, and its "eyeless golden idols," signifying false worship—the worship of power, so like the Romans' worship of their empire and their emperors—are driven "into the dark" (313).

Yeshua's death reveals precisely what has so enraged Matthu: that the one God in whom Yeshua believes is not a God of power, of earthly sway, whose intervention determines events below, rewarding the good and punishing the wicked *in this life*. He is not a God who buys worshippers with favors. He is genuine goodness, stripped of all worldly advantage, goodness for its own sake. Awaiting the Messiah, the Jews in Jerusalem are expecting one who will lead them in a revolt against the Roman occupation. In Bulgakov's view, they have misunderstood: Yeshua is the messiah who would have led them against the Roman *idea*—namely, the worship of power itself—and he would have done it not through revolution but through enlightenment. The widespread belief that change is impossible through such methods is Woland's achievement.

The decoying and murder of Yehudah at Pilate's command is a betrayal that repeats Yehudah's betrayal of Yeshua. Pilate dreams of ascending the ribbon of moonlight to continue his conversation with the "ragged wanderer." Yeshua assures him, "Now we shall always be together," and he is filled with joy (332). But his awakening to reality is bitter. Like a "wolf," he listens to the details of Yeshua's burial, Judas's murder, and Kaiyapha's embarrassment at the return of the thirty pieces of silver (336). But like Matthu, he cannot assuage his anguish with petty victories.

Woland and his crew must leave Moscow before Easter Sunday. Setting fire to the apartment (in earlier drafts of the novel it was the whole city), they finally depart amid chaos and confusion. Koroviev and Behemoth linger long enough to flounce into Griboyedov's, order a snack, and reduce the place to ashes. These gestures point toward the apocalypse for which they hunger.

Woland and Azazello sit on a rooftop at sunset awaiting the others. Matthu Levi arrives with instructions from Yeshua and addresses Woland as "spirit of evil and ruler of shadows." Woland claims that all things cast shadows (which we know to be false) and asks, "What would your good be doing if there were no evil?" (368). Matthu calls Woland "old Sophist." This is apt, because the argument is an old one, but a false one, in Bulgakov's view. The possibility of evil must exist in order for humans to be morally free to choose, but evil is no less evil for all that.

The intervention of Yeshua here indicates that the Master and Margarita have made mistakes. All that Yeshua can ask for on their behalf is "rest"; they have not earned "light," only peace (369). Azazello is sent by Woland to "arrange everything"—to kill the Master and Margarita with poisoned wine.

Margarita is "haunted" by the "golden idols" of Herod's palace—and no wonder, for she has succumbed to them in accepting Woland as her savior. We hear, obscurely, that the lovers' "psyche had undergone great changes" (372) and that both have headaches that indicate demonic influence. Margarita is delighted to see Azazello, and the two mortals die drinking "Woland's health" (374). Though they emerge as spirits, accusing Azazello, "Poisoner!" they are easily persuaded that this is a necessary transition to their new existence. Since they still think, Azazello argues, they must exist (*cogito ergo sum*); therefore, they have not been harmed. This is duplicitous, since their deaths encourage them to believe that their destiny is concluded and they need do nothing more.

Margarita's spirit form is restored to humanity, and her witch characteristics vanish. However, this is not Woland's doing; it is the truth of her life choices made manifest. Margarita says, "Great Woland! His solution is so much better than anything I could have thought of" (376), but it is very easy to believe this when she does not glimpse any higher possibilities. Woland has precluded thought.

Their magnificent ride over Moscow on coal black horses is interrupted by a visit to Ivan at the clinic. Ivan, the "disciple," is invited to continue the story of Pilate and Yeshua, for the Master "shall be busy with other things" (379). This evasion is never examined, but we may recognize it as an abandonment of purpose. The dead body of the Master is discovered in room 118, while his spirit journeys on with Margarita's to the edge of the abyss.

The rainbow that arches over Moscow evokes God's forgiveness and his promise, which Bulgakov believes Yeshua fulfills. The Master, gazing at the city he will never see again, feels his excitement at the demon ride turn "into a sense of profound and mortal wrong" (382). Instinctively he recognizes that he has been driven and tricked onto the wrong path, that Woland has stolen the earthly future of his novel and perverted his destiny. Moscow and its persecutions, together with Woland and his terrors, have deprived him of his true purpose. But this awareness is fleeting. It gives way "for some strange reason to a proud indifference" (always a sign in this novel of a demonic state of mind) "which in turn was replaced by premonitions of eternal peace" (382). "Eternal" is a lying word here; the Master may require rest, but it need not and should not be eternal. He can regenerate himself and regain his dedication to serve the light even after death. But Woland does not want him to realize this; he wants him to believe his strivings are over, that "it is finished" (382). These words, also spoken by Christ on the cross, are not spoken by Bulgakov's Yeshua and do not apply to the human struggle for enlightenment.

The next chapter begins with an elegiac evocation of weariness and the ease of death. The words "night," "evening," "black," "mists," and "darkness" are repeated, as "enchantment" drops away and the demons are revealed as they really are. Koroviev is joyless and self-engrossed. Behemoth is a demon jester. Azazello is a conscienceless killer—"the demon of the waterless desert" from Leviticus 16:8–10 (384).[18] Woland (himself not described) rides a "hulk of darkness" with a bridle of chains, perhaps symbolic of human enslavement by the illusion of necessity.

When they reach the place of Pilate's imprisonment, Margarita, beholding his suffering, insists that 12,000 moons is too long and cries, "Let him go!" (386). But Yeshua has already called for him, and the Master is given the chance to "finish your novel with a single phrase," as Woland puts it, freeing Pilate. However, this is not the true end of the story, which Woland insists, deceitfully, "is already finished" (387). Speaking "softly and persuasively," Woland enjoins the Master to think of nothing but the delights of his "eternal refuge," which is like a scholar's retreat in a Romantic novel. "Don't you want to sit," Woland asks slyly, "like Faust, over a retort, hoping to create a new homunculus?" However, it is not Faust but his unimaginative assistant Wagner who creates the homunculus, a being that can never leave the retort in which it was formed. Like the Master's unfinished novel, it is trapped in a semi-life and cannot grow anymore than the Master and Margarita can evolve in Woland's pleasant asylum.

Woland and his demons plunge "into the abyss" (388). The Master and Margarita see "the promised dawn" and enter their new home, much like Adam and Eve's leaving Eden for the larger world, only in reverse. The reader will never know for certain what becomes of them, but in this novel, nothing is ever finished.

In the epilogue Ivan, now a professor of history and philosophy, has a vision. His wife still gives him injections to cure his terrible dreams on the nights of the spring full moon. At first he dreams of the crucifixion, but after the injection he dreams of Pilate and Yeshua conversing, of Yeshua's complete forgiveness—he assures Pilate the execution never took place. For Yeshua, evil belongs to the realm of shadows, and being ultimately illusory, it has no eternal reality. Then Margarita and the Master pay a dream visit to Ivan. Perhaps they have already worked their way free of their "eternal" refuge. Margarita kisses Ivan—a form of blessing or encouragement—and then she and the Master recede into the full moon, the realm of the spirit. The novel is enigmatic about their fate. Are they, like Pilate, with Yeshua now, or is this only Ivan's imagination? We cannot know if Ivan will recover enough to fight off Woland's influence and complete the story. This novel, like Yeshua's conversation, suggests that nothing important is ever finished.

Bulgakov's Yeshua is one-half of the internal dialogue through which we exercise our freedom. He cannot be authoritatively defined, because he defies authority. After the crucifixion, he is spiritual and points to the spiritual; yet, paradoxically, he is most himself when incarnated in an endless succession of human thoughts and deeds. He is the face of the ideal self for which we must strive, in order not to despair; without an ideal of the good, we are forced to inhabit reality on all fours. He is the simple antidote to the poison of meaninglessness. His interventions are spiritual, not material, and so he cannot rival Caesar or Stalin for earthly dominion; he cannot prevent them from seizing power. Instead, he offers a way to live within their rule without succumbing to it. While human beings are often broken by fear and suffering, for Yeshua their being broken, even their cowardice, is never unforgivable. Bulgakov's Yeshua cannot contravene eternal justice, but he will harrow hell until the last soul is saved. Thus, he is a Jesus whose path is hard indeed to follow but whose mercy is infinite.

When Bulgakov served in the White Army, late in 1919–1920, he was appointed as the medical officer to the Terek Cossack regiment in Piatigorsk. During this time, as is well documented, he witnessed the vicious beating and brutal murder of a number of innocent and defenseless civilians, most of them Jews.[19] Afraid for his own safety, he did not intervene; like Pilate, his actions were dictated by cowardice, though on other occasions he displayed notable courage. As a consequence of these experiences, he was haunted by intense shame and guilt for the rest of his life. A number of his works contain references to these atrocities and to the cowardice of onlookers who fail to act. Clearly, the story of Pilate and his moral failure is directly related to Bulgakov's own. Thus, Bulgakov's Satan is primarily the agent of fear, particularly the fear of material suffering and death. His Jesus must therefore stand for the means by which that fear is transcended and tyranny is resisted, or, failing that, through whom atonement is possible, no matter how dire the crime. Ultimately, this is a work about inventing Jesus. Bulgakov clearly believes that Jesus existed as a historical figure and also that he exists eternally as a spiritual force. However, he focuses in this novel on the need—at the level both of the individual and the society—to reinvent, subjectively and through the communion of art, the particular Jesus that is necessary for salvation.

NOTES

1. Bulgakov labored on his own novel from 1928 until he died in 1940, leaving it to his wife to publish. Many features of *The Master and Margarita* reflect the events of Bulgakov's own life.

2. For Bulgakov's persecution by Soviet critics, and his relations with Stalin, see A. C. Wright, "Bulgakov, Stalin, and Autocracy," in *Bulgakov: The Novelist-Playwright*, ed. L. Milne (Luxembourg: Harwood Academic Publishers, 1995), 38–49; M. Ginsburg, translator's introduction to *The Master and Margarita* (New York: Grove, 1967); N. Natov, *Mikhail Bulgakov* (Boston: Twayne, 1985), 7–21.

3. All quotations from the text are from M. Bulgakov, *The Master and Margarita,* trans. M. Ginsburg (New York: Grove, 1967). I have also consulted M. Glenny's translation (London: Collins Harville, 1967).

4. R. H. Pittman, *The Writer's Divided Self in Bulgakov's* The Master and Margarita (Oxford: Macmillan, 1991), 124–25; and G. Krugovoy, *The Gnostic Novel of Mikhail Bulgakov* (Lanham, MD: University Press of America, 1991), 32–38.

5. A. Barratt, *Between Two Worlds* (Oxford: Clarendon, 1987), 181–97.

6. Krugovoy, *Gnostic Novel of Mikhail Bulgakov,* 36–37.

7. J. Milton, *Paradise Lost,* Book III, line 339.

8. S. Kierkegaard, *Fear and Trembling, and The Sickness unto Death,* trans. W. Lowrie (Princeton NJ: Princeton University Press, 1954), 79–80.

9. R. H. Pittman, "Dreamers and Dreaming in M. A. Bulgakov's *The Master and Margarita,*" in Milne, *Bulgakov,* 158.

10. M. V. Jones, "The Gospel according to Woland and the Tradition of the Wandering Jew," in Milne, *Bulgakov,* 113. He adds, "This inversion reinforces our sense that the key to the whole text, otherwise difficult to decode, is in the realistic, historical, demythologized version of the Gospels present in turn as Woland's narrative, Bezdomny's dream and the Master's novel" (113).

11. Natov (*Mikhail Bulgakov,* 98) notes that "Matthew Levi is sent to Voland by Yeshua . . . much in the tradition of the Book of Job, where the Lord converses with Satan and gives him power over his servant Job (Job 1: 8–14)." This does not indicate Manichaeanism.

12. Krugovoy (*Gnostic Novel of Mikhail Bulgakov,* 10) claims that a metaphysical *gnosis* is symbolically encrypted in the novel but that it is entirely Christian, though Gnostic in flavor. For him, Bulgakov's Satan is the "principal rival and antagonist of God" (16), not a minister of his will. He argues that while Bulgakov's world at first seems Manichaean, it becomes clear that Satan's evil is slowly but inexorably reversed. On this Gnosticism being beyond doctrinal Christianity, see A. Barratt, *Between Two Worlds* (Oxford: Clarendon, 1987), esp. 160–77, 223.

13. See E. C. Ericson Jr., *The Apocalyptic Vision of Bulgakov's* The Master and Margarita (Lewiston, ME: Edwin Mellen Press, 1991).

14. See Kierkegaard, *Fear and Trembling,* and *The Sickness unto Death,* 170–75.

15. Krugovoy (*Gnostic Novel of Mikhail Bulgakov,* 12–24) provides an extensive discussion of numerology in the novel.

16. L. Skorino, cited in Barratt, *Between Two Worlds,* 16–17. Skorino wisely notes that the novel is antimaterialist.

17. Krugovoy (*Gnostic Novel of Mikhail Bulgakov,* 109–13) discusses the complex parallels between Bulgakov, Gogol, and the Master.

18. Ibid., 47.

19. Ibid., 223–24.

5 | The Existential Turn

Refiguring Christ from Kazantzakis to Scorsese

STEVEN TAUBENECK

> I wanted to renew and supplement the sacred Myth that underlies the great Christian civilization of the West. It isn't a simple "Life of Christ." It's a laborious, sacred, creative endeavor to reincarnate the essence of Christ, setting aside the dross—falsehoods and pettinesses which all the churches and all the cassocked representatives of Christianity have heaped upon His figure, thereby distorting it.
>
> Nikos Kazantzakis

The figure of Jesus Christ raises many problems for interpretation.[1] We can begin with Christ as a historical problem: did he actually, historically exist?[2] Quickly an even more pressing problem arises: that of his human qualities. To identify Christ's humanity, we would have to have a sense of human nature in the first place, for how does a god become human? What would constitute the humanity or the divinity of such a figure, and how could these qualities be represented? Though many people have for a long time developed different understandings of the figure of Christ, in this essay I want to focus on a particular phase of interpretation, one I will call "the existential turn."[3] The exemplary text I will use to distinguish this phase is Nikos Kazantzakis's *The Last Temptation of Christ* (1951).[4] My argument is that, although Kazantzakis set out to represent Christ in an existential way, by freeing the figure from the "falsehoods" he saw in it, he ultimately repeated many of the traditional features. These include the essentialism evident in the quotation given at the beginning of this essay, and features of what I will call "idealistic asceticism." Kazantzakis's idealistic asceticism is further evident in the 1988 film adaptation of the book directed by Martin Scorsese. Although both works caused a scandal at the time of their release, neither goes far enough in imagining an existentially recognizable, human figure of Christ. Indeed, with these two works as evidence, I will suggest that a consistently humanized, existential Christ has yet to be imagined. Despite these two attempts and similar attempts to humanize Christ from more recent times, such as Dan Brown's *The Da Vinci Code* (2003)[5] and Mel Gibson's *The Passion of the Christ* (2004), the Christ figure we have today is still in many ways hardly recognizable as a human being.

Nikos Kazantzakis was born on the island of Crete in 1883 and died in the University Clinic in Freiburg, West Germany, in 1957. Throughout his life he struggled to give his own personal interpretation to the figure of Christ, and as a highly educated reader he sought to deepen this interpretation by mixing in the perspectives of several other prominent writers. One of the most important writers for Kazantzakis was the German philosopher Friedrich Nietzsche. It is not known for certain when Kazantzakis began his study of Nietzsche, though he was probably influenced by his studies with Henri Bergson in Paris in 1908. In any case, by 1909 Kazantzakis had completed his thesis on "Nietzsche in the Philosophy of Law." Though the critical reception of Nietzsche's work had already begun in the late 1880s, this thesis is actually one of the earliest comprehensive scholarly responses to Nietzsche. Kazantzakis's response to Nietzsche can be seen in the context of the earliest, cultlike phase in Nietzsche reception. The intellectual historian Steven E. Aschheim, in *The Nietzsche Legacy in Germany 1890–1990*, cites one of the eulogies given at Nietzsche's death in 1900: "Nietzsche was the guide to a new human future, a man whose stature was comparable only to Buddha, Zarathustra, and Jesus Christ. These were men whose visions encompassed whole nations and whose effects could be measured only in aeons."[6] In agreement with the exaggeratedly heroic depiction of Nietzsche's early reception, Kazantzakis projected a figure of Christ mixed with Nietzschean qualities in *The Last Temptation of Christ*. Though it may seem strange for Kazantzakis to have drawn on Nietzsche for his depiction of Christ, given Nietzsche's many critical comments about Christianity in *Twilight of the Idols*, for example, Kazantzakis clearly saw parallels between the two figures.[7]

There has been considerable discussion of Nietzsche's influence on Kazantzakis, most notably in McDonough's *Nietzsche and Kazantzakis*,[8] but I would argue not so much for Nietzsche's "influence" but for the view that Kazantzakis took specific examples from Nietzsche's life and work and used them to create his own imaginative depictions. Kazantzakis recognized his affinities with Nietzsche, as well as Nietzsche's affinities with other historical figures, and made use of Nietzsche for the exploration of his own distinctive concerns. The result in *The Last Temptation* is a peculiarly hybrid representation of Christ, a Christ with decidedly Nietzschean features. One of Kazantzakis's central issues, which he highlights in the prologue to the novel, involves his sense of two opposing "forces" within himself:

> My principal anguish and the source of all my joys and sorrows from my youth onward has been the incessant, merciless battle between the spirit and the flesh.
>
> Within me are the dark immemorial forces of the Evil One, human and pre-human; within me too are the luminous forces, human and pre-human, of God—and my soul is the arena where these two armies have clashed and met. (*LTC*, 1)

This description characterizes a kind of anguish from the life of a polarized, self-divided seeker. Kazantzakis describes himself as someone who has experienced the same type of "battle" that he will depict for Christ. The battle is dualistic, "between the spirit and the flesh" or the spirit and the body, and linked to this struggle is the conflict between good and evil, or God and Satan. Further, these are experiences that "every man" has: "Every man partakes of the divine nature in both his spirit and his flesh. That is why the mystery of Christ is not simply a mystery for a particular creed: it is universal" (*LTC*, 1). Kazantzakis argues that the dualistic conflict between the spirit and the flesh is essentially the same for Christ, himself, and everyone.

There are indeed many examples from earlier writers to support this claim, including Nietzsche's Zarathustra, a character modeled on the Persian prophet Zoroaster, the founder of Zoroastrianism.[9] Zoroaster was the prophet of darkness and light, good and evil, and Nietzsche had returned to this figure to address the very source of dualistic thinking itself. Not only did Kazantzakis write on Nietzsche for his thesis, but later he worked on translations of both *The Birth of Tragedy* and *Thus Spoke Zarathustra* into Greek. In order to create his figure of Christ, Kazantzakis took advantage of Nietzsche's dualistic Zarathustra in relation to his own personal experience. The examples of Zarathustra and Nietzsche confirmed for Kazantzakis the belief that the dualism of spirit and flesh is widespread. Kazantzakis's Christ thus becomes a patchwork figure, patched together from various sources and traditions. In their book *A Thousand Plateaus:*

Capitalism and Schizophrenia, Gilles Deleuze and Felix Guattari give a useful definition: "Patchwork, in conformity with migration, whose degree of affinity with nomadism it shares, is not only named after trajectories, but 'represents' trajectories, becomes inseparable from speed or movement in an open space."[10] As a patchwork, migratory, and nomadic figure, Kazantzakis's Christ is not an especially Christian one, in the sense of a compassionate, sympathetic healer, but a figure resembling an embattled seeker. This Christ carries the features of, perhaps, John the Baptist, transposed into Nietzsche's Zarathustra. The humanity of Kazantzakis's Christ consists in the extremity of his internal struggle, the extent to which he is being torn apart from inside.

Yet Kazantzakis goes still further and suggests that the battle between the body and soul will lead men in an ascending direction as they follow what is allegedly their "duty":

> Struggle between the flesh and the spirit, rebellion and resistance, reconciliation and submission, and finally—the supreme purpose of the struggle—union with God: this was the ascent taken by Christ, the ascent which he invites us to take as well, following in his bloody tracks.
>
> This is the Supreme Duty of the man who struggles—to set out for the lofty peak which Christ, the first-born son of salvation, attained. How can we begin? (*LTC*, 2)

Kazantzakis uses the image of a struggling, ascending figure who could be linked to an entire tradition of struggling or striving figures: from John the Baptist to Nietzsche's Zarathustra, Goethe's Faust, and Camus's Sisyphus.[11] The process of a "struggle between the flesh and the spirit" is characterized by contrasting sets of oppositions, on the way to "union with God." Kazantzakis imagines an ascending, uplifting process of supreme effort aimed at joining with a transcendental figure for the purpose of salvation. In logical, structural terms, Kazantzakis follows the pattern of dialectical sublimation, whereby it is only through the struggle of opposites that a new level or a higher synthesis is reached. His is a kind of neo-Romantic, neo-Hegelian vision, whereby the seeker ascends to salvation through a dialectical process of self-critique and self-overcoming. We can already see from these opening remarks to the novel how Kazantzakis has taken the material from the Bible and Nietzsche and turned it in a certain direction. On the one hand, the figure of Christ will be essentially human, according to Kazantzakis: a struggling, driven character seeking release. But on the other hand, he will be pursuing an idealistic goal: seeking "union with God," a goal that Nietzsche would surely have put into question. According to this account,

Kazantzakis's Christ embarks on a journey that will transcend Nietzsche's in the direction of salvation.

Although he uses language reminiscent of Nietzsche, Kazantzakis is much more committed to the idea of a meaningful, fulfilling struggle for redemption and salvation than Nietzsche would have supported. There is no sense of the "will to power" in Kazantzakis's vision; rather, the entire purpose of human struggle is to ascend toward salvation through a union with the divine. What Kazantzakis envisions here is much closer to, for example, Dante than to Nietzsche, a claim supported by the fact that Dante's *Divine Comedy* was also among Kazantzakis's earlier and more successful translations and that he referred to Dante as his "Fellow Traveler" as late as 1949.[12] It would help to understand Kazantzakis's representation if we were to see him writing a modernized version of Dante's pilgrim's struggle toward salvation. This is very different from Nietzsche's perspective, and it should certainly qualify Kazantzakis as one of the great recent visionaries of a modern Christ. The Christ in Kazantzakis's book is reinterpreted through Nietzsche into a modern version of Dante's seeker. This Christ consists of elements from the Bible but also from Kazantzakis's own life and readings, specifically from Nietzsche and Dante. The Kazantzakis Christ is a patchwork, a collage consisting of bits from various other writers and his own concerns. Under the pressure of the Dantesque elements in his picture of Christ, the Nietzschean elements are bent in the direction of a transcendental journey. Kazantzakis takes the emphasis in Nietzsche on this world, on this life and its importance for the individual, and turns it toward the next world, the supernatural, and salvation. In this way Kazantzakis bends the existential elements in Nietzsche toward a more essentialist, idealistic view that stresses the asceticism of Christ.

This is, in other words, a quasi-existential representation. Even though Kazantzakis had studied with Bergson, had read and corresponded with Sartre and Camus, and was well aware of existentialism as a contemporary movement, his depiction of Christ retains many features from older traditions. What distinguishes existentialism, by contrast, is the insistence that the older, traditional categories are no longer relevant to understanding human beings. According to Sartre, for example, humans should not be understood as beings with essential or fixed qualities, but rather as changing, malleable beings who actually transform themselves from one situation to another. In his famous lecture from October 1945, "Existentialism Is a Humanism," Sartre argued that "*existence* comes before *essence*,"[13] an argument suggesting that the situations in which we find ourselves are more important than our essential nature. Further, since it is our existence that we respond to primarily, we are free to create ourselves anew: "Man is nothing but that which he makes of himself. That is the first principle of existentialism" (*BW*, 29). Sartre's depiction of a being that chooses to change, develop, or become other to itself is quite at odds with the depiction of Christ in *The Last Temptation* as a figure driven by idealistic asceticism. Indeed, Sartre's antiessentialism, which was taken further by Simone de Beauvoir in her book *The Second* Sex, would dispense with the idea of "human destiny" altogether.[14] For both Beauvoir and Sartre, we are much freer than we traditionally believe, and this freedom is neither tied to a transcendental figure, nor to salvation, nor to any particular state of mind or emotion. Our freedom is open to us to pursue, and that is what makes us worried.

From this more antiessentialist perspective, anyone who rejects Kazantzakis's vision as heretical is missing the point. Kazantzakis's aim was to endorse Christ, not to reject him: "I am certain that every free man who reads this book, so filled as it is with love, will more than ever before, better than ever before, love Christ" (*LTC*, 4). Here Kazantzakis specifically endorses the role of love in his characterization. His idea is that if we are free to imagine Christ as the particular type of hybrid that he himself has imagined, combining disparate features depicted with love, then the reader, too, will come to "love Christ," "better than ever before." Clearly this is not a text directed against Christ but rather one that seeks to renew the figure of Christ through a distinctive combination of features created out of various representations. Kazantzakis wanted his readers to think about their representations of Christ, for themselves and from their own experiences. He was seeking a more personal relation to the figure, just as writers from Kierkegaard to Luther to Dante to Augustine and to Paul have done. Kazantzakis identified with Christ, but in his own revisionist ways, just as many others have done over the last two thousand years. These may not be the more familiarly Christian ways, but they certainly aim to celebrate Christ.

Beyond the dualisms of spirit and flesh, good and evil, God and Satan, which he borrowed in part from Nietzsche but also from others, Kazantzakis comments that he has taken over some of Nietzsche's concepts while overcoming some of his problems: "We must add to the essence of life, express the summit of our desire. In the grip of a superhuman will, we must surge forward. There is no moral problem binding us. This has been solved for us, whereas for Nietzsche it was insoluble and extremely painful" (*NKB*, 56). From this passage we see the essentialist vitalism from Nietzsche's philosophy of life, the concept of a "superhuman will" from his theory of the superman, and the reflection on the "moral problem" that Nietzsche had been unable to solve. The dualistic struggle between spirit and flesh reaches heightened or intensified form in theories of life, the superman, or persistent moral dilemmas. Kazantzakis believed that he had solved the moral problem, whereas Nietzsche had not. In *The Last Temptation of Christ* Kazantzakis offers his solution: to embrace the "ascetic ideal," which Nietzsche had explicitly criticized in the third essay of his *On the Genealogy of Morality*, called "What Do Ascetic Ideals Mean?"[15] Nietzsche's point is that the "ascetic ideal" has in fact several meanings, depending on the context and the people involved. It is not at all to be promoted as the greatest quality of the human, but simply as a "basic fact of the human will, its *horror vacui*: it needs a goal" (*GM*, 67). For Nietzsche, ascetic idealism could mean many things, with the most positive or the most negative consequences.

Nietzsche's problem, from Kazantzakis's point of view, was that he had lived as an ascetic idealist at the same time as he criticized this very type of behavior. Early in 1915, Kazantzakis described in his notebooks his faith in the ascetic life and how that was linked for him to Dante: "I shall conquer everything through asceticism. To summarize a throng of thoughts in a vigorous, striking image. To give the creatures of the imagination the same relief possessed by living reality, like Dante" (*NKB*, 57). Later that same year, he noted his feelings in church and his growing identification with Christ: "Great feeling in the church. The crucified Christ seemed to belong to me more, to be more my own self. I was profoundly aware of the 'suffering God' inside me, and I said, 'with perseverance, love, and endeavor may the Resurrection come'" (*NKB*, 58). Nearly thirty-five years before he wrote *The Last Temptation*, Kazantzakis had identified with the figure of Christ, proclaimed the values of asceticism, and pursued the writings of both Dante and Nietzsche. Though it may seem at first as if Nietzsche's work, or a more consistently realized existentialist perspective, might lead to a wholesale rejection of Dante and Christ, Kazantzakis had already begun to combine these traditions in his distinctively hybrid interpretation. In the first place, this peculiar combination was meant to be for himself, his own personal guide to self-transformation through struggle, but his unique combination of art, religion, and philosophy was evidently also meant for the public as well. Kazantzakis disseminated his vision of Christ through Dante and Nietzsche by means of a patchwork image, and this image culminated in *The Last Temptation*.

In addition to his interests in art, religion, and philosophy, Kazantzakis developed a lifelong involvement with politics.[16] As part of the odyssey he made before he came to write *The Last Temptation*, he traveled to Paris, Berlin, Vienna, Madrid, Rome, and Cairo, among other places, to live for short periods and to write, but perhaps most importantly to Moscow. Kazantzakis had become fascinated by the Russian Revolution, and especially by the figure of Lenin. For Kazantzakis, Lenin himself was one of the great ascetics in human history, but someone who also had a powerfully transformative vision of society. Kazantzakis was even invited to the tenth anniversary of the revolution by the Soviet government (*NKB*, 165). By this time, however, he had grown impatient with the actual course of Soviet politics and had written a longer essay called "Metacommunism" (*NKB*, 155). His idea was to combine into a new religion the strengths of Communism, in social terms, with the drive to ascetic self-overcoming he had derived from Christ, Dante, and Nietzsche. By the time he came to write *The Last Temptation*, his image of Christ had been shaped by art, religion, philosophy, and politics. This distinctive patchwork informs the book and continued in different ways in the reception of the book. Kazantzakis clearly had a lifelong fascination with Christ, marked by both existential and metaphysical concerns, yet the existential qualities are consistently turned in the direction of the metaphysical, religious search.

The story line of the novel follows the broad outline of the story of Christ from the New Testament. But Kazantzakis adds various dimensions to the story from beginning to end. This process of grafting on different dimensions to the story creates a fuller picture of the figure of Christ than the one given by Matthew, Mark, Luke, or John. Kazantzakis even shows Matthew writing down his account of Christ's life, as if to substantiate the source of his own version in the novel. I see this as part of his commentary on the story, and in this Kazantzakis is doing what many other writers have done before him. Kierkegaard, for example, in *Fear and Trembling*, created a similar revision of the story of Abraham.[17] What joins Kierkegaard and Kazantzakis is not only their involvement in the tradition that came to be known as "existentialism" but also their technique of taking well-known figures from the Bible and adding richer, more psychological dimensions to them. Such writings are best seen as thought experiments. Kierkegaard gave a more psychological and ethical account of Abraham, whereas Kazantzakis is recommending that we imagine the Christ figure through the perspectives of art, religion, philosophy, and politics. Both are mainly adding to the discussion of sacred figures, not denying their sacred qualities. In my view the important issue here is not whether such projects are heretical or not, but whether they are convincing. It is clear that Kazantzakis was trying to reinvigorate the sacredness in the figure of Christ while preserving the human features, but how convincing is his version? To address this question we have to turn more closely to the book.

Kazantzakis begins his depiction with an image of possession: "A cool heavenly breeze took possession of him" (*LTC*, 5). This first sentence introduces a number of elements that are crucial for the story. Christ, the "him" imagined here, is a figure under "possession." This psychological, somewhat mystical or occultist term suggests that Christ is not a deliberate, fully self-aware or self-controlled figure, but someone driven by conflicting forces. The notion that Christ was "possessed" gives a different slant to the figure than the one more commonly imagined, but it follows the idea of "visitation," for example, from the story of Mary's pregnancy, or it reminds us of the image of possession from the stories of Greek gods like Dionysus. From the outset Christ is possessed by nature: in this first sentence of the novel Kazantzakis plays with the double meaning of the word "heaven." The "breeze" is "heavenly," suggesting that a breeze came from the heavens. With the image of "possession" by more natural forces, Kazantzakis tries from the beginning to ground his depiction of Christ in this world, with experiences that are plausible for all of us. His Christ is not supernatural but split between the world of human experiences with nature, or the body, and another world, namely, the "heavenly" world of the spirit. The split in this Christ is the split between the earth and the sky, the body and the spirit, the human and the divine. It is as if the split itself, the alienation in the figure based on the division between the spirit and the flesh, were what Christ shares with everyone. Ultimately, it will be the resolution of this split that makes him a transcendent figure, someone who surpasses the more familiar divisions in human nature.

The opening blends a description of the setting with the internal monologue of the character:

> Above, the blossoming skies had opened into a thick tangle of stars; below, on the ground, the stones were steaming, still afire from the great heat of the day. Heaven and earth were peaceful and sweet, filled with the deep silence of ageless night-voices, more silent than silence itself. It was dark, probably midnight. God's eyes, the sun and the moon, were closed and sleeping, and the young man, his mind carried away by the gentle breeze, meditated happily. (*LTC*, 5)

In this description, "heaven and earth" are joined in a "peaceful," "sweet" connection that intoxicates "the young man." He meditates "happily," in harmony with his environment. The picture is of a happy union between the man and nature. Kazantzakis thus begins his story with a neo-Romantic image. The alienation between the body and the spirit is soothed, softened by the power of "the gentle breeze."

Midway through the paragraph, however, the scene changes and introduces another, more sinister yet equally universal, set of elements:

> But as he thought, "What solitude! What Paradise!" suddenly the wind changed and thickened; it was no longer a heavenly breeze but the reek of heavy greasy breaths, as though in some overgrown thicket or damp luxuriant orchard below him a gasping animal, or a village, was struggling in vain to sleep. The air had become dense, restless. The tepid breaths of men, animals and elves rose and mixed with a sharp odor from sour human sweat, bread freshly removed from the oven, and the laurel oil used by the women to anoint their hair.
>
> You sniffed, you sensed, you divined—but saw nothing. (*LTC*, 5)

The "wind" changes from a "heavenly breeze" to "heavy greasy breaths"—suddenly the air has moved from the heavens to the earth. "God's eyes" have disappeared and been replaced by the "breaths of men, animals and elves," the "odor from sour human sweat," "bread," and "laurel oil used by the women." In a strikingly dialectical reversal, the air from heaven is transformed into the emanations from the earth, and now humans as well as "elves" are linked with animals and food. The elfin reference creates links to fairy tales and mythology, and the displacement of women—there is only the smell of their oil—subordinates the women to a remote location. It is not clear why Kazantzakis would have included "elves" in this depiction, and it certainly seems that he should have promoted a more positive image of women. But perhaps the "elves," at least, were the product of the translator's alchemy. In "A Note on the Author and His Use of Language," translator P. A. Bien promotes the idea that Kazantzakis was a champion of "the peasant imagination" (*LTC*, 502). According to Bien, Kazantzakis preferred the language of "the demotic," as against "the unimaginativeness of pedantic intellectuals," or the "forces of newspaper jargon and faulty composition courses in the schools" (*LTC*, 503). The "elves," from this perspective, would have arisen from folk traditions of storytelling. In any case, the concatenation of ingredients ultimately reaches your nose—"you," who can smell the mixture, but can see "nothing." Kazantzakis's narrator draws a large ring of participants into the story of Christ, extending even to the reader, with this all-embracing "you" who is involved as a participant and an onlooker from the beginning. The reader is drawn in, and will continue in the story from both inside and outside the events of the narrative. It is as if Kazantzakis took the ingredients of the birth scene in the manger in Bethlehem and transposed them into Christ's adulthood. There are no angels in this version, but the "elves" and the "deep silence of ageless night-voices" accompany the sleeping figure.

At the same time, this reconstructed Christ suffers from psychological, social, and spiritual torments. He had dreamt the opening scene, his dream is interrupted by nightmare images, and when he awakes he is lying on wood shavings. His father is paralyzed, his mother is bitter and despondent, and he blames himself for having sent Magdalene into prostitution. This Christ is the son of a carpenter, but he is also the maker of crosses for the Romans. Suddenly his waking stupor is interrupted by the angry figure of Judas, a "redbeard" and a "Zealot," who has been sent to kill Christ for his collaboration with the Romans. Here Christ has another visitation, this time from a vengeful Judas who is determined to do violence to him. Judas demands of him, "How will you ever pay for all those sins, poor devil?" (*LTC*, 19). Christ answers by evoking their brotherly relationship: "'With my life, Judas, my brother,' he finally managed to say. 'I have nothing else'" (*LTC*, 19). For Kazantzakis, Christ and Judas have a brotherly relationship: throughout the text the one provokes the other by attacking, giving way, criticizing, and cajoling. This is not the occasional but painful relationship imagined in other versions of the Christ story. In this version Christ and Judas have an ongoing struggle with each other that culminates in crucifixion and its aftermath. Kazantzakis clearly juxtaposes the apparently weaker and more human Judas with the presumably stronger and more transcendent Christ, in order to profile Christ's distinctive characteristics. Christ resembles Judas but is stronger; he is a more supernatural human being. Judas is a kind of *Doppelgänger*, an alter ego, in Kazantzakis's version. This Judas is angrily political, even protorevolutionary, and Christ's involvement with him adds a somewhat political edge to the depiction.

There are many other events along Christ's journey in Kazantzakis's version, but for the purposes of my argument I will turn to the ending, to what constitutes the "last temptation" predicted by the title. At the end of the twenty-ninth chapter, Christ is depicted on the cross being crucified by angels: "A multitude of angels had come down from heaven, holding hammers and nails in their hands. They flew around Jesus, swung the hammers happily and nailed the hands and feet; some tightly bound the victim's body with stout cord so that he would not fall; and a small angel with rosy cheeks and golden curls held a lance and pierced Jesus' heart." Instead of the "heavenly breeze" from the opening, now Christ is tormented by the angels themselves, presumably the messengers from God.

But just as he is about to die, Christ calls out the beginning of his famous last line: "Eli . . . Eli . . ." (*LTC*, 443). He then drops his head and faints. From chapter 30 to the end of chapter 33, he faces his "last temptation." Kazantzakis makes use of the presumed length of Jesus' ministry, from age thirty to thirty-three, to organize the ending. In this interlude, which lasts for nearly three chapters and involves about fifty pages in the English edition, Kazantzakis adds his most sensational twist to the biblical version.

During this section of the book, Christ enjoys the possibility of another life, as if he had had the chance to choose another, more familiar kind of existence. Here Kazantzakis returns to the problems of human existence and decides in favor of the ascetic ideal. Most significantly, the problems of human existence are linked to women, sexuality, childbearing, and fathering a family. Kazantzakis's version considers the possibility that Christ might have become a father, even a bigamist, but ultimately decides in favor of the ascetic.

Christ wakes up from the cross and finds himself leaning on a tree. He is met by a "guardian angel" (*LTC*, 445) who leads him to meet Mary Magdalene (*LTC*, 450). Christ then follows a path that leads him in a different direction from the one that led him to the cross: "The road by which the mortal becomes immortal, the road by which God descends to earth in human shape. I went astray because I sought a route outside the flesh; I wanted to go by way of the clouds, great thoughts and death. Woman, precious fellow worker of God, forgive me. I bow and worship you, mother of God" (*LTC*, 450). Christ embarks on a journey into the flesh, into this world, and one that is involved with women. He is no longer the fierce ascetic who spurns women, but he rejoices with them and accepts women into his life. His "last temptation," in the version constructed by Kazantzakis, is the possibility of a life on earth, with women, that includes the pleasures and pains of the flesh. Christ is tempted here by the opposite of the ascetic ideal, and for a time he pursues this way.

In this version of the nonascetic life, Magdalene dies and Christ begins relations with two other women, Martha and Mary (*LTC*, 460). These women embrace him and have children with him. In addition, his "guardian angel" turns "into a Negro boy" (*LTC*, 459), someone from "Ethiopia" (*LTC*, 464) who accompanies and guides Christ in this new life. The "angel" encourages Christ to see the two women as different sides of the same figure: "There is only one woman in the world; one, with innumerable faces. One of those faces is coming. Get up to greet it. I am leaving" (*LTC*, 466). After he has left the cross, Christ learns to accept and embrace the world of the flesh—of sexuality, childbearing, and fathering a family. It is as if the repressed, physical side of the figure were brought out and explored in the Kazantzakis version.

For the "last temptation" of Christ, in other words, Kazantzakis imagines a more unrepressed and openly sexual incarnation of the figure. This unrepressed version could be compared with the figures in D. H. Lawrence's novels, for example, but certainly should be related to Sigmund Freud's work.[18] (By all accounts, too, Kazantzakis himself was involved intimately with many women during his life.) The version of the Christ story that now emerges is one of a figure fully involved with the pleasures of the flesh, the home life, and the domestic realm. Christ even becomes a kind of entrepreneur when he establishes a business for himself with the two women. By pairing the emphasis on sexuality with an emphasis on business, Kazantzakis clearly imagines a neo-Freudian–proto-Marxian combination for this last temptation. Now, presumably, this Christ figure tastes the temptations of a more familiar existence, a human existence marked by pleasure and pain, old age, sickness, and domestic issues such as sex and money.

It is disturbing that Kazantzakis would place women, Africans, and money on the side of "the Devil" (*LTC*, 496) in the picture representing the last temptation for his Christ figure. Beyond the sexism and racism he might be accused of at this point, the links he suggests between women, Africans, and Satan also reveal the extent to which this version is still largely committed to the basic assumptions underlying the biblical account. Though he spent a great deal of effort developing a more psychological, somewhat tormented depiction of Christ, in the end the last temptation imagined by Kazantzakis reinforces the very values he was presumably criticizing from the outset. This Christ turns against the potentially existential character he might have become, and instead becomes a reincarnation of the ascetic he has so often been. Kazantzakis's Christ finally does not differ very much from the biblical figure.

The crux of the matter appears at the very end of the text. At this point, Christ wakes up on the cross again and has his final epiphany:

> The moment he cried "Eli Eli" and fainted, Temptation had captured him for a split second and led him astray. The joys, marriages and children were lies; the decrepit, degraded old men who shouted coward, deserter, traitor at him were lies. All—all were illusions sent by the Devil. His disciples were alive and thriving. They had gone over Sea and land and were proclaiming the Good News. Everything had turned out as it should, glory be to God! He uttered a triumphant cry: "It is accomplished!" And it was as though he had said: Everything has begun. (*LTC*, 496)

The celebratory language here points to the emphasis wanted by the narrator, recognized by the character, and ultimately promoted by the author. There is not much ironic distance here between the author, Kazantzakis in this case, and the narrator or the character of Christ. Indeed, the emphasis is rather the other way around: Kazantzakis the author evidently wanted his own perspective, at least as recorded in the prologue and supported by the biography, to merge with the perspectives of the narrator and the character. In this version, relations with women, children, old men, the aging body, the "guardian angel," and the "Negro boy" are implicitly denounced as "illusions sent by the Devil," temptations this Christ figure must overcome. He overcomes these temptations by dying on the cross, by embracing the ascetic life, and by beginning a new religion. The potentially existentialist figure of Christ has been transformed through ascetic idealism into a version much closer to the martyred, self-sacrificing, and biblical one familiar from two thousand years of religious tradition.

The self-overcoming reversal carried out on the text by itself—or perhaps it would be better to think of this transformation as a process carried out by the author on his text, his vision, and himself—can be measured by comparing this ending with the ending of Nietzsche's *On the Genealogy of Morality* and by Freud's suggestions in *Civilization and Its Discontents*. Nietzsche's point is that the ideals of chastity, humility, and poverty are self-destructive and therefore not helpful for the improvement of human life. As he writes at the end of his analysis, "We would much rather will *nothingness* than *not* will," suggesting that human beings spend a great deal of their energy investing in self-destructive activities rather than constructive ones (*GM*, 118). Though he clearly recognized that he himself was subject to the charge of being an ascetic idealist, Nietzsche showed a great deal more skepticism and critique toward the complex than Kazantzakis did in his book. Moreover, Kazantzakis evidently thought that these ideals were the best, highest, and noblest ones for improving human life. This position brings him, in my view, directly opposed to Nietzsche's view, even to Kierkegaard's view, let alone in contrast to later existentialists such as Sartre and Beauvoir. Furthermore, the touches of sexism and racism that appear in the ending of the novel would have been antithetical to Beauvoir and Sartre as well.

Of course, I am not suggesting that existentialism was a movement in which one single position dominated. Most of the existentialists rejected the very claim that it was a movement; they even rejected its name and each other. Kazantzakis's position brings him closer to the view of, for example, Albert Camus, with his figure of Sisyphus, and Walter Kaufmann, the translator of Nietzsche and one of the most prominent early writers in English on existentialism.[19] In his book on Nietzsche entitled *Nietzsche: Philosopher, Psychologist, Antichrist*, but also in the translations and in the commentaries he appended to them, Kaufmann consistently developed a reading of Nietzsche as a figure of self-overcoming or self-surpassing.[20] *Nietzsche* first appeared in 1950, at about the same time as Kazantzakis was writing *The Last Temptation of Christ*, though there was no contact between Kazantzakis and Kaufmann as far as I know. In his analysis, Kaufmann is at pains to distinguish Nietzsche from his reception by the Nazis. Mainly he wanted to show that Nietzsche would never have had anything to do with such a mass movement, not only because he was committed to a more individual view in the first place, but also because he was recommending self-overcoming so forcefully. At every place where he could in his translations, too, Kaufmann used the notion of self-overcoming or related notions to characterize Nietzsche's account. Certainly the emphasis on an un-Nazi Nietzsche was positive and important. But Kaufmann went too far in the direction of creating a neo-Christian figure for his Nietzsche. His self-overcoming Nietzsche resembles an ascetic idealist as well, because he is continually interested in turning against his own appetites. The side of Nietzsche that represents the "will to power," as a result, is blocked out, pushed aside, or denied. The result is similar to Kazantzakis's Christ. On both accounts, true heroism or the true "superman" arises when individuals turn against themselves so much that they endorse the ascetic ideal. Individuals, from this perspective of self-overcoming, overcome themselves into nothingness. Surely this is not the kind of strength that Nietzsche had in mind.

In contrast, I argue that Nietzsche's view was that humans should find new, healthier, and more self-constructive ways of self-transformation than what the Judeo-Christian tradition recommends. These ways would connect more directly with Sartre's recommendation in his essay "Existentialism Is a Humanism": "You are free, therefore choose—that is to say, invent" (*BW*, 34). A more existentialist view is not an ascetic, self-denying view, but a more life-enhancing, self-creating view. This certainly includes the kind of life that Kazantzakis's Christ rejects as linked to the devil.

In fact, if Freud's arguments were included as well, it could be seen that accepting a sexually active, unrepressed life with a family would be far healthier than the repressed, neurotic life promoted by the ascetic ideal. Freud even went so far as to propose in *Civilization and Its Discontents* that the only way out of the violence gathering around him in the

1930s was through a more open, unrepressed sexuality. Of course, at the same time he saw that a completely unrepressed humanity might tend toward more violent impulses. In any case, Freud saw that repression leads to neurosis, whereas Kazantzakis suggests that the ascetic ideal leads to salvation. My point is that Kazantzakis finally turned in his novel against the potential of the more existentialist, post-Freudian Christ he had created. The "battle" that Kazantzakis evoked in the prologue to his novel was eventually decided in the direction of the spirit, not the flesh, with the spirit representing the ascetic and idealistic view. Kazantzakis's picture actually repeats and supports the most traditional view of Christ as a suffering, self-sacrificing martyr who gave up his life for humanity on the cross.

Not surprisingly, the 1988 film by Martin Scorsese envisions the last temptation in ways similar to Kazantzakis's version. The main difference in the 1988 film is the depiction of Christ as a variation on a figure from the 1960s. As played by Willem Dafoe, Scorsese's Christ figure resembles a visionary hippie. He treats the women as if they were in a commune together, and he gathers his followers as if they were believers in a counterculture. When Scorsese's Christ turns against the last temptation, it is as if he turns against a materialistic deformation of the alternative lifestyle. But this turn is just what Nietzsche decried as following from ascetic idealism; the conclusion of the film resembles very closely the conclusion of the book and the scenario Nietzsche had criticized. In Kazantzakis's version Christ comes to resemble a hermit/prophet/social revolutionary, whereas in Scorsese's version Christ comes to resemble a figure from the 1960s counterculture, or what is now called "the hippie generation"—those people who resisted the Vietnam War, dropped out of the mainstream culture, moved back to the land, and began living in communes. Despite their differences in terms of characters and setting, neither version differs substantially from the Christian view, so that ultimately neither version offers a significant alternative to the biblical one.[21]

In sum, perhaps a more fully articulated, existentialist Christ still remains to be imagined. Perhaps there is more to both the figure of Christ and the movement of existentialism that could be combined more successfully in the future. In my view this would not be a figure of ascetic idealism, but one that would precisely recognize and recommend the kind of life that is rejected in the book and the film. For the divine potential of the human can only be realized in this world, within history and subject to the vagaries of time and chance.

NOTES

Epigraph. N. Kazantzakis, *Nikos Kazantzakis: A Biography Based on His Letters,* trans. Amy Mims (New York: Simon & Schuster, 1968), 505. Further references to this text will be noted with *NKB.*

1. The study of interpretation, or hermeneutics, was promoted by many in the Christian tradition, including Augustine, *On Christian Teaching,* trans. R. P. H. Green (Oxford: Oxford University Press, 1999), and P. Melanchthon, *Orations on Philosophy and Education,* ed. Suchiko Kusukawa, trans. C. Salazar (Cambridge: Cambridge University Press, 1999), until it was expanded into other areas, for example, by M. Heidegger in *Ontology: The Hermeneutics of Facticity,* trans. J. van Buren (Bloomington, IN: Indiana University Press, 1999).

2. One of the more useful recent works on "the historical Christ" is by S. C. Evans, *The Historical Christ and the Jesus of Faith: The Incarnational Narrative as History* (Oxford: Oxford University Press, 1996).

3. There has been considerable debate about the concept of existentialism; see, for example, Ç. Guignon and D. Pereboom, eds., *Existentialism: Basic Writings* (Indianapolis: Hackett, 2001).

4. N. Kazantzakis, *The Last Temptation of Christ,* trans. P. A. Bien (New York: Simon & Schuster, 1960).

5. D. Brown, *The Da Vinci Code* (New York: Doubleday, 2003). Christ barely appears in either this novel or the film version, directed by Ron Howard (2006), though both suggest that he started a family with Mary Magdalene, a suggestion also made by *The Last Temptation of Christ.*

6. S. E. Aschheim, *The Nietzsche Legacy in Germany, 1890–1990* (Berkeley, CA: University of California Press, 1992), 23.

7. F. Nietzsche, *Twilight of the Idols,* trans. R. J. Hollingdale (Middlesex, England: Penguin, 1968).

8. See B. T. McDonough, *Nietzsche and Kazantzakis* (Washington, DC: University Press of America, 1978).

9. See the latest version in English: F. Nietzsche, *Thus Spoke Zarathustra,* trans. Graham Parkes (Oxford: Oxford University Press, 2005).

10. See G. Deleuze and F. Guattari, *A Thousand Plateaus: Capitalism and Schizophrenia,* trans. B. Massumi (Minneapolis: University of Minnesota Press, 1987), 477.

11. See J. W. von Goethe, *Goethe's Faust,* trans. W. Kaufmann (New York: Viking, 1967); and A. Camus, *The Myth of Sisyphus and Other Essays,* trans. Justin O'Brien (New York: Knopf, 1955).

12. H. Kazantzakis, *NKB,* trans. Amy Mims (New York: Simon & Schuster, 1968), 482. For a good recent translation of Dante's epic poem into English, see Dante Alighieri, *The Divine Comedy,* trans. C. H. Sisson (Oxford: Oxford University Press, 1998).

13. From *Jean-Paul Sartre: Basic Writings,* ed. S. Priest (London: Routledge, 2001), 27. Passages from this text will be cited with *BW.*

14. S. de Beauvoir, *The Second Sex,* trans. and ed. H. M. Parshley (New York: Vintage, 1989).

15. See F. Nietzsche, *On the Genealogy of Morality,* trans. M. Clark and A. J. Swensen (Indianapolis: Hackett, 1998), 67–118. Passages from this text will be noted by *GM.*

16. See P. A. Bien's account of Kazantzakis's life and writing in terms of his "politics of the spirit" in Bien, *Kazantzakis: Politics of the Spirit* (Princeton, NJ: Princeton University Press, 1989).

17. See S. Kierkegaard, *Fear and Trembling,* trans. H. V. and E. H. Hong (Princeton, NJ: Princeton University Press, 1983). Though the concept of existentialism was only promoted

after Sartre's lecture in 1945, both Kierkegaard and Nietzsche have often been considered important forerunners. See, for example, the influential account by W. Barrett, *Irrational Man: A Study in Existential Philosophy* (Garden City, NY: Doubleday, 1958).

18. See, e.g., D. H. Lawrence, *Women in Love* (Oxford: Oxford University Press, 1998); and S. Freud, *Civilization and Its Discontents*, in *The Standard Edition of the Complete Psychological Works*, vol. 21 (London: Hogarth, 1953), 57–146.

19. See, for example, W. Kaufmann, *Existentialism: From Dostoevsky to Sartre* (New York: Penguin, 1975).

20. W. Kaufmann, *Nietzsche: Philosopher, Psychologist, Antichrist* (Princeton: Princeton University Press, 1974).

21. On August 12, 1988, the *New York Times* carried articles both supporting and condemning the film for its vision of Christ's story. A fuller and more balanced account of the controversy around the film can be found in R. Riley, *Film, Faith, and Cultural Conflict: The Case of Martin Scorsese's* The Last Temptation of Christ (Westport, CT: Praeger, 2003).

6 | D. H. Lawrence's Risen Jesus

ROSS LABRIE

In *The Man Who Died* (1931), D. H. Lawrence reconstructed the scriptural story of Jesus by creating a mythic figure who, Lawrence felt, would be more accessible and meaningful to twentieth century persons.[1] In 1927 Lawrence wrote to a correspondent that the message of the resurrection of Jesus failed to play a vital role in modern culture. If only, he wrote, "one saw a chink of light in the tomb door."[2] In spite of the sexual pun that underlies the story of the fighting cock that dominates the first half of *The Man Who Died*, Lawrence makes it clear that an awakened sexuality is only part of the reconstructed figure of Jesus. Thus, while he altered the spiritual and mythic character of the biblical story, Lawrence was reluctant to discard the sacred import of the story of the resurrection. Indeed, in 1914 he had confided in a letter to Edward Garnett that he was "primarily" a "religious man" and that his fiction was written from the "depth" of his religious experience.[3]

Lawrence's reconstructing of the biblical story of the risen Jesus essentially involved making Jesus into a figure imbued with the culture of Romanticism, not unlike Lawrence himself. As a Romantic writer, Lawrence especially reflected the influence of Blake, whose embracing of sexuality within a religious vision and whose visual art he had in part emulated.[4] In infusing the story of Jesus with Romantic values, Lawrence merged the Christian story with the pre-Christian myth of Isis, a myth that he thought would appeal to modern consciousness. Isis is referred to at one point as "our lady" by a slave associated with the temple of Isis, a veiled reference to Mary, the mother of Jesus, and at another point the unnamed Jesus figure in *The Man Who Died* addresses her as "thou greater than the mother unto man," a reference to the biblical Eve.[5] In joining the myths of Jesus and Isis, Lawrence hoped to overcome what he thought of as the most significant limitation of the resurrection story, namely, its ontological narrowness and incompleteness.

In a letter written in May 1927, Lawrence outlined his intention in reconstructing the resurrection of Jesus in *The Man Who Died*: creating a Jesus who awoke to find "what an astonishing place the phenomenal world is, far more marvelous than any salvation or heaven" and who gave thanks that he didn't have a "'mission' any more."[6] The "mission" of Jesus, from Lawrence's point of view, involved a celibate asceticism that put him out of reach of most of humanity. Also at issue for Lawrence were the ambiguous appearances of the biblical, risen Jesus in which Jesus seemed to have a sort of apparitional form rather than a solidly physical one.[7] Lawrence dealt with these issues by depicting Jesus' resurrection as indisputably "in the flesh," as he wrote to a friend: "Of course if there is any point whatsoever in the resurrection it was the resurrection of the body."[8] By this Lawrence meant a resurrection of the body in the time immediately after the resurrection rather than some future and indistinct resurrection of the dead such as he found in Christian doctrine. As with Blake, Lawrence's idea of resurrection involved a seizing and transforming of the present moment as is indicated in his poem "The Risen Lord," which was published in 1929:

> Now I must conquer the fear of life,
> The knock of the blood in my wrists,
> The breath that rushes through my nose, the strife
> Of desires in the loins' dark twists.[9]

Lawrence set about his reconstruction by creating two plots with different sets of characters bridged by the figure of Jesus. The first plot involves the escape of a gamecock from its peasant owner in an area just outside of Jerusalem at the time of Jesus' resurrection. The two events are synchronized to bring the story of the tethered cock and the tethered Jesus into alignment with each other. Jesus is tethered in the sense that he has been bound in burial robes and in the sense, from Lawrence's point of view, that he had been imprisoned prior to his death in an ascetic and arid spirituality. Ironically, the risen Jesus intercepts the escaped cock and returns the bird to its owner, a narrative symbol of the habitual, repressive spirituality that continues to dominate his thinking shortly after his rising. Through the first half of *The Man Who Died*, Lawrence shows Jesus' increasing consciousness of the intense vitality of the bird until he acquires the bird from the peasant and then gives it away to an innkeeper whose prize cock the escaped cock had just killed in a mortal fight. By then Jesus has assented to what the bird symbolizes, including its violent fight to the death.

The second plot, which is set in the area of Sidon in ancient Phoenicia on the present-day Lebanese coast, draws the Jesus figure into a sexual encounter with a priestess of Isis, who worships the Egyptian fertility goddess at a temple overlooking the Mediterranean. Lawrence felt that the union with Isis enlarged Jesus' humanity as the Gospels' portrayal of Jesus had not. Lawrence's risen Jesus is depicted as a fertility god whose generative mission slowly dawns on him.[10] Complementing this awareness, Isis, in search of the scattered remains of Osiris, is drawn toward the spiritual awareness present in Jesus. The primordial sacredness of Lawrence's risen Jesus is underscored by the rhetoric of *The Man Who Died* with its incremental procession of sentences, sentences in which the visual detail moves with partial repetition and with slow dignity. Moreover, not infrequently, the sentences are given a sustained balance by the repeated, rhythmic use of the word "and" between clauses, evoking the sort of formal symmetry that one associates with the opening chapter of the book of Genesis.

The setting of the Isis plot, like that involving the escaped cock, is vividly related to nature as both a symbolic parallel to the development of the Jesus and Isis figures and as the matrix of their spiritual journeys. The cock leads the way for the gaunt figure of Jesus, for example, in being a "shabby little thing, but which put on brave feathers as spring advanced, and was resplendent with arched and orange neck by the time the fig-trees were letting out leaves from their end-tips" (9). Similarly, the second plot begins with the winter sun and moves through the seasonal year, whose fertility is paralleled by the priestess's conception of a child (Horus in the Isis myth), who symbolizes a tangible participation by Jesus in humanity in a way that the celibate Jesus of the Bible, in Lawrence's view, does not.

Literary critic and cultural historian Northrop Frye observed that whereas the main thrust of New Testament typology is set into the future and into the eternal world, *The Man Who Died* fits Jesus into the "revolving cycle of nature."[11] The point is consistent with Lawrence's dampening of the supernatural elements in the biblical story. Lawrence's Jesus insists, for example, that in all likelihood he had not been dead when he was put in the tomb even though, somewhat inconsistently, he later admits that he "had died" or "had been killed" (25). The inconsistency may reflect Lawrence's difficulty with the Gospel evidence that Jesus was indeed dead on the cross, but in any case he wanted to deflect attention away from the supernatural in order to emphasize the enormous significance of patterns of resurrection from within the natural. Thus, he evokes the seasonal *eter-nality* of nature in describing the emergence of spring creatures: "They came like crests of foam, out of the blue flood of the invisible desire, out of the vast invisible sea of strength, and they came coloured and tangible, evanescent, yet deathless in their coming" (34).

As has been intimated, even if nature is not associated with the theistic in *The Man Who Died*, it nevertheless transcends a conventional concep-tion of physicality and temporality and becomes the final point of refer-ence for Lawrence's Jesus. The spiritually expansive role of nature in *The Man Who Died* is thus similar in its grandeur to that suggested in great Romantic poems like Shelley's "Mont Blanc," where nature is essentially identified with the creative intelligence behind and immanent in all of being. Similarly, in Coleridge, the great theorist of English Romantic poetry, one finds in poems like "Dejection: An Ode" an understanding of nature filled with ontological intelligibility. The reason is that, as M. H. Abrams has pointed out, the heightened mind of the observer in Roman-tic writing dissolves in a unity of "self and non-self."[12]

This merging of self and non-self and of mind and matter that is so characteristic of Romanticism tends to cause the reader to revise rational-istic definitions. In *The Man Who Died*, for example, the vitality of the cock is taken by Jesus as representing not only life in the physical and organic sense but as signifying "virtue" (69). Here the usual semantic sig-nificance underlying the word "virtue," especially its moral content, becomes absorbed by a more inclusive set of meanings in which vitality, including physical and sexual vitality, is the first attribute of virtue. At the edges of such a use of language, it must be admitted, is a certain amor-phousness, and the same may be said of Lawrence's formulation of ulti-mate reality in *The Man Who Died*. In a summing up of such reality, Lawrence's Jesus spaciously declares, for example, that behind all of being are "destinies of splendour" and a "greater power" (129).

The precise nature of that power is of course difficult to determine, and in a sense, within the culture of Romanticism, to try to do so is to attempt to stretch the mind beyond its ability to formulate reality. Nonetheless, there are Romantic ideas that Lawrence employs that help the reader to understand the ontology of *The Man Who Died*. In Romanti-cism generally, because of its connection to Neoplatonism, the idea of wholeness is central, especially in writers like Blake and Coleridge. Jerome McGann has pointed out that Romantic writers strive to "pass through the multiplicity of particulars to the single reality, the 'One Life' underlying them all."[13] Allied with the idea of wholeness in Romantic thought is that

of cosmic unity. Lilian Furst has noted that Romantic writers were fascinated by correspondences between physical and immaterial reality "at the
bottom of which lay the assumption that the cosmos was ontologically
united."[14] Similarly, McGann has remarked on Wordsworth's quest for the
recovery within human consciousness of the "idea of unity."[15] The
Romantic view of the universe was *organic*, as one sees in Coleridge's view
of society as an organism with the parts "subserving" the whole.[16] In connection with the idea of wholeness, in a letter to Lady Cynthia Asquith in
1915, Lawrence deplored the ascetic, penitential atmosphere that over-
shadowed the resurrection of Jesus, the "Gethsemane Calvary and Sepulchre stages," as he put it. Instead, he asserted the need for a resurrection
that had "sound hands and feet and a whole body and a new soul."[17] Similarly, to another correspondent he insisted that Christian doctrine ostensibly taught the resurrection of the body, and "if that doesn't mean the
whole man, what does it mean? And if man is whole without a woman—
even Jesus—then I'm damned."[18]

The inclusion of the Isis myth in the second part of *The Man Who Died*
allowed Lawrence to focus on themes of separation and fragmentation
and on the need for wholeness and unity. At one point the priestess of Isis
reflects:

> She was looking for the fragments of the dead Osiris, dead and scattered
> asunder, dead, torn apart, and thrown in fragments over the wide world.
> And she must find his hands and his feet, his heart, his thighs, his head, his
> belly, she must gather him together and fold her arms round the re-assem-
> bled body till it became warm again, and roused to life, and could embrace
> her, and could fecundate her womb. (86–87)

Later, she reflects that in union with the man who died she herself
would be "whole" (141). As is evident in the relationship between Jesus
and the priestess of Isis, sexuality is clearly a significant part of the wholeness idealized by Lawrence, and sexuality is presented as much more than
"personal feeling." Lawrence regretted the Christian severing of sexuality
from the "rising and the setting of the sun," as he put it, its separation from
the "magic connexion of the equinox."[19] As this quotation suggests, the
portrayal of unity in *The Man Who Died* is organic and cosmic, in contrast
to the interpersonal unity of love called for and practiced by the biblical
Jesus.

Regarding the theme of unity in *The Man Who Died*, Jill Franks has
argued that Lawrence wanted to resurrect the "dark gods" of the self, the
instinctual and the unconscious, as against the rational and conscious.[20]
Extending the range of this observation, one might argue that it was

Lawrence's bold affirmation of the instinctual in *The Man Who Died* that contrasts sharply with the biblical Jesus' conscious and purposeful mission. Lawrence's linking of the unconscious and the sacred is evident in much of his writing, as in the uncollected poem "Resurrection of the Flesh:"

> To take it off, this clothing of a man,
> This content of my consciousness, this very me
> Which I am still and have been all I can
> And am and was, shed it all thoroughly.
>
> To come at last to nothingness, and know
> Nothing and nothing any more, and so
> Not even dream, not even pass away
> Nor cease to be: dark on the darkness stay.
>
> And then within the night where nothing is,
> And I am only next to nothingness,
> Touch me, oh touch me, give me destinies
> By touch, and a new nakedness.
>
> I want to know no more.[21]

The emphasis on knowing no more is a rejection of the sovereignty of rational consciousness, a rejection that is typical of Romantic writers. Lawrence made this rejection amply clear in his own case in a letter to Lady Cynthia Asquith in 1915 in which he characterized the "conscious life" as a "masquerade of death," in contrast to the "living unconscious life" in which will be found "reality in the darkness."[22] In some ways Lawrence is disingenuous in disowning consciousness in this way since he and his central characters tend to pursue consciousness, particularly the consciousness of being, assiduously. What Lawrence cautioned against was the exaltation of a consciousness that had become severed from the rich, dark waters in the self that lay beneath it and that in fact supported it. In spite of the conventional, semantic linking of purpose with conscious intent, Lawrence points repeatedly in *The Man Who Died* to the existence of a "resoluteness" in the unconscious sources of the self that lay "deeper even than consciousness" (27). In the poem "Resurrection of the Flesh" as well as in *The Man Who Died*, Lawrence clearly believes that the unconscious resolve of nature is beneficial and that this natural resolve is preferable to that of the biblical Jesus because it is inclusive, affirming areas of the self traditionally suppressed by Christianity. Taking the matter further, the bloody cockfight encouraged by Lawrence's risen Jesus would seem to suggest a Nietzschean and Blakean view of nature. Both Nietzsche, whose influence on Lawrence has been generally recognized, and Blake affirmed the energy of being as a protest against the conventional, self-denying meekness of the Christian ethic.

Allied with the distrust of the rational in *The Man Who Died* is the problematic status accorded to language as the voice of the rational. Thus, Lawrence's Jesus says, "Now I have passed the place where words can bite no more and the air is clear, and there is nothing to say, and I am alone within my own skin, which is the walls of all my domain" (61). This doubtfulness about language would seem to have no parallel in the case of the biblical Jesus, who uses language with conscious power and purpose. Also noteworthy in the above passage is the emphasis on touch (as opposed to ratiocination), a theme that is important in *The Man Who Died*. The matter of touch is portrayed by Lawrence as an aspect of the biblical Jesus' pathology, his inability, because of the all-consuming pressure created by his message and mission, to relate naturally and instinctively to other human beings (59). What *The Man Who Died* affirms is the natural life informed by spontaneity, itself a strong Romantic value, as Lilian Furst has pointed out, one that allows the "true self to respond to the subject at hand before the intervention of the rational mind with its discourse of impersonal argumentation."[23]

The idea of touch as a source of cognition is used by Lawrence as a foil to the traditional, well-known words of the risen Jesus to his followers in the Gospels: "Do not touch me." These familiar words, it is now generally believed, are a mistranslation of Jesus' caution to his disciples. In the New Jerusalem Bible's translation of John 20:17, for example, the words of Jesus are translated as, "Do not cling to me, because I have not yet ascended to the Father." Jesus' intention, then, is not to dissuade people from touching him but to prepare his followers to become more self-reliant for the journey ahead. Nonetheless, Lawrence seizes on the traditional translation, whereby the risen Jesus eschews being touched, in order to focus on a failing, as he saw it, in the biblical Jesus—namely, a cold asceticism. Thus, when Lawrence's Jesus approaches sexual union with the priestess of Isis, he confesses to being more afraid of touching her than he was of death (130). Such a touching, however, is crucial to the risen Jesus' healing and completeness.

Lawrence is, however, careful not to identify the instinctual solely or even primarily with the physical. Throughout the narrative, those characters who are immersed in the physical world, like the peasant and his wife, and the slaves of the priestess of Isis, are treated with condescension and even disdain by the risen Jesus and the priestess of Isis. The resurrection slated for the peasant, for example, is seen by Jesus as of a lowly kind: "Why, then, should he be lifted up? Clods of earth are turned over for refreshment, they are not to be lifted up" (38). Similarly, the peasant's wife is portrayed as mercenary and mean, and although Jesus is conscious that the woman is attracted to him, he recoils from her "little soul" and her body with its "little greed" (53). He cannot accept the woman because her life is mundane and merely "personal" (53). Similarly, the priestess of Isis feels alienated from the "servile class" and awaits a lover, an Osiris, of a superior stamp (101). Slaves, she muses, were "embedded in the lesser life," leading her to retreat from their world into her "dream" (102–3).

The priestess's dream is equivalent in kind to the larger vision held by Lawrence's Jesus, a vision forever out of reach of the crude majority. Thus, Jesus reflects that unless the "little day, the life of the little people" is drawn up into the "greater day" so that the "little life" is set within the "circle of the greater life," all will be "disaster" (122). What Lawrence points to here is the need for a transcending of the physical world while continuing to inclusively recognize the value of that world. Nevertheless, one is aware of the elitist ideology that informs Lawrence's narrative, in contrast to the communal and relatively egalitarian attitude of the biblical Jesus. The reason for the difference is that Romantic thought emphasizes individual consciousness as the most elevated of human attributes, a consciousness intuitive enough to share something of the creative intelligence of the cosmos. Lawrence places Jesus and Isis high on the ladder of consciousness, and indeed, because of the tableau-like presentation of the narrative, they often seem to belong to no other world. The reader becomes aware of this when Jesus and the priestess, from distinct vantage points, watch with fascination as a young male slave seizes and rapes a young female slave, the two onlookers eventually turning their attention and consciousness toward each other (81). Romantic writing privileges consciousness over active involvement, as is evident in well-known poems like Wordsworth's "Solitary Reaper" or Keats's "Ode to a Nightingale."

All the same, embedded in Romanticism is a tension between the desire for wholeness and unity and the need for solitude and contemplation. In *The Man Who Died,* there is such a tension, and the result is that wholeness and unity, except for the relatively brief relationship between Jesus and the priestess of Isis, are centered on wholeness and unity *within the self.* Lawrence's risen Jesus is a solitary contemplative, who is more than ever dedicated to the solitary life following his death and resurrection: "I am apart! And life bubbles variously. Why should I have wanted it to bubble all alike? What a pity I preached to them! A sermon is so much more likely to cake into mud, and to close the fountains, than is a psalm or a song" (65). Scorning the limitations of general solutions offered for all, Lawrence's risen Jesus moves through thought with intuitive perceptions whose value to the reader lies in their suggestion that the journey through being must be an individual one. In this search, Lawrence's Jesus celebrates his solitude, his "pure aloneness," through which in the proliferation of consciousness he arrives at "one sort of immortality" (62). Similarly, Lawrence himself wrote to a correspondent in 1911 that there is a "decree" for each human being: "thou shalt live alone."[24]

In spite of his sexual intimacy with the priestess of Isis, Lawrence's Jesus does not seek a continuing relationship but rather approaches union with any woman with the requirement that his "aloneness" be left unimpaired (66). Similarly, the priestess of Isis unites with Jesus under the impression that he is Osiris, and she wishes to know "no more" about him (149). Janice Harris has suggested that each approaches the other not as an *other* but solely within the frame of each's "respective dream."[25] While Jesus goes away at the end of the narrative, promising to return in the springtime, it is doubtful that he shall return, not only because of his fear of the Roman authorities and of the mother and slaves of the priestess, but because more than anything he desires his solitary state. All of this contrasts with the biblical Jesus, who returns not only in person for a time but returns providentially in the granting of extraordinary powers to his followers, a sign of his continued and faithful presence with them through the ages (Mark 16:19–20).

The distance between the biblical Jesus and Lawrence's Jesus is probably most visible in relation to love. G. K. Chesterton once remarked that there is a world of difference between the Romantic conception of unity and the Christian conception of love, arguing that "union itself is not a noble thing. Love is a noble thing; but love is not union."[26] Chesterton distinguished between the structural, metaphysical unity of being sought by Romantic writers and the personal commitment of will and of support to others advocated by the biblical Jesus. Lawrence was characteristically ill at ease with the topic of love, saying on one occasion that he didn't want anyone to love him because love was too "possessive."[27] With a similar, emotional distancing, Lawrence's Jesus, perceiving that the priestess of Isis has an illusory view of himself, reflects with detachment that this didn't matter since her "life and her death were different from his" (136). Significantly, when intimidated by the fear of a second death, Lawrence's Jesus turns not to human or to divine love but to a "law of the sun" for protection (129).

Erotic love would seem to be at the core of *The Man Who Died*, with its insistence on the need for the body and the unconscious, but in fact the lovers are curiously distant and cerebral in their relationship with each other. There is, for example, the matter of the priestess's attraction to the suffering of Jesus: "There was a beauty of much suffering, and the strange calm candour of finer life in the whole delicate ugliness of his face" (101–2). While the priestess is attracted to Jesus in part because of his suffering, the attraction is of an aesthetic and metaphysical kind. It is as if she recognizes that he has endured suffering and thereby come to understand the depths of human experience, a vicarious knowledge that she herself wants. Lawrence's Jesus in turn is repelled by the kind of sacrificial love he sees reflected back at him by his follower, Madeleine (the biblical Mary of Magdala): "He looked at her, and saw she was clutching for the man in him who had died and was dead, the man of his youth and his mission, of his chastity and his fear, of his little life, his giving without taking" (57–58). Jesus' *taking* of love, as things turn out, is of a restrained and ritualistic kind, and the only love he seems capable of by his own admission is "compassion" (62). His compassion, though, like pity in Graham Greene, has a quality of condescension and abstractness about it that contrasts with the concrete love specified by the biblical Jesus in, say, the Beatitudes (Matt 5:1–12).

What disturbed Lawrence about Christian love was that it was prescribed. In his poem "Commandments" he wrote:

When Jesus commanded us to love our neighbour
he forced us either to live a great lie, or to disobey:
for we can't love anybody, neighbour or no neighbour, to order,
and faked love has rotted our marrow.[28]

In a sense, Lawrence raises an important objection to the mandate of love issued by Jesus and by Christians. One cannot expect people to be attracted to those who for one reason or another fail to attract them. On the other hand, Lawrence gives scant value to that other meaning of love espoused by Christians—*caritas*. Here the Christian is enjoined to love his or her fellow human beings by *caring* for them whether or not attraction is felt. Lawrence has little sympathy with such sacrificial love because he feels that it denies the part of the self that wants to receive, often a part of the self that is physical and instinctual. In *The Man Who Died*, such sacrificial love is termed by the risen Jesus as a "corpse" of love, a love that denies the body and passions and that associates happiness vaguely with a shadowy afterlife (137). In rejecting the sacrificial aspect of love, Lawrence struck at the essence of Jesus' sacrifice and of Christian theology. As biblical scholar

Paula Fredriksen has noted, Jesus' sacrifice on the cross was understood as the "ultimate sign" of God's love for humanity just as love itself quickly became the "theological lodestone" of early Christianity.[29]

Lawrence's Jesus is then a radically different figure from the biblical Jesus. In *The Man Who Died*, the reader is given a sustained opportunity to compare the spiritual character and claims of both Christianity and Romanticism. Historically, because of the tension between the pantheism of Romanticism and the theism of Christianity, reconciling the two has been successful only infrequently, with William Blake and Gerard Manley Hopkins being ready examples. Typically, Romantic writers have veered toward one extreme or the other, as in the case of Wordsworth and Coleridge, who initially moved away from Christianity and toward Romanticism but then returned later in life to orthodox Christianity. Like the second generation of the great English Romantic poets—Keats, Shelley, and Byron—Lawrence moved toward Romanticism as a system of belief sufficient, he believed, in itself. If this is the case, the austere and cheerless atmosphere that pervades *The Man Who Died* is perplexing. In spite of its beauty, the world of Lawrence's risen Jesus is lacking in delight. While attempting to present a more inclusive Jesus, Lawrence in effect created a tradeoff. In return for an ethic of self-wholeness and self-development, Lawrence rejected not only Christian asceticism but also the communal and mutually supportive values so strongly set forth by the biblical Jesus. Furthermore, even within the most ascetic traditions of Christianity, figures such as Julian of Norwich, Meister Eckhart, and Thomas Merton make one aware of the centrality within Christianity of the pursuit and achievement of *happiness*. In contrast, Lawrence's somber, risen Jesus, absorbed by the expansion of consciousness, would appear to regard happiness under any other name as superfluous.

Notes

1. The earliest form of *The Man Who Died*, a story entitled "The Escaped Cock," appeared in the United States in *Forum* 79 (February 1928): 286–96. A revised and expanded version of the story was published in Paris by the Black Sun Press in 1929. The final version authorized by Lawrence and the first English edition of what had evolved into a novella was published by Martin Secker in London in 1931 under the title *The Man Who Died*.

2. Lawrence to Trigant Burrow, August 23, 1927, in The *Letters of D. H. Lawrence*, ed. J. Boulton et al. (Cambridge: Cambridge University Press, 1991), 6:113.

3. Lawrence to Edward Garnett, April 22, 1914, in *Letters*, 2:165.

4. Lawrence to Lady Ottoline Morrell, April 3, 1929, in *Letters*, 7:235.

5. Lawrence, *The Man Who Died* (London: Martin Secker, 1931), 96, 108. Further references will be internalized in the text.

6. Lawrence to E. H. Brewster, May 3, 1927, in *Letters*, 6:50.

7. See Paul's distinction between the earthly and heavenly bodies of those who are resurrected in Jesus (1 Cor 15:47–49).

8. Lawrence to Maria Chambers, April 24, 1928, in *Letters*, 6:378.

9. Lawrence, "The Risen Lord," in *The Complete Poems of D. H. Lawrence*, ed. V. de Sola Pinto and W. Roberts (New York: Viking, 1971), 461.

10. Lawrence's risen Christ and cock have been identified with Asclepius's cock and with phallic worship by E. Hinz and J. Teunissen in "Savior and Cock: Allusion and Icon in Lawrence's *The Man Who Died*," *Journal of Modern Literature* 5 (1976): 279–96.

11. N. Frye, *The Great Code: The Bible and Literature* (New York: Harcourt Brace Jovanovich, 1982), 96.

12. M. H. Abrams, *The Correspondent Breeze: Essays in English Romanticism* (New York: Norton, 1984), 102.

13. J. McGann, *The Romantic Ideology: A Critical Investigation* (Chicago: University of Chicago Press, 1983), 134.

14. L. Furst, *Romanticism in Perspective*, 2nd ed. (London: Macmillan, 1979), 172.

15. McGann, *Romantic Ideology*, 40.

16. On this view by Coleridge, see A. S. Byatt, *Wordsworth and Coleridge in Their Time* (London: Nelson, 1970), 154.

17. Lawrence to Lady Cynthia Asquith, November 28, 1915, in *Letters*, 2:454.

18. Lawrence to Laurence Pollinger, January 7, 1929, in *Letters*, 7:122.

19. Quoted in J. C. Oates, *The Hostile Sun: The Poetry of D. H. Lawrence* (Los Angeles: Black Sparrow, 1973), 59.

20. J. Franks, *Revisionist Resurrection Mythologies: A Study of D. H. Lawrence's Italian Works* (New York: Lang, 1994), 22.

21. Lawrence, "Resurrection of the Flesh," in *Complete Poems*, 738.

22. Lawrence to Lady Cynthia Asquith, November 28, 1915, in *Letters*, 2:455.

23. Furst, *Romanticism in Perspective*, 244.

24. Lawrence to Helen Corke, March 14, 1911, *Letters*, 1:240.

25. J. H. Harris, *The Short Fiction of D. H. Lawrence* (New Brunswick, NJ: Rutgers University Press, 1984), 248.

26. G. K. Chesterton, "What Is Right with the World?" in *A G. K. Chesterton Anthology*, ed. P. J. Kavanagh (San Francisco: Ignatius, 1985), 346.

27. Lawrence to Lady Ottoline Morrell, April 3, 1929, in *Letters*, 7:235.

28. Lawrence, "Commandments" (1932) in *Complete Poems*, 654.

29. P. Fredriksen, "Love," in *The Oxford Companion to the Bible*, ed. B. Metzger and M. Coogan (New York: Oxford University Press, 1993), 468.

7 | "Ben-Yosef Is a Jewish Son"

Jewish Portrayals of Jesus—Dialectic
Reclamation of Preservation and
Transformation

DAPHNA ARBEL

That Jesus was a Jew is evident from the Gospels. Despite this fact, until the modern era Jesus was considered as an "other" (literally, *otoh ha-ish*, a disapproving term for "that man") in most classical Jewish theological teachings, as well as in the collective Jewish cultural memory. From such perspectives, Jesus has been looked upon as a dissenter, who subverted the traditions of Judaism and whose teachings were used by his followers as a justification for the persecution of the Jewish people over the centuries.[1] From the eighteenth-century onward, however, a new understanding of Jesus has gradually emerged among Jewish intellectuals when they have separated him from the church and portrayed him as a Jew among Jews.

This study seeks to discern specific characteristics of these contemporary Jewish depictions of Jesus. In particular, it maintains that the figure of the Jewish Jesus has been treated in Jewish circles in two distinct and contrasting manners. On the one hand, Jewish scholars have focused primarily on the figure of Jesus in his historical setting. In these works, Jesus is examined in the context of the authentic social, cultural, and religious frameworks in which he lived. On the other hand, Jewish writers and artists have typically depicted an image of Jesus that transcends both his historical identity and authentic reality. In these works, Jesus is situated in a variety of different settings and treated as an ahistorical figure who embodies diverse and shifting Jewish concerns of both collective and personal nature.

This dialectic of preservation and transformation of the Jewishness of Jesus is the focus of the following discussion. First, it offers a brief survey of characteristic treatments of Jesus' historical heritage in Jewish scholarship. Second, it examines several literary depictions of Jesus by contemporary Jewish and Israeli writers and poets. Third, it investigates select pictorial portrayals of Jesus by the Jewish artist Marc Chagall that, I suggest, represent paradigmatic perceptions of Jesus that are shared by other contemporary Jewish artists.

I argue that these textual and pictorial examples illustrate the dialectical manner in which the image of the historical Jesus has been both maintained and transcended in the Jewish contemporary cultural imagination by scholars, writers, and artists.

Jesus in Jewish Scholarship: A Brief Survey

The challenge of resituating Jesus in his authentic milieu and reconstructing his historical Jewish context was undertaken by Jewish scholars from as early as the eighteenth century. For instance, the eighteenth-century German rabbi Jacob Amden presented Jesus not as a heretical figure, as he was perceived by earlier generations, but as a teacher, who presented Judaism to the Gentiles.[2] In 1838, Joseph Salvador examined the figure of Jesus in a historical Jewish context in his *Jesus-Christ et sa doctrine*.[3] Moses Mendelssohn depicted Jesus as a law-abiding member of the Jewish faith in his *Jerusalem* (1838): "Jesus of Nazareth was never heard to say that he had come to release the House of Jacob from the law. Indeed, he said, in express words, rather the opposite."[4] Subsequent studies likewise treated Jesus' Jewish identity and the social-historical context in which he lived. These works drew attention to various features of the context of Jesus' ministry, such as first-century Galilee; the temple, Sanhedrin, and synagogue; Jewish scriptures, festivals, and customs; theological and ethical teachings; Pharisaic traditions; Jewish liturgy; and contemporary apocalyptic movements.[5]

Heinrich Graetz explored these topics in detail in his *History of the Jews* (1853–1875).[6] Abraham Geiger, the founder of Reform Judaism, reclaimed Jesus' Jewish legacy in a very clear manner in his *Judaism and Its History* which he published in 1866: "He was a Jew, a Pharisean Jew with Galilean coloring. He did by no means utter a new thought; nor did he break down the barrier of nationality."[7] The examination of the "Jesus of history" within the context of early Judaism was developed further in Joseph Klausner's thorough study *Jesus of Nazareth: His Life, Times, and Teaching*, which appeared in 1922.[8]

Critical investigations of Jesus and of his Jewish background, education, mandate, and teachings have continued to develop in modern Jewish scholarship. For instance, Hans-Joachim Schoeps published his account of the *Life of Jesus* in 1945.[9] In 1948 the Jewish philosopher Martin Buber characterized Jesus as his "elder brother" in the introduction to his *Two Types of Faith*, in which he examined the relationship of Judaism and Christianity.[10] Asher Finkel discussed the impact of Judaism on the content and style of Jesus' message and ministry in *The Pharisees and the Teacher of Nazareth* (1964).[11] Schalom Ben-Chorin published his *Brother Jesus* in 1967.[12] David Flusser's historical study, *Jesus*, appeared in 1968.[13] The significant examinations of Jesus in Geza Vermes' trilogy, *Jesus the Jew, Jesus and the World of Judaism*, and *The Religion of Jesus the Jew*, beginning in 1973, provided a substantial analytical examination of Jesus' Jewish identity.[14] By situating Jesus within the context of the authentic Jewish society that was his own natural environment, these studies have contributed to the extensive academic examination of the historical Jesus in recent years.[15]

As these and other parallel studies demonstrate, Jewish scholars have examined the figure of Jesus in relation to the Jewish context of his day, not in isolation from it. Accordingly, they have treated Jesus as a historical figure who was not apart from but connected to the Jewish life of his time. He is described, for instance, as a Pharisee involved in the debate between the schools of Hillel and Shamai, a *hasid* who operated in Galilean charismatic Hasidism, and as a revolutionary apocalyptic figure.[16] By applying various methodologies, Jewish scholars have characterized Jesus as a first-century Galilean Jew in diverse manners, attributing different ideologies to him. These studies, nonetheless, have commonly emphasized the significance of the historical, social, cultural, and religious context in which Jesus' thought and teachings were formulated in Second Temple Judaism.

Jesus Imagery in Jewish and Israeli Literature and Poetry

In tandem with academic studies, various contemporary Jewish literary depictions portray Jesus as distinctly Jewish through employing a variety of literary methods of characterization. Other aspects of Jesus' personality, teachings, and authentic historical setting, however, are excluded from these presentations. By emphasizing Jesus' Jewish identity as his single dominant trait, these presentations may draw indirect links to the "historical Jesus." Noticeably, however, the image of the Jewish Jesus has also been completely divorced from his authentic historical setting and from the social, cultural, and theological concerns of this time. Instead, the Jewish Jesus has been incorporated into divergent contemporary Jewish historical realities and perceived as a long-lasting but ever-changing Jewish icon upon which various concerns could be projected.

Several depictions seem most characteristic. First, the image of the Jewish Jesus has been situated at the center of such devastating events as blood libels, pogroms, and the Holocaust in Europe, to convey notions of Jewish suffering and martyrdom. Second, the Jewish Jesus has been associated with national emancipation, renewal, and the formation of new identities, such as the biblical exodus and the establishment of an independent state of Israel in 1948. In this role he embodies notions of hope, liberation, and freedom. Finally, the Jewish Jesus has been appropriated by Jewish and Israeli writers and artists to express notions of personal searching and salvation. These depictions of Jesus are expressed both explicitly and implicitly in a variety of works. I will examine a cross section of these portrayals in turn.

SUFFERING AND MARTYRDOM: BLOOD LIBELS, POGROMS, AND THE HOLOCAUST

Sholem Asch's short story "In a Carnival Night," published in 1909, is my first example.[17] The story describes a papal procession in sixteenth-century Rome, which is marked by the brutal spectacle of eight Jews being chased and beaten. The story then depicts Jesus climbing down from the cross at St. Peter's Cathedral to become one of the helpless Jewish victims. The narrative removes Jesus from his authentic Jewish milieu. Nonetheless, it clearly emphasizes the Jewishness of Jesus by depicting him flogged half-naked, along with other Jews, through the side streets of Rome. Asch's Jewish Jesus bears the suffering and humiliation with his fellow Jews. In contrast, his Christian persecutors, who bow down to Jesus' image, are portrayed as ignoring his basic teachings of compassion, love, and piety.

Another example is Uri Zvi Greenberg's poem "Uri Zvi in Front of the Cross," published in 1922. This Yiddish poem was originally printed in the shape of a cross, over which appeared the capital letters typically found above the Christian crucifix: INRI, the Latin initials for "Jesus of Nazareth, King of the Jews." Here Greenberg reclaims Jesus' Jewish identity by depicting him as his brother, who has remained nailed to the cross. At the same time, Greenberg also projects the image of the Jewish Jesus into the contemporary Jewish experiences of the pogroms in Eastern Europe by describing him as watching a pogrom from the top of Golgotha: "For two thousand years you've been tranquil on the cross, brother Jesus. All

around you the world expires. Damn it! You've forgotten everything! . . .
Beit Lechem [Bethlehem] is a Jewish town. Ben-Yosef [son of Joseph] is a
Jewish son."[18]

Other Jewish writers and poets have similarly projected the image of the
Jewish Jesus into the historical reality of World War II and especially the
Holocaust. For instance, the Yiddish writer Der Nister symbolically places
Jesus with all the "Jews on the cross."[19] In his story "Der Tseylem" ("The
Cross"), Lamed Shapiro identifies Jesus with a Jewish victim of a pogrom by
depicting the latter with the mark of the cross on his forehead.[20] In *Night*, Elie
Wiesel identifies Jesus with a young, innocent boy who is hung by the Nazis:

> And I, who believed that God is love, what answer could I give my young
> questioner, whose dark eyes still held the reflection of that angelic sadness
> which had appeared one day upon the face of the hanged child? What did I
> say to him? Did I speak of that other Israeli, his brother, who may have
> resembled him, the Crucified, whose cross has conquered the world?[21]

In a similar vein, in his poem "Does David Still Play before You?" the
Israeli poet Moshe Dor portrays Jesus as a Jew, bearing the Yellow Star: "And
among curls of incense, does still to forgive and love plead the face, paler than
a cloud, of Jesus with the Yellow Star?"[22] Raising questions about the moral
meaning of the suffering of the Jews, Dor's Jesus is placed in a German death
camp, as a model of all Jewish victims during the Holocaust.

RENEWAL AND HOPE AND NATION BUILDING: THE JEWISH WORLD AFTER WORLD WAR II

The figure of the Jewish Jesus has not only been associated with experiences
of horror and persecution. In a variety of works, Jesus has also been situated
at the nexus of modern renewal, especially in the aftermath of World War II.
In reaction to new political realities and emerging ideologies such as nationalism and Zionism, as well the establishment of Israel as an independent and
internationally recognized Jewish state in 1948, the figure of Jesus has been
associated with traditional Jewish heroes and role models.

For example, Jesus has been associated with Judah the Maccabee, who led
the Maccabean revolt against the Seleucid Empire in the second century BCE.
In a similar manner, Jesus has been equated with Simeon Bar-Kokhba, the
Hebrew leader of the major revolt against Rome under the emperor Hadrian
in 132–135 CE. Presented as an icon of Jewish freedom, resistance, and heroism, Jesus is reconstructed in these presentations as a figure who combats the
devastation and displacement suffered by the Jews in the old world.

Jesus is also associated with notions of renewal, salvation, and the
long-awaited Jewish sovereignty on Israeli soil. In Greenber's "Oracle to

Europe," for example, Jesus is portrayed as a participant in the Bar-Kokhba revolt as the figure of Ahasver, the "Wandering Jew."[23] In contrast to the traditional legend of the Wandering Jew, however, in Greenberg's presentation, Jesus/Ahasver is not condemned to wander the earth for rejecting the Christian savior. Instead, he is the only survivor of the Bar-Kokhba revolt and is ordered to carry the message of Jewish political autonomy from one generation to another. From another perspective, the Israeli poet Yehuda Amichi introduces Jesus into the idyllic reality of the united independent Jerusalem after the Six Days' War (1967). Associating him with hopeful prophetic seekers of sacredness, known and unknown, Amichai, in his poem "From Jerusalem 1967," describes him as follows:

> I climb up the Tower of David
> a little higher than the prayer that ascends the height:
> halfway to heaven. A few of
> the ancients succeeded: Mohammed, Jesus,
> and others.[24]

These depictions of Jesus vary. Yet they all demonstrate a common perception of Jesus as a model of Jewish courage, rebirth, and hope in the new historical realities after World War II.

INNER SEARCH AND SALVATION: "PERSONAL SITES" OF INDIVIDUAL WRITERS

From the late 1960s to the present, the literary atmosphere in Israel has been characterized above all by strong interests in the individual rather than the collective.[25]In this context, Jesus has been incorporated into the Israeli literary landscape as an icon that expresses, in universal terms, notions of the existential human condition, individual search, personal anxiety, and spiritual transformation. For instance, in his novel *Life as a Parable*, the Israeli author Pinhas Sadeh symbolically embraces Jesus' passion as a model of personal redemption and a new, inner path of life. Here Jesus is associated with a secular protagonist who lives in modern-day Israel, who longs for the kingdom of heaven. Amos Oz's novella *Crusade* and Yithak Orpaz's novel *Daniel's Trial* also follow the model of Jesus' passion in order to express ideas of inner spiritual salvation in the context of secular, modern-day Israeli life.[26]

A similar depiction of Jesus is found in Benjamin Shvili's *Descent from the Cross*, which presents a story of his search for God by using the figure of Jesus as a personal symbol.[27] The book opens with a description of Jesus appointing the author as his messenger. The author is requested to "liberate" Jesus by removing him from the cross and reinstating him among the Jewish people, from whom he was cut off. In Shvili's story, these acts of liberating Jesus are presented through a personal prism; Jesus is equated with the author himself, who is set free and subsequently gains his own inner renewal, self-realization, and spiritual elevation.

As these literary examples demonstrate, contemporary Jewish depictions often treat Jesus as an ahistorical Jewish figure. Unlike Jewish scholarly depictions, which focused mainly on the historical Jesus in his authentic context, literary presentations often dissociate Jesus from his original setting and role. Consequently, Jesus is presented as the Jewish Ben-Yosef, who is placed in the center of changing, historical times in order to embody diverse Jewish concerns and aspirations, both collective and personal.

Marc Chagall's Imagery of Jesus

Jewish artists have presented various depictions of Jesus as a Jew from the late 1930s on. For instance, Mark Antokolsky produced his painting entitled *Ecce Homo*, or *Christ before the People* in 1873; Max Libermann depicted Jesus as a Jewish child in *The Twelve-Year-Old Jesus in the Temple* in 1879; Max Band exhibited portraits of a bearded Jew as the *Ecce Homo* in 1937 and 1944; Maurycy Gottlieb painted Jesus with prayer shawl and earlocks, speaking in synagogue to his fellow Jews, in his unfinished *Jesus Preaching at Capernaum* in 1878–1879. In a similar vein, Josef Foshko depicted the crucifixion of an old Jew in 1940, and Mathias Goeritz produced his series of crucifixions entitled *Redeemer of Auschwitz* in 1950–1953.[28]

Marc Chagall, the Russian-born Jewish artist (1887–1985), depicted Jesus as one of his major themes as early as 1908. One of the leading figures in Jewish art, Chagall has produced wide-ranging depictions of Jesus, which illustrate, for this study, diverse perceptions of him.[29]

An analogous presentation that simultaneously maintains and transcends the figure of the Jewish Jesus characterizes the complex depictions of Jesus in the work of Chagall. While emphasizing the historical Jewish identity of Jesus as a fixed characteristic, Chagall places him, in a rather fluid manner, in contemporary historical realities to embody current Jewish concerns. In many of Chagall's depictions, Jesus is not the Christ of the church.[30] Rather, various visual icons emphasize his Jewish identity. These include, for instance, the Jewish prayer shawl (*tallith*), which covers Jesus' loins, the phylacteries (*tefillim*) he wears on his head and arm, the Torah scroll he holds, and the Hebrew letters that identify him. Yet at the same time, Chagall often treats Jesus as an ahistorical Jewish iconic figure and therefore is able both to continuously appropriate his image and to place him in various historical situations significant to the

Jewish people. Analogous to the way the Jewish Jesus is depicted in literature and poetry, in Chagall's paintings this figure is projected into similar realities: the chaos and destruction before and during World War II, situations of national rebirth and renewal after the war, and the private reality of the artist's inner world.

SUFFERING AND MARTYRDOM: BLOOD LIBELS, POGROMS, AND THE HOLOCAUST

In early 1944, Chagall explained his perception of the figure of Jesus as follows:

> For me Christ has always symbolized the true type of the Jewish martyr. That is how I understood him in 1908, when I used this figure for the first time. . . . It was under the influence of the pogroms. Then, I painted and drew him in pictures about ghettos, surrounded by Jewish troubles, by Jewish mothers, running and holding their children in their arms.[31]

Chagall's *White Crucifixion* (1938) illustrates this perception clearly.[32] Here an appeal to the historical Jesus is made by distinctive, visible symbols, which convey Jesus' Jewishness with certainty. Around his loins he wears a Jewish prayer shawl, with two black stripes as a loincloth, and at his feet burns the seven-branched menorah, the oldest symbol of Judaism. The traditional lettering about his head states in Aramaic, "Jesus King of the Jews," making a clear reference to the crucifixion of the historical Jesus. This figure of Jesus, however, is depicted alongside familiar images of terror in Eastern Europe: revolutionary mobs attack the Jews (left), the Jewish village and synagogue burn (right), Jews flee a pogrom on foot and by boat (left), and the Torah scroll, signifying the Jewish sacred tradition, is devoured by flames (right). Strong Jewish responses to these catastrophes are conveyed by typical symbols: Jewish matriarchs and patriarchs weep from above, a mother clutches her baby at her breast, and an old Jewish man weeps. In the center is the crucified Jesus, who is not depicted as a savior and rescuer. Instead, he himself is a Jewish victim, defenseless and powerless, bound to the cross.

For Franz Meyer, the classic biographer of Chagall,

> this Christ's relation to the world differs entirely from that in all Christian representations of the Crucifixion. There . . . all suffering is concentrated in Christ, transferred to him in order that he may overcome it by his sacrifice. Here instead, though all the suffering of the world is mirrored in the Crucifixion, suffering remains man's lasting fate and is not abolished by Christ's death.[33]

In a similar vein, David Roskies has suggested that in Chagall's *White Crucifixion* Jesus does not abolish the suffering around him. Instead, he represents the Jewish people, whose pain is not redeemed. In this chaotic world

Hunt, William Holman (1827–1910). *The Light of the World*, c.1851–53 Keble College, Oxford, UK/The Bridgeman Art Library, BAL2561.

Rouault, Georges (1871–1958) © ARS, NY. *The Passion* (Ecce Homo). Oil on canvas mounted on panel, 83.8 x 56.5 cm. Location: Musee National d'Art Moderne, Centre Georges Pompidou, Paris, France. Photo credit: CNAC/MNAM/Dist. Réunion des Musées Nationaux/Art Resource, NY, ART325304.

Chagall, Marc (1887–1985). *White Crucifixion.* 1938. Oil on canvas, 154.3 x 139.7 cm. Gift of Alfred S. Alschuler, 1946.925. Reproduction, The Art Institute of Chicago, IL, E09176.

Chagall, Marc (1887–1985) © ARS, NY. *The Yellow Crucifixion,* 1942. Location: Musee National d'Art Moderne, Centre Georges Pompidou, Paris, France. Photo credit: Art Resource, NY, ART127086.

Chagall, Marc (1887–1985) © ARS, NY. *Resistance*, 1937–1948. Oil on canvas. Photo: Gerard Blot. Location: Musee National message biblique Marc Chagall, Nice, France. Photo credit: Réunion des Musées Nationaux/Art Resource, NY, ART146064.

Chagall, Marc (1887–1985) © ARS, NY. *The Exodus*. 1952–1966. Oil on linen canvas. 130 x 162.3 cm. AM 1988–81. Photo: Philippe Migeat. Location: Musee National d'Art Moderne, Centre Georges Pompidou, Paris, France. Photo credit: CNAC/MNAM/Dist. Réunion des Musées Nationaux/Art Resource, NY, ART173823.

Chagall, Marc (1887–1985) © ARS, NY.
The Soul of the Town, 1945. Oil on canvas,
107 x 82 cm. Location: Musee National
d'Art Moderne, Centre Georges Pompidou, Paris, France. Photo credit:
CNAC/MNAM/Dist. Réunion des Musées
Nationaux/Art Resource, NY, ART325210.

Chagall, Marc (1887–1985) © ARS, NY.
Autoportrait à la pendule (Self-portrait
with Clock). 1947. Oil on canvas, 86 x 70.5
cm. Photo credit: Banque d'Images, ADAGP/Art
Resource, NY, ART325547.

Jesus, alongside all the Jews, is crucified as both victim and martyr, a casualty of brutality and destruction. Ziva Amishai-Maisels has described the contemporary historical context that affected Chagall's imagery in *White Crucifixion*. It was "inspired by specific events: the German *Aktion* of June 15, 1938 in which 1,500 Jews were taken to concentration camps; the destruction of the Munich and Nuremberg synagogues on 9 June and 10 August 1938; the deportation of Polish Jews at the end of October 1938 and the outbreak of pogroms in November including Kristallnacht (9–10 November, 1938)."[34]

Chagall's *Yellow Crucifixion* (1943) conveys a similar conception.[35] Here Jesus' Judaism is made plain, as he wears the phylacteries of a devout Jew on his head and arm while an open Torah scroll covers his right arm. Once again, Jesus is treated as an ahistorical figure and is situated in the contemporary Jewish world of terror. The fear and exile of the war years are emphasized by images of suffering (right), a burning village (right), and a sinking boat and drowning Jews (left). Here Jesus is obviously not the Christian Messiah who overcomes all suffering by his sacrifice, but is himself a Jewish victim. As Amishai-Maisels has explained, the *Yellow Crucifixion* that Chagall began sketching in 1942 was clearly inspired by the sinking of the *Struma* in the Black Sea in February 1942 and the drowning of 769 Jewish refugees.[36] By placing Jesus in the center of events, Chagall suggests that everyone is abused and all Jews are innocent victims.

In The *Martyr* (1940–1944), which Chagall began painting during the German invasion of France in the early 1940s, the crucified Jesus is portrayed as a present-day Russian Jew who wears the phylacteries on his arms and the prayer shawl around his body.[37] Yet as Roskies has noted, here Chagall has placed Jesus in his own village, Vitebsk, the Jewish *shtetl* in which he grew up.[38] This *shtetl* becomes the locus of destruction, representing numerous burning villages all over Eastern Europe from which Jews escaped. Bound to the stake, Jesus becomes a symbol of Jewish martyrdom during Eastern European pogroms. He is surrounded by images of destruction: a flaming village (right); the Wandering Jew escaping the destruction (right); a patriarchal figure holding a menorah, which emerges from the leg of a flying goat; a fiddler with half of his face missing (left); and a mother and child seated in the street of a burning village (right). Chagall's own father appears (lower right), as well as the artist himself, who is hardly noticeable in the corner. All undergo the Jewish experience of fear, devastation, and pain.

In *The Crucified* (1944), Jesus is unmistakably identified with all Eastern European Jews who were killed during the Holocaust.[39] The portrayal of the Jews hanging on a series of crosses distinctly conveys this conception.

The Jews are depicted as bearing a smudged sign around their necks: *Ich bin Jude.* The desolate sky and earth convey the sense of desecration. The town is covered by snow, a corpse lies on the doorstep (right), and there is also a slaughtered hen (center) and a dead mother with a child at her breast (left). Roskies has interpreted this depiction as a reversal of the Passover tradition and its message of salvation. Unlike in the Passover Haggadah, in *The Crucified* the angel of death does not pass over the Jewish houses but instead kills the Jews one by one.[40] As Amishai-Maisels has noted, particular contemporary events during the dark days of the war inspired Chagall's imagery. In particular, he was struck by the news of the liquidation of the ghettos, which was published in 1943 and 1944. Chagall was also reacting to the failure of the Warsaw Ghetto uprising, which he mentioned in a speech in April 1944, as well as to news about the destruction of his hometown, Vitebsk, to which he responded in an article written in February 1944 for a Yiddish paper.[41]

RENEWAL AND HOPE AND NATION BUILDING: THE JEWISH WORLD AFTER WORLD WAR II

From another perspective, Chagall also integrates Jesus into his visions of renewal and of the formation of new national identities such as in the biblical exodus and the establishment of the state of Israel. Chagall associates Jesus with biblical heroes such as King David, the prophets, and especially with Moses. In Chagall's eyes, "Moses is the source from which all springs, even Christ."[42] Emphasizing the affinity between Jesus and the modern Jewish people, Chagall expressed his views regarding the UN and its decisions concerning the establishment of the state of Israel in a statement that shed light on his images: "No world of conferences can be successful until the Jewish people are taken down from the cross on which they have been crucified for two thousand years."[43]

Two of Chagall's paintings, *Resistance* and *Resurrection*, illustrate his words. The source of these paintings was a single large work titled *Revolution*, which Chagall began in 1937 and divided into a triptych in 1942 (with the third section titled *Liberation*). *Resistance* was exhibited in November 1948, during the Israeli War of Independence.[44] In this piece, Jesus is characterized as a Jew by his loincloth and is depicted as both a spectator of a pogrom and a Jew who embraces the Jewish anticipation for salvation.[45] Jesus is placed among Jewish refugees who are fleeing the horrors of pogroms and the Holocaust, helped by partisans and fighters and directed by a supernatural white calf (top).[46] Below him is the fallen ghetto in which Chagall has represented his own corpse laid out with palette in hand. A ray of light illuminates the refugees and also the upper part of Jesus' body as he turns hopefully toward them. Moreover, Amishai-Maisels suggests, Jesus is identified with the Jewish people in their struggle, "his body arching against the cross as he too resists his fate."[47]

In *Resurrection,* Jesus is also situated in the center of events that suggest the possibility of renewal. In this piece the viewer's attention is drawn not toward the world of the past, represented by a burning village (right), but toward a group of Jewish people who join partisans and fighters in celebration. Images of light, a torch and a lantern, are prominent in this composition. These are echoed by the luminous body of Jesus wrapped with the prayer shawl/loincloth, as well as the shining face of the Jewish man who is not fleeing but solidly holding the Torah scroll (right). In contrast to *Resistance,* in *Resurrection* the figure of the artist with his easel almost merges with Jesus, an identification that seems to convey his renewed creativity and symbolic participation in the resurrection of Jesus and the Jewish people.

Chagall's *Resurrection by the River* (1947) alludes to notions of redemption in the new state of Israel, according to Amishai-Maisels.[48] In this depiction the Jewish Jesus, identified by a *tallith* loincloth, is soaring toward heaven, while below him are images suggesting hope, renewal, homecoming, and deliverance. Next to a boat of people crossing a flaming river, Chagall portrays those who have already found refuge on a near shore (right). Among them are the artist and his easel, a couple at a Sabbath table lit by candles, people holding bouquets of flowers, several musicians, and a mother holding her child, her face lit by candlelight.

In *Exodus,* which Chagall began in 1952 and completed only in 1966, Jesus participates in both biblical and modern journeys to liberation and freedom, as he becomes one of the Jewish people.[49] Moses is depicted with the tablet of the Ten Commandments (lower right) guiding a group of refugees, who leave behind a burning village to join the biblical exodus. A flying fish leads displaced people and a drowning mother and child away from the sinking *Struma* to join the contemporary emigration to the promised land. A huge figure of Christ rises above the crowd, taking part in this Jewish exodus to liberation.

INNER SEARCH AND SALVATION: CHAGALL'S "PERSONAL SITES"

From another perspective, Chagall's paintings demonstrate his perception of the Jewish Jesus as a universal teacher who offers a personal message. "For me Christ was a great poet," he said, "the teaching of whose poetry has been forgotten by the modern world."[50] Portrayed as Jewish by the familiar symbol of his prayer shawl/loincloth, Jesus is often projected into the artist's inner reality as a personal icon with whom Chagall identifies. For instance, in a poem that Chagall wrote for his wife Bella, he explains how he envisions Jesus as a personal model, an internalizing of his own self: "Like Christ, I am crucified, fixed with nails to the easel."[51]

Chagall made this identification as early as 1912 when, in *Calvary*, he depicted himself as a child on the cross, mourned by his Jewish parents at the foot of the cross.[52] In *The Descent of the Cross* (1941), Jesus has become a personal model for Chagall as demonstrated by his replacing the historical "INRI" with his own personal name, "Marc Ch.," above the figure of Jesus.[53] Here Chagall unites himself with Jesus, thereby alluding to his own salvation, which is depicted through Jesus' descent from the cross. Here again, Jesus is a Jew, who is removed from the cross and held by a bird-headed woman. In a similar manner, Chagall evokes the Jewish Jesus in *The Soul of the Town* (1945) by portraying himself as a two-faced artist sketching the image of a Jewish Jesus and a Torah scroll in the sky.[54] In a similar vein, Chagall situates Jesus in his own personal landscape in *Self Portrait with Wall Clock* (1947). By depicting himself as a sad-eyed goat who sketches his own self-portrait as the Jewish Jesus clothed with the *tallith* loincloth, Chagall clearly reinforces his identification with Jesus.[55]

The paintings examined here reveal that the Jewishness of Jesus is central to Chagall's work, as it is to the Jewish and Israeli writers discussed earlier. At the same time, Chagall's Jesus transcends the authentic historical setting of early Judaism. In Chagall's various depictions, Jesus often becomes a Jewish icon. As such he is situated in shifting contemporary historical times, in order to represent various Jewish collective and personal concerns.

Conclusion

Unlike in previous generations, it is clear that contemporary Jewish academic, literary, and artistic treatments of Jesus have reclaimed the Jewishness of Jesus as his primary characteristic. Yet, as I have demonstrated, there is not a unified depiction of this figure. Instead, the image of Jesus has been treated in a dialectical manner that both maintains and transcends his Jewish identity.

On the one hand, academic studies have often emphasized the original historical setting of Jesus, drawing attention to various features of Second Temple Judaism, in which the "Jesus of history" lived and taught. On the other hand, various literary and artistic depictions have presented Jesus as an ahistorical Jewish figure. Transcended from his authentic historical setting,

Jesus has been situated in contemporary and shifting historical times to become the Jewish Ben-Yosef, who has been constantly appropriated in Jewish literature and art to convey new webs of Jewish collective and personal meaning.

NOTES

1. For surveys on Jewish conceptions of Jesus, see S. Sandmel, *We Jews and Jesus* (New York: Oxford University Press, 1965); W. Jacob, *Christianity through Jewish Eyes* (Cincinnati: Hebrew Union College, 1974); J. Jocz, *The Jewish People and Jesus Christ*, (Grand Rapids: Baker, 1981); D. Hanger, *The Jewish Reclamation of Jesus* (Grand Rapids: Zondervan, 1984); M. Goldstein, *Jesus in the Jewish Tradition* (New York: Macmillan, 1950).

2. See H. Falk, "Rabbi Jacob Emden's Views on Christianity," *Journal of Ecumenical Studies* 19 (1982): 107–8.

3. On Joseph Salvador and his views, see Y. Klausner, *A History of Modern Hebrew Literature* [in Hebrew] (Jerusalem: Ahiasaf, 1952), 1:81; J. Fleishmann, *The Problem of Christianity in Modern Hebrew Thought* [in Hebrew] (Jerusalem: Magness Press, 1964), 20–21.

4. M. Mendelssohn, *Jerusalem, or On Religious Power and Judaism*, trans. A. Arkush (Hanover, NH: University Press of New England, 1983), 134.

5. See the discussion of various views in D. Hanger, *The Jewish Reclamation of Jesus* (Grand Rapids: Zondervan, 1984).

6. H. Graetz, *History of the Jews* (Philadelphia: Jewish Publication Society of America, 1956), 2:150–71.

7. A. Geiger, *Judaism and Its History*, trans. M. Mayer (London: n. p., 1866). For a discussion of his position, see S. Heschel, *Abraham Geiger and the Jewish Jesus* (Chicago: University of Chicago Press, 1998).

8. J. Klausner, *Yeshu ha-Notzri*, 2 vols. (Jerusalem: Stybel, 1922); ET, *Jesus of Nazareth: His Life, Time, and Teaching*, trans. H. Danby (London: Macmillan, 1925; 3rd ed., 1952).

9. H.-J. Schoeps, *Das Leben Jesu: Versuch einer historischen Darstellung* (Frankfurt: Eremiten, 1954).

10. See M. S. Freedman, *Martin Buber: The Life of Dialogue* (New York: Harper, 1955), 279. Cf. D. Berry, "Buber's View of Jesus as Brother," *Journal of Ecumenical Studies* 14 (1977): 203–18.

11. A. Finkel, *The Pharisees and the Teacher of Nazareth* (1964; reprint, Leiden: Brill, 1974).

12. S. Ben-Chorin, *Bruder Jesus: Der Nazarener in jüdischer Sicht* (Munich: List, 1967); ET, *Brother Jesus: The Nazarene through Jewish Eyes* (Athens, GA: University of Georgia Press, 2001).

13. D. Flusser, *Jesus in Selbstzeugnissen und Bilddokumenten*, Rowohlts monographien (Reinbek bei Hamburg: Rowohlt, 1968); ET, *Jesus*, trans. R. Walls (New York: Herder & Herder, 1969).

14. G. Vermes, *Jesus the Jew: A Historian's Reading of the Gospels* (London: Collins; Philadelphia: Fortress, 1973); Vermes, *Jesus and the World of Judaism* (London: SCM Press, 1983; Philadelphia: Fortress, 1984), rev. and repr. as *Jesus in His Jewish Context* (Minneapolis: Fortress, 2003); Vermes, *The Religion of Jesus the Jew* (London: SCM Press; Minneapolis: Fortress, 1993). See also Vermes, *The Authentic Gospel of Jesus* (London: Allen Lane, 2003).

15. For studies of the Jewish character of Jesus by Christian scholars see, for example, E. P. Sanders, *Jesus and Judaism* (London: SCM Press; Philadelphia: Fortress, 1985); H. Falk, *Jesus*

the Pharisee: A New Look at the Jewishness of Jesus (New York: Paulist Press, 1985); B. F. Meyer, *The Aim of Jesus* (London: SCM Press, 1979); A. E. Harvey, *Jesus and the Constraints of History* (London: Duckworth, 1982), C. A. Evans, *Jesus and the Victory of God* (London: SPCK, Minneapolis: Fortress, 1996); C. A. Evans and B. D. Chilton, *Jesus in Context: Temple, Purity, and Restoration*, Arbeiten zur Geschichte des antiken Judentums und des Urchristentums 39 (Leiden: Brill, 1997); J. H. Charlesworth, *Jesus within Judaism* (Garden City, NY: Doubleday, 1988). See Peter Schäfer's important new study *Jesus in the Talmud* (Princeton: Princeton University Press, 2007), which examines references to Jesus found in the Talmudic-Midrashic literature.

16. On Jesus as an orthodox Jew and the Pharisaic struggle between the schools of Shamai and Hillel see, e.g., H. Falk, *Jesus the Pharisee: A New Look at the Jewishness of Jesus* (New York: Paulist Press, 1985). On Jesus as a *hasid* see studies by G. Vermes in note 15 above. On Jesus' revolutionary apocalyptic message see, for example, A. Segal, "Jesus, the Jewish Revolutionary," in J. H. Charlesworth, *Jesus' Jewishness: Exploring the Place of Jesus within Early Judaism* (New York: Crossroad, 1991), 199–225.

17. S. Asch, "In a Carnival Night," in *From the Shtetl to the Wide World*, ed. S. Rozansky (Buenos Aires: Musterverk fun yiddisher literature, 1972). See also Roskies, *Against the Apocalypse*, 264–65.

18. U. Z. Greenberg, "Uri Zvi in Front of the Cross," published originally in Yiddish in *Gezamlte verk* 1 (1923): 304–7. This citation is taken from D. G. Roskies, *Against the Apocalypse: Responses to Catastrophe in Modern Jewish Culture* (Cambridge, MA: Harvard University Press, 1984), 270. See H. Rosenbloom, "Theological-Historical Conflict with Christianity in Uri Zvi Greenberg's Poetry," in *Perakim: Organ of the American Hebrew Academy* 4 (1966): 263–320.

19. For discussion and terminology, see Roskies, "Jews on the Cross" [in Hebrew] in *Against the Apocalypse*, 258–310.

20. L. Shapiro, "The Cross," in *The Jewish Government and Other Stories*, ed. and trans. C. Leviant (New York: Twayne, 1971). See discussion in Roskies, *Against the Apocalypse*, 262.

21. E. Wiesel, *Night*, trans. S. Rodway (New York: Hill & Wang, 1960), 10–11. For an analysis of imagery from a Christian perspective, see F. Mauriac's foreword, 9–12.

22. M. Dor, *Sirpad umatekhet* (Ramat Gan: Massada, 1965), 155. Translation is from D. Johnson, *Crossing the River: Selected Poems* (Oakville, Ontario: Mosaic, 1989), 55.

23. On the "Oracle to Europe," see Roskies, *Against the Apocalypse*, 271–72.

24. Y. Amichai, "Jerusalem 1967," in *Poems of Jerusalem: A Bilingual Edition*, by Y. Amichai. trans. S. Mitchell (New York: Schocken, 1987).

25. See D. H. Weinberg, *Between Tradition and Modernity: Haim Zhitlowski, Simon Dubnow, Ahad Ha-Am, and the Shaping of Modern Jewish Identity* (New York: Holmes & Meier, 1996); Y. Zerubavel, *Recovered Roots: Collective Memory and the Making of Israeli National Tradition* (Chicago: University of Chicago Press, 1995).

26. P. Sadeh, *Hahayim Kemashal* (1957; reprint, Tel Aviv: Schoken, 1984); A. Oz, *Ad Mavet* (Tel Aviv: Am Oved, 1969); Y. Orpaz, *Masa' Daniel* (Tel Aviv: Am Oved, 1969). See Y. Schwartz, "The Person, the Path, and the Melody: A Brief History of Identity in Israeli Literature," *Prooftexts* 20, no. 3 (2000): 318–39.

27. B. Shevili, *Ha-Yeridah min ha-Tselav* (Jerusalem: Schocken, 2000).

28. For a discussion of Jesus portrayals by Jewish artists, see Z. Amishai-Maisels, "The Jewish Jesus," *Journal of Jewish Art* 9 (1982): 86–99.

29. On Chagall in the context of contemporary Jewish art, see A. Kahof, *Chagall to Kitaj: Jewish Expedience in 20th Century Art* (New York: Praeger, 1990); J. Chatelain, *The Biblical Message: Marc Chagall* (New York: Tudor, 1973).

30. See P. Provoyeur, *Marc Chagall, Biblical Interpretation* (New York: Alpine Fine Arts Collection, 1983). Compare Chagall's statement: "God, perspective, color, the bible, form,

lines, traditions, the so-called humanism, love, caring, the family, the school, education, the prophets, and Christ himself have fallen into pieces," in Amishai-Maisels, "Jewish Jesus," 103.

31. Cited in Amishai-Maisels, "Jewish Jesus," 103.

32. On *White Crucifixion* see S. Alexander, *Marc Chagall: A Biography* (New York: Putnam's Sons, 1978), 311–17, 320–21; A. Kagan, *Marc Chagall* (New York: Abbeville, 1989), 67–68, 178; Amishai-Maisels, "Jewish Jesus," 85; Amishai-Maisels, *Depiction and Interpretation: The Influence of the Holocaust on the Visual Arts* (Oxford: Pergamon, 1993), 22–23.

33. F. Meyer, *Marc Chagall: Life and Work*, trans. Robert Allen (New York: Harry Abrams, 1963), 414–15; see also 416, 435.

34. Roskies, *Against the Apocalypse*, 286–87.

35. Amishai-Maisels, "Jewish Jesus," 101.

36. On *Yellow Crucifixion* see Meyer, *Marc Chagall*, 446; Alexander, *Marc Chagall*, 476; Amishai-Maisels, "Jewish Jesus," 85–86; Amishai-Maisels, *Depiction and Interpretation*, 168.

37. Amishai-Maisels, *Depiction and Interpretation*, 184; see also Kagan, *Marc Chagall*, 69.

38. On *The Martyr* see Meyer, *Marc Chagall*, 418; Alexander, *Marc Chagall*, 476; Kagan, *Marc Chagall*, 68–69; Amishai-Maisels, "Jewish Jesus," 101.

39. Roskies, *Against the Apocalypse*, 286.

40. On *The Crucified* see Kagan, *Marc Chagall*, 69; Amishai-Maisels, "Jewish Jesus," 86; Amishai-Maisels, *Depiction and Interpretation*, 185. On the crucifixion theme in Chagall's art, see Alexander, *Marc Chagall*, 475.

41. Roskies, *Against the Apocalypse*. 289.

42. Amishai-Maisels, "Jewish Jesus," 102; Amishai-Maisels, *Depiction and Interpretation*, 184.

43. Meyer, *Marc Chagall*, 508.

44. See Chagall's speech, delivered in New York in 1945, on the celebration of the end of World War II in Europe, in *Marc Chagall on Art and Culture*, ed. B. Harshav (Stanford, CA: Stanford University Press, 2003), 103.

45. This painting was entitled *Ghetto* when it was first exhibited in 1948, in order to show its connection to the Warsaw Ghetto revolt. See Amishai-Maisels, "Jewish Jesus," 102; Amishai-Maisels, *Depiction and Interpretation*, 326. On *Revolution—Resistance, Resurrection, Liberation* see Alexander, *Marc Chagall*, 317–18, 386–87; J. Cassou, *Chagall* (London: Thames & Hudson, 1965), 244; Amishai-Maisels, *Depiction and Interpretation*, 326–27; E. Pacoud-Reme, "Resistance, Resurrection, Liberation," in *Marc Chagall. Catalogue Published by the San Francisco Museum of Modern Art with Association with Harry N. Abrams, INC Publishers* (New York: Harry Abrams, 2003), 172–75.

46. Amishai-Maisels, "Jewish Jesus," 102.

47. According to Amishai-Maisels, here Chagall identifies the partisans with Israeli fighters for independence in the new state. See Amishai-Maisels, *Depiction and Interpretation* 102–3. See her citation of Chagall's speech from 1944: "Let not the world think that the Jewish people today are the same as those who before inhabited the ghettoes. . . . New young people appear and with them . . . a new consciousness has grown. . . . In light of history the new Jews appear more like partisans than like wanderers with sacks over their shoulders. . . . Their brothers and fathers fought in the ghettos of Warsaw and other cities. Their crucifixion in the street of Vitebsk and other places took on the tragic appearance of the crucified Christ himself."

48. Amishai-Maisels, *Depiction and Interpretation*, 102.

49. Ibid., 326.

50. On *Exodus* see Amishai-Maisels, *Depiction and Interpretation*, 327.

51. Cited in Amishai-Maisels, "Jewish Jesus," 103; cf. Alexander, *Marc Chagall*, 320.

52. On *Calvary* see Amishai-Maisels, "Origins of the Jewish Jesus," *Journal of Jewish Art* 11 (1985): 51–86; Cassou, *Chagall*, 242; J. B. Teshuva, *Chagall: A Retrospective* (Westport, CT: Hugh Lauter Levin Associates, 1995), 301–2.

53. On *The Descent of the Cross* see Cassou, *Chagall*, 247–48.

54. On *The Soul of the Town* see Alexander, *Marc Chagall*, 376, 476; J. J. Sweeney, *Marc Chagall* (New York: Museum of Modern Art, 1946), 71.

55. On *Self Portrait with Wall Clock* see Kagan, *Marc Chagall*, 72.

8 | Crossing Cruci-fictional Boundaries

Transgressive Tropes in Chaim Potok's *My Name Is Asher Lev*

ROBERT A. DAUM

Chaim Potok's highly successful novel *My Name Is Asher Lev* (1972) portrays the protagonist as a world-class painter growing up in an observant Hasidic family in Brooklyn in the period during World War II and its aftermath.[1] From the safety of the Diaspora, Asher Lev's family and community agonize over the fate of relatives and friends trapped in Europe and the Balkans. Separated by oceans, Jewish communities become increasingly aware of the scale of destruction of the war and the Holocaust. During and after the war, the enormity of the catastrophe causes various personal, psychological, and theological crises for the novel's characters, including the members of Asher Lev's family.[2]

The conflict between Asher Lev's artistic talent and his family's religious culture is the central theme in this novel. In order to portray this psychic pain and articulate his theme of cultural conflict, Potok's artist employs a singularly controversial, symbolic vocabulary: he depicts his own and his family's pain and suffering by painting the Hasidic Jewish mother, father, and son as the three figures in two crucifixion scenes and also in other works inspired by Michelangelo's *Florentine Pietà*.[3] In the most dramatic paintings, entitled *Brooklyn Crucifixion I* and *Brooklyn Crucifixion II*, his mother occupies the central position of Jesus, and he

and his father flank her on each side. In the months leading up to the creation of this body of work, Asher struggles to suppress it. Inspired by and yet
resisting the challenges of the *Pietà* and the *David*, Asher begins to see himself in the role of Jesus in the Passion narrative. (Only later does he paint his
mother's image at the center of the Christian Passion narrative in the role of
Jesus.) This identification, however, is only hinted at; more explicit is his
identification of his mother with the figure of the Virgin Mary:

> That night, I sat at the window and looked out at the lights of the city and
> found I could not stop thinking of the *Pietà* and the *David*. The next day, on
> the swiftly moving train to Rome, I drew the *Pietà* from memory, and discov-
> ered that the woman supporting the twisted arm of the crucified Jesus bore a
> faint resemblance to my mother. I stared at the drawing in horror and
> destroyed it. (314)

Eventually he stops resisting, and the work emerges:

> During breakfast, I drew on the tablecloth the contour of the Duomo *Pietà*
> with the vertical figure eliminated. I made the two side figures into bearded
> males, giving them the same robes as those worn by the Marys. I looked at the
> drawing. The dread was gone. I had no strength left for fighting. I would have
> to let it lead me now or there would be deeper and deeper layers of the weary-
> ing darkness. And I dreaded that darkness more than I did anything I might
> do with canvas and paint. (316–317)

Like his (and Potok's) hero Michelangelo, and like the protagonist in
James Joyce's *A Portrait of the Artist as a Young Man*, Potok's artist eventually refuses to compromise his creative vision.[4] In this contest between his
particular Jewish sensibilities ("his Hasidic essence," as S. Lillian Kremer
puts it[5]) and the Western artistic tradition, art wins:

> I returned to the apartment and sat at the table and thought of the *David* and
> its spatial and temporal shift. I looked at the painting of the old man with the
> pigeons that stood against a wall. And it was then that it came, though I think
> it had been coming for a long time and I had been choking it and hoping it
> would die. But it does not die. It kills you first. I knew there would be no
> other way to do it. No one says you have to paint ultimate anguish and tor-
> ment. But if you are driven to paint it, you have no other way. The prelimi-
> nary drawings came easily then. After a while, I put them away. It was
> Passover, and I rested. (327)

As Kremer notes, an important difference between Stephen's and
Asher's choices is that "whereas Stephen's growth as an artist has included
rejection of his heritage, Asher's has been the process of discovering a
form to convey his." Kremer points out that in *Ulysses* Dedalus comes to
an understanding closer to that of Asher.[6]

As in his other novels exploring what Potok referred to as "core-core cultural confrontation," the conflict is depicted as a binary opposition between cultural essences or centers. I shall analyze the assumptions behind, and the constructedness of, Potok's cultural confrontation model. I shall argue that the simultaneous displacement of the figure of Jesus from the cross and the replacement of that figure by the image of an Orthodox Jew is both a representation and at the same time a *production* of two powerful, authoritative motifs. That is, the painting both assumes and contributes to the production of the semiotic significance of, on the one hand, the crucified Christ as the quintessential Christian symbol and, on the other hand, the (suffering) Orthodox Jew as the quintessential Jewish symbol. The semiotic coherence and power of the former serves to enhance the semiotic coherence and power of the latter; this reciprocal effect masks the constructedness of Potok's (Asher's) selection of the suffering Hasidic Jew as the signifier for Judaism's core.

I shall not enter into a discussion here of the extent to which the image of Christ on the cross may be contested as a signifier for Christianity *tout court* or for suffering in the tradition of Western figurative art. I do contend, however, that the image of the Orthodox Hasidic Jew as the signifier of the quintessential (suffering) Jew is a problematic motif—and this not simply because of its juxtaposition with the motif of the cross or its metonymic displacement of the figure of Jesus from that cross.[7] That is, I shall interrogate the core-core culture confrontation model and also the constructedness of Potok's representation of the core of Jewish culture in the binary pairing upon which the novel is based.

Transgressive Juxtapositions

In an immigrant community in which Talmudic scholarship, piety, and service to community are highly valued, Asher's artistry would have been frowned upon in any event. In the context of the war's massive destruction and the anguish of his family and community regarding the events across the ocean, Asher's passion for figurative art strikes his father and most of his community as narcissistic and trivial at best, and as idolatrous at worst. Already as a schoolboy Asher had committed the transgression of taking time away from the performance of *mitzvot* (commandments) in general, and the study of Torah in particular, in order to draw. In spite of tremendous communal and familial pressures, however, the creative power of Asher's artistry will not be denied. A great strength of the novel is Potok's evocation of the immensity of Asher's talent in this unlikely place. As a fictional biography of a great artist, the novel is very effective.

The central character experiences, and provokes in his family and community, a range of personal and religious crises, as he and they find it increasingly difficult to reconcile the implications of a world-class artistic talent in the body of a young Hasidic Jewish man. Inevitably, the well-informed rebbe himself hears of Asher's great gift, and, to Asher's father's dismay, the rebbe places the young man under the tutelage of a famous older Jewish artist, Jacob Kahn, who is affiliated loosely with the sect. The rebbe's hope is that the young man will remain an observant Jew. He does, as far as he and Potok are concerned. The artist does not wish to reject his community, but his community perceives his behavior as a fundamental repudiation of its mores and collective identity. Its response is to shun him, but from its perspective, his actions forced them to do so. Determining precisely who rejected whom in this context misses the point; the conflict is a mutual production, even if the artist made the first move. Kremer observes, "The artist declares that his relationship with God will be of his own design and one true to the larger Judaic tradition, a voluntary bond of creative association." This characterization of "the larger Judaic tradition" as "a voluntary bond of creative association" is, of course, a representation to which members of Asher Lev's community would take exception.[8] The catalyst for the final breach is his public display of two paintings in a prominent Manhattan gallery.[9] As the titles—*Brooklyn Crucifixion I* and *II*—suggest, the paintings juxtapose the motif of the crucifixion with portraits of Asher's own family.

Following Potok himself, scholarship on this novel has interpreted the fictional painter Asher Lev's provocative, even scandalous, use of the crucifixion motif to depict his Hasidic family's pain as the illustration of a "core-core culture confrontation" between figurative art and traditional Judaism. The notorious paintings are emblematic of the author's rhetorical strategy, and they mark the decisive rupture between the painter and his family, community, and rabbi after years of tension. As the rebbe puts it, "Your naked women were a great difficulty for me, Asher. But this is an impossibility" (366). The artist struggles to resist transgressing this boundary, but he finds himself incapable of doing so:

> I remember that the first time I saw the Michelangelo *Pietà* in the Duomo I could not draw it. It was the fifth day of July. I stared at its Romanesque and Gothic contours, at the twisted arm and bent head, at the circle formed by Jesus and the two Marys, at the vertical of Nicodemus—I stared at the geometry of the stone and felt the stone luminous with strange suffering

and sorrow. I was an observant Jew, yet that block of stone moved through me like a cry, like the call of seagulls over morning surf, like—like the echoing blasts of the shofar sounded by the Rebbe. I do not mean to blaspheme. My frames of reference have been formed by the life I have lived. I do not know how a devout Christian reacts to that *Pietà*. I was only able to relate it to elements in my own lived past. I stared at it. I walked slowly around it. I do not remember how long I was there that first time. When I came back out into the brightness of the crowded square, I was astonished to discover that my eyes were wet. (310)

Although the central displacement in the plot is the exchange of Jewish figures for Christian figures in an iconic Christian scene, the novel enacts a whole series of displacements and juxtapositions engendering and enacting tension and/or conflict.[10] On a broader scale, the distant World War and Holocaust are witnessed helplessly from the Brooklyn Diaspora. The Eastern European Hasidic sect, having been safely removed from the setting of the war, is now resettled as a highly observant but insecure Jewish minority within a large, diverse Jewish community. The broader Jewish community (which is actually a multiplicity of communities) exists as a minority within the dominant, variegated Christian and secular American culture. A broad theme within the novel is the negotiation of the boundaries between these various cultural constellations by American Jews in the temporal context of World War II and the Holocaust, yet at a spatial remove from the field of war itself.[11]

The novel's physical locations are depicted as heterogeneous, if not necessarily incompatible. Potok's New York and Paris are inhabited both by Hasidic Jews and also by secular Jewish (and other) gallerists and collectors. Asher eats in kosher restaurants or homes in European cities bursting with Christian-inspired artwork. He wears a generic cap to cover his head, which allows him to observe traditional Jewish strictures without marking himself explicitly as a Jew in the eyes of non-Jews in Paris, Rome, or Florence. In Asher's words, he spends "hours in a Renaissance city lived by a man born in a Brooklyn street, a man wearing a red beard and ritual fringes and a fisherman's cap" (310).[12]

The device of spatial displacement also plays out within the walls of Asher's family home. The artist is growing up in the wrong place—that is, his talent is seemingly in the wrong body. The boy's father is rarely home, due to his constant traveling around the world as an emissary for the sect's rabbi.[13] The purpose of these travels is to establish Hasidic schools, which will serve as incubators of young Jewish scholars to replace some of those who perished in the Holocaust. Asher's mother is also out of place. She never recovered from the shock of the murder of her brother, and the constant absence of her husband drives her to the edge. That is to say, she is psychologically fragile, and she stands for hours at the window of their apartment.

Asher is obsessed with the image of his mother looking anxiously and fearfully out the window. He is also painfully aware of the pain that personal loss and the growing conflict between his father and himself have caused his mother. This pain is inscribed on her body, and it torments Asher. The catharsis for the artist is the representation of his family's pain, dominated by his mother's suffering, using the symbolic imagery of Western figurative art. As a result of the dominance of Christianity in the development of the European artistic tradition, the most prevalent motif in Western figurative art to represent pain, suffering, and forbearance is martyrdom. The foundational Christian martyrdom is, of course, the passion of Jesus. Like real Jewish artists such as Marc Chagall, the fictional painter Asher Lev finds himself incapable of expressing his ideas fully without making use of these traditions. As Asher explains:

> For dreams of horror, for nights of waiting, for memories of death, for the love I have for you, for all the things I remember, and for all the things I should remember but have forgotten, for all these I created this painting—an observant Jew working on a crucifixion because there was no aesthetic mold in his own religious tradition into which he could pour a painting of ultimate anguish and torment. (330)

Chaim Potok was also an amateur painter, and he created a version of the *Brooklyn Crucifixion*. Other Jewish artists painted crucifixion scenes before Potok and (the fictional) Asher Lev, including versions with figures explicitly marked as Jews on the cross.[14] The best known was Marc Chagall, who used the motif a number of times.[15] The art historian Sed-Rajna notes how the sculptor Jacques Lipschitz justified his creation of a Virgin for the Church of Assy (1947–1953). On the back of the sculpture Lipschitz wrote the following: "Jacob Lipschitz, Jew, faithful to the religion of his ancestors, has made this Virgin for the better understanding of human beings on this earth so that the Spirit may prevail."[16]

The Stickiness of Binaries: Problematizing Potok's Notion of Core-Core Culture Confrontation

Lipschitz's apologetic inscription attests to the challenge facing Asher Lev and to the cultural conflict underlying Potok's plot. As noted above, Potok characterized this conflict in binary terms. Binarism in rhetoric about cultural, social, philosophical, or political conflicts is hardly an invention of

Hegelian historiography. It can be seen in the "two ways" trope of Greco-Roman antiquity and the ancient Near East. The undermining of the "Athens versus Jerusalem" binary approach to Jewish history is common-place of contemporary scholarship; nevertheless, this approach more or less frames Potok's cultural confrontation model. An approach to Jewish history as a series of rigid conflicts between, for example, rationalism and mysticism, halakhah and kabbalah, assimilation and fidelity to tradition, continuity and change, and so forth, is now seen as reductive, but reductive binary conflicts lend themselves to popular fiction.

At the same time, of course, there is abundant literary evidence of polemical discourse framed in precisely these reductive patterns. This is to be expected, given the nature of polemical discourse. To some extent Potok's reliance on this model is due to the fact that he wrote the work in 1972. This was before the critical theoretical work of Roland Barthes and Jacques Derrida—which interrogated binary, centering, and mar-ginalizing discourse—had entered the academic mainstream. Another gap to consider is the one between critical theory and popular culture, or at least the gap between critical theory and the lived experience of people in ideologically orthodox cultures or subcultures, in which reductive polemical discourse thrives.[17] This is the sociological context in which Asher Lev (and, in a rather different sense, Chaim Potok) "lived" in the early 1970s.

The novel's dramatic climax—the exhibition of the *Brooklyn Crucifix-ion* series in Manhattan—is generated not merely by the artist's transgres-sive use of figurative art, but by his integration of the elements of the symbol systems of seemingly incompatible cultures. On the surface the body of work in his exhibition challenges the overdetermined demarcation between Judaism and Christianity, but this act of rebellion also represents the (albeit controversial) expression of his autonomous renegotiation of his identity as a Jew and an artist.[18] As Kremer notes, long before he created these particular works, the artist cut off some of the physical marks of his particular Jewish identity: his earlocks. In this liberating act, the artist declares that his relationship with God will be of his own design and will be true to the larger Judaic tradition, a voluntary bond of creative associa-tion.[19] Potok applied this cultural model in other works as well.[20] Like many binary oppositions, these are legitimate and useful to a point, but such reductions are also misleading and historically inaccurate. Both the art versus Judaism binary and the Christianity versus Judaism binary can be better understood as dynamic dialectics in which the elements consti-tuting both binary terms are continuous *and* unstable. The opposition between these binaries is culturally produced, not essential. Of course, the broad parameters defining each element as fundamentally oppositional are largely continuous—that is, Christianity has not been Jewish since late antiquity (and even less so since the early Middle Ages), but the *precise* significations of the terms "Christianity" or "Judaism" have never been stable. To a large extent Potok was aware of this, but recent research in Jewish and Christian origins has sharpened our understanding of the fluidity of these phenomena.

I am making more than a passing reference here to nominalist approaches to discourse. My point is that the assertion or reliance on a model of a cultural "core" is a practice of knowledge production, and the archaeology of that particular culture (and its core) is a phantasm, whose "reality" is indirectly conjured by means of its juxtapositioning over and against another culture's supposed cultural core. The notion of "core-core cultures confrontation" need not imply that the elements constituting the binary are essential, stable, and continuous, but Potok's repeated employment of the model serves to essentialize, stabilize, and historicize these elements. The problem is that his model suggests that cultures are more rather than less unitary and that a culture's core is identifiable and, therefore, largely stable. I should like to insist that a cultural core is *always* discursively produced and that identifications of a cultural core are gestures of power even in works of fiction.[21] One might think that while the core of a culture is relatively stable, only the boundaries are fluid, or that the boundaries are subject to renegotiation and resistance more than the core. There may be some truth to this, in that a core would seem to represent a consensus, but this is illusory, as any particular articulation of a culture's core, or of its "essence," is a culturally produced (and resisted) discursive production. That some discursive productions may resonate more than others in principle may be sociologically significant, assuming that one can measure such a thing, but this does not make it any more "real"—nor, for that matter, any less real—than any other nominalist practice.[22]

The designation of a particular values hierarchy to signify the core of one's culture is not the only power gesture implied by the employment of a binary model. Identifying the core of the other culture, against which one's own cultural core is fundamentally in conflict, is another critical component of the discourse of cultural construction. The process is (at least) bidirectional. This is a crucial factor to consider in an analysis of Potok's cultural confrontation model.[23]

Placing Asher Lev's family within a crucifixion scene represents the clash of traditional Judaism and Western figurative art and Christian theology. This particular juxtaposition, like those of Chagall, Motka, and other artists, is also predicated on the selection of an ultra-Orthodox, Hasidic Jewish figure (in this case, a family of mother, father, and son; moreover, a suffering family) to represent, indeed to inhabit, the core of Judaism against the core of Christianity and of Western figurative art. The displacement of the figure of Jesus from the cross and his replacement by an ultra-Orthodox Jewish woman represents Potok's notion of the core-core cultures clash. This is a problematic juxtaposition, in that it seeks perforce to elevate to a transcendent level on a par with the epitome of Christian symbology the image of a Hasidic Jew. The binary pairing of the crucified Christ and a crucified Hasidic Jew implicitly mobilizes the discursive authority of the crucifixion scene—arguably the quintessential Christian motif—in order to amplify the discursive authority of the ultra-Orthodox Hasidic family as representative of the quintessence of Jewish culture. As should be evident at this point, I wish to question the selection of a twentieth-century figure (or family) from a minority subculture originating no earlier than the late eighteenth century to signify the core even of twentieth-century Jewish culture.

At the risk of overgeneralizing, I suggest that, notwithstanding the fact that Christian iconography remained alienating (or at least unappealing) for most Jews in twentieth-century America, Michelangelo's *Pietà* would have been seen as a great work of art. Moreover, I am not persuaded that the artistic dimension of the cultural conflict thematized in the novel would have been felt by most American Jews in the 1970s, particularly given the use of the crucifixion motif by Chagall, Wiesel, Gross, and others. The designation of an orthopractic subculture of twentieth-century Jews—who certainly would have been alienated not only by the Christian iconography but also by much else in Western culture—to represent the core of Jewish culture in opposition to the core of two thousand years of Christianity (or of Western figurative art) is reductive, to say the least. It essentializes Jewish culture as fundamentally incompatible with the material art of Western culture. The Jewish element in the binary pairing is far less representative vis-à-vis its culture than the Christian (or "Western") element in respect of its culture.[24]

Reassessing the Assumptions behind Potok's Binary Poles

Having questioned the theoretical basis and noted some of the problematic implications of the use of Potok's model of core-core culture confrontation more generally, I turn now to a brief critique of the constitutive elements of the binary itself. Several of the elements constituting this symbolic system have been destabilized in the academic world, if not quite at the popular level, since the publication of the book in 1972.[25] A variation on the theme of the aforementioned Athens versus Jerusalem binary is a reconstruction of all of Jewish history as an undifferentiated, uninterrupted period of absolute hostility to any form of representational art. Recent scholarship on the place of art in Jewish culture has unsettled some of the assumptions behind Potok's use and the public's reception of the notion of a fundamental opposition between Judaism and any form of representational art.

To be sure, representation of the human form is prohibited in Jewish law, and while the contrast has been overdrawn, it is correct to say that in general, the Jewish approach to representational art is closer to the aniconic approach of Islam than to the very different approach of Roman Catholic or Eastern Orthodox Christian churches.[26] Nevertheless, Potok's statements on the fundamental opposition between what he has called "Mosaic monotheism" and the world of art—an opposition that forms the very basis of the novel's central plot—are inaccurate. A few examples should suffice. In a transcript of an address, Potok stated:

> Anything having to do with pagan worship is anathema to monotheism, and fundamental to pagan worship was idolatry, the representation of God in human form. Therefore Jews have never participated in art of any kind that was connected to worship.[27]

While essentially correct in his assertion that "anything having to do with pagan worship is anathema to monotheism," the rest of this statement requires correction. Leaving aside nonplastic art forms (liturgy, instrumental and vocal music, dance), there is ample archaeological evidence of synagogue art, not to mention decorative ritual objects, well into the modern period. While material representations of God in human form are not found in Jewish contexts after the Byzantine period, the "representation of God in human form" at a symbolic level is a significant component of Jewish religious practice down to the present day.[28] Potok has drawn the opposition too simplistically.

Similarly problematic is the following statement:

> All through the middle ages, as far as Jewish law is concerned, Christianity was essentially an idolatrous religion because of it's [sic] iconography. Because of this, religious Jews never participated in the art of that civilization, which was intimately connected to that form of worship. So we have a situation of two thousand years of Jewish wandering throughout the western side of our planet, contributing to everything except art. There has not been a single instance, until the modern age, of any religious Jew who has partici-

pated in any significant way at all in this extraordinary adventure we call modern art. . . . Because Jews did not participate in the mainstream of Western art, there are no Jewish motifs in Western art.[29]

The claim that "Christianity was essentially an idolatrous religion" is an imprecise representation of the more nuanced position of important medieval Jewish authorities. Christianity and Islam were explicitly *not* classified as idolatrous, but rather as underdeveloped forms of monotheism provided by the Deity as a means to draw Gentiles closer to pure monotheism.[30] At a more popular, polemical level, as well as among medieval kabbalists, there is evidence of a more negative attitude. One of the most widely read texts of the Middle Ages was a work entitled *Sefer Toldot Yeshu*, a parodic Hebrew life of Jesus written after the ninth century.[31] At any rate, the divinity of Jesus in Christian theology, not to mention anthropomorphic Christian iconography, was certainly incompatible with classical rabbinic or medieval halakah.

Having noted the fundamental opposition in Jewish law toward various aspects of Christian religious culture, Potok's statement that "religious Jews never participated in the art of that civilization, which was intimately connected to that form of worship," calls for comment. It appears that Potok did not mean to say only that "religious Jews never participated in the art of that civilization" in cases when that art "was intimately connected to that form of worship"; rather, he seems to be saying that the art of Western civilization for two thousand years "was intimately connected to that form of worship" and, therefore, that religious Jews simply never participated in its production. I agree that there is ample evidence that a great deal of the (surviving) art of Western civilization, particularly at the elite level, was intimately connected to Christianity, but as the rabbinic texts below will show, some Jews, including "religious" Jews—a rather nebulous and reductive term to describe Jews in the past and in the present—may well have been involved in the production of Western art and even of objects intimately connected with "idolatrous" worship.

Regarding art, including representational imagery, there is ample textual support in Jewish sources both for aniconic attitudes and for resistance to such attitudes in the biblical, Hellenistic, Roman, and Byzantine periods.[32] A few texts will serve to demonstrate that even classical rabbinic tradition adopted a complex, nuanced approach to figurative representation, the production of images (and idols!), and social pressures. The Mishna in *Avodah Zarah* 3:4 contains a famous representation of a confrontation between R. Gamaliel and Proklos:

Proklos the son of Philosophos asked Rabban Gamaliel in Acre while he was bathing in the Bath of Aphrodite: "It is written in your Torah: 'Let nothing that is banned stick to your hand' (Dt. 13:18). Why, then, do you bathe in the Bath of Aphrodite?" He said, "(We) don't answer (questions about Torah) in the bath." And when he came out, he said to him: "I did not come within her domain, she came within mine. People do not say, 'Let us make a bath as a decoration for Aphrodite'; rather, they say, 'Let us make an Aphrodite as a decoration for the bath.'"[33]

The text continues with another, perhaps more vulgar, argument against the notion that the goddess's image is an object of worship for the rabbinic bathers by pointing out that the bathers are naked, are ritually impure from a seminal emission, and are urinating in front of the statue. The Mishna contrasts Torah and "pagan" culture in various ways, beginning with R. Gamaliel's demonstrative refusal even to discuss Torah while naked; this is contrasted with the nudity, ritual impurity, and urination of the bathers in the presence of Aphrodite's image. Gamaliel argues that the idol's image is only a decoration, not an object of worship. The even sharper, subsequent comment ridicules pretensions of the idol's sanctity. Note that R. Gamaliel does not appear to be bothered in the least by the presence of Aphrodite's image.

A hint of the socioeconomic context can be seen in the Mishna in *Avodah Zarah* 4:4, in which R. Ishmael argues that, whereas the idols of Gentiles are prohibited only once they have been the objects of worship, a Jew's idol is forbidden from the moment of its manufacture. In contrast, R. Aqiba takes the opposite, more lenient position, which is endorsed by the Mishna's editors: a Gentile's idol is forbidden upon its manufacture, but a Jew's idol is forbidden only after it has been the object of worship. R. Aqiba's response is not intended to defend the religious use of idols by Jews, but rather the decorative use and even the production of various images found in Jewish homes, towns, and bathhouses.

The Yerushalmi preserves a teaching prohibiting the images of kings, but not of local officials. Similarly, imagery per se is not prohibited, but iconography associated with emperor worship is. The Babylonian Talmud records a similar approach in which worship of the image is seen to be the crux of the problem; there is a difference of opinion regarding the production of idols in cities, but "all" authorities are said to agree that idols are forbidden in villages, where they are likely to be the objects of worship. By the modern period, centuries after Christianity and Islam were at least explicitly classified as monotheistic faiths, the halakhic position, albeit with differences, still captured the tensions represented in the early classical rabbinic sources treated above.[34]

Some of the horror expressed by the characters in *Asher Lev* when they are confronted by Asher's provocative paintings is due to the historical experience of compulsory conversion, apostasy, and martyrdom, in which Christian iconography, theology, liturgy, and leaders were prominent.[35] Of course, the motif of individual and collective Jewish martyrdom predates Christianity. In addition to extra-canonical cases, such as 2 Maccabees 7 (Hannah and her seven sons), exemplary martyr stories in classical Jewish sources include that of "the ten sages" who perished during the Hadrianic persecution; the tale of Hananiah, Mishael, and Azariah (Dan 3) and its midrashic and Talmudic treatments;[36] and the various narratives pertaining to the conquests of Jerusalem and the destructions of the temples.[37] The halakhic sources on martyrdom are developed in the context of persecutions by Sassanian Zoroastrian, Byzantine Christian, Visigothic Christian, Muslim (especially Almohade and Almoravid), and later medieval Christian regimes, not to mention the Crusades.

To some extent, medieval Jewish legal teaching regarding martyrdom in the face of the worship of idolatrous images can be differentiated more or less geographically between an Ashkenazi approach advocating martyrdom, or "sanctification of the (Divine) Name" (*kiddush ha-Shem*), even in the face of a demand to worship an image privately, on the one hand, and an alternative approach advocated by Maimonides writing in Fatimid Egypt, on the other hand. Maimonides privileged survival over martyrdom in the face of compulsory apostasy, if one were faced with such a choice.[38]

Jewish liturgical practice is rife with the motif of martyrdom, most prominently the observance of the Ninth of Av in commemoration of the destruction of the Temples and the "martyrology" component of the High Holy Day prayers. While much is made of the contrast between the Jewish and Christian Passion narratives, so to speak—that is, Isaac is not sacrificed by his father, whereas Jesus is sacrificed by his—there is abundant evidence of the extent to which both medieval Christians and Jews, particularly after the First Crusade, produced liturgical and exegetical texts in which martyrdom featured prominently.[39]

Framing the Transgressive Trope

Like Potok's/Asher's hero, Michelangelo, whose transgressive image of David ultimately had to be moved indoors, Asher's *Brooklyn Crucifixion* provokes a storm of controversy inflamed to some extent because of its spatial configuration.[40] The author's transgressive acts constitute a series of related displacements and spatial tensions. The most dramatic of these is Asher's displacement of the de-Judaized figure of Christ from its cross— the center of the christological symbol system—and its replacement by a figure signifying, at least in popular Jewish culture in 1972, the quintessential remnant of the world destroyed in the Holocaust. The motif of the suffering Jew is also a venerable if not an unproblematic one. Moreover, in the context of post-Holocaust discourse in the early 1970s, the projection of a Jew signifying Eastern European Hasidic Orthodox culture onto the template, as it were, of the Christian Passion narrative in *Brooklyn Crucifixion* is one with precedents, including Jewish ones.[41]

One major problem, as I see it, is that the juxtapositioning of these motifs creates a contrived and incommensurate binary pairing. I am questioning the semiotic rather than the aesthetic strength of the fictional painting. I am also drawing attention to the constructedness of Potok's rendering of Judaism's core—a Hasidic Orthodox Jewish man or woman on a cross—even if Potok (also) meant to suggest that Judaism's core was aniconic "Mosaic monotheism." Even if the contours of Jesus and Mary are effaced from the crucifixion scene, the elements in this semiotic contest are incommensurate.

Potok's selection of a crucifixion scene to represent the core both of Christian culture and of the depiction of suffering in the tradition of Christian-dominated, European painting is transgressive, although not unprecedented. It is also reasonably coherent. Although the image of Christ on the cross is an overdetermined signifier[42] and, to be sure, there are Christians (and others) who might propose various other (also contestable) "core" images to represent Christianity, nonetheless in the tradition of Western figurative art and in Christian cultures this motif has no serious rival.[43] So too, the image of the suffering Jew is a salient one,[44] and in the aftermath of the Shoah it gained new currency.

At the same time, however, the metonymic displacement of the crucified Christ by a crucified Hasidic Jew for the purpose of signifying two apposite cultural cores masks the constructedness of Potok's model of Jewish and also, of course, of Christian culture. Potok's *Asher Lev* not only narrativizes a contrast between cultural aesthetics; however, it also promotes a particular, reductive representation of those cultural aesthetics. In addition, his cultural model reifies *a particular sort of Jew* as a signifier for all Jews "who are at the very heart of their Judaism"[45] by placing that figure in tension with the crucified Christ, who can arguably be situated at the semiotic heart, as it were, of Christianity. The notion of cultural confrontation is not without value, as James Joyce, Potok, and other writers from antiquity to the present clearly have demonstrated. Moreover, *Asher Lev* is a compelling *Bildungsroman* that depicts a young man's conflicted fashioning of his own identity. What I have attempted to interrogate and problematize here is the way in which Potok's *Brooklyn Crucifixion* draws upon the discursive power of the motif of the crucified Christ as the very heart of Christianity in order to offer the reader the metonym of the crucified Orthodox Hasid as the very heart of Judaism. This displacement— actually a series of semiotic displacements—engenders a reification of a particular, constructed model of Jewish culture, whose core is both hostile to Western aesthetics and inhabited by a particular form of (Orthodox) Jew. As a metonym for Jewish culture as a whole, the model is inadequate.[46]

NOTES

1. Modern-day Hasidim are a subset of what are popularly known as "ultra-Orthodox" Jews (*haredim*, connoting "fervently observant" in Hebrew). The Hasidim are people who belong to any of a number of Orthodox Jewish sects led by rabbinic dynasties; generally speaking, these dynasties trace their origins back to the circle of followers of the founder of a particular type of traditionalist Judaism in eighteenth-century Eastern Europe—Israel Baal Shem Tov (1720–1760). For a fine recent survey of East European Jewish culture in the modern period, see D. Biale, "A Journey between Worlds: East European Jewish Culture from the Partitions of Poland to the Holocaust," in *Cultures of the Jews: A New History*, ed. David Biale (New York: Schocken, 2002), 799–854, and the ample bibliography provided there. For a helpful survey of scholarship on East European Jewry in modernity, see M. Stanislawski, "Eastern European Jewry in the Modern Period: 1750–1939," in *The Oxford Handbook of Jewish Studies*, ed. M. Goodman (Toronto: Oxford University Press, 2002), 396–411.

2. I wish to thank Paul Burns for inviting me to participate in the project that resulted in this chapter, as well as the colleagues who participated in the workshop at the Northwest Pacific Regional Conference of the AAR/SBL in 2004. I am indebted to Frederick Fajardo for his astute comments, and I am grateful to my graduate student, Tracy Ames, for her bibliographic assistance.

3. Note that my formulation does not presuppose a simplistic model of Christian appropriation of Jewish motifs, nor of two fully formed phenomena in the first century: "Christianity" and "Judaism." The religious cultures of early and medieval Judaism and Christianity were diverse, complex, fluid, and interrelated. Systematic theological formulations in early medieval texts do not prove the existence of homogeneous, undifferentiated, hegemonic religious societies or cultures in the early Middle Ages, not to mention centuries earlier (or later, for that matter). Moreover, the "appropriation" model itself is highly reductive, inasmuch as it rests on an assumption of prior ownership. The crucifixion motif at the dramatic center of this novel is a combination of a series of appropriations, or metonymic displacements, including elements of the trial of Abraham and the binding of Isaac in Gen 22, traces of the servant motif in Isaiah, aspects of Mediterranean mystery religions, components of ancient Near Eastern deicide narratives, features of the son of God motif associated particularly with Augustus, and other

biblical and extrabiblical tropes. Religious mythology, like cultural production generally, combines elements particular to a given cultural context as well as compelling figures from a broad semiotic pool. Were it to do otherwise, the result would be incoherent and incomprehensible. For a nuanced recent treatment of some of these themes in respect to the formation of Judaism and Christianity, see D. Boyarin, *Border Lines: The Partition of Judaeo-Christianity* (Philadelphia: University of Pennsylvania Press, 2004). See also G. N. Stanton and G. G. Stroumsa, eds., *Tolerance and Intolerance in Early Judaism and Christianity* (Cambridge: Cambridge University Press, 1998); J. Barclay and J. Sweet, eds., *Early Christian Thought in Its Jewish Context* (New York: Cambridge University Press, 1996); M. Hirshman, *A Rivalry of Genius: Jewish and Christian Biblical Interpretation in Late Antiquity*, trans. B. Stein (Albany, NY: SUNY Press, 1996). For an analysis of Jewish polemical discourse regarding Christianity in the medieval West, see R. Chazan, *Fashioning Jewish Identity in Medieval Western Christendom* (Cambridge: Cambridge University Press, 2004). For an analysis of rabbinic rhetoric and authority construction, see R. Daum, "Describing Yavneh" (PhD diss., University of California, Berkeley, 2001).

4. For a fine analysis comparing Joyce's *Portrait* and Potok's *Asher Lev*, see S. L. Kremer, "Daedelus in Brooklyn: Influences of *A Portrait of the Artist as a Young Man* on *My Name Is Asher Lev*," *Studies in American Jewish Literature* 4 (1984): 26–38.

5. Kremer, "Daedelus in Brooklyn," 37.

6. Ibid., 37–38.

7. By "metonymic displacement," I mean a transference or shifting of signifiers or symbols, without however implying that these significations or symbol systems are fixed, universal, or stable.

8. Kremer, "Daedelus in Brooklyn," 32.

9. This breach is not quite "final." The artist's ties to his community are strained almost to the point of no return, but lines of communication do remain open, and in a subsequent work, the thread of the plot nearly brings Asher home.

10. The original Christian figures in the Passion narrative would have been Jewish, or at least Judean. There is, therefore, some irony in Potok's replacement of first-century Jewish figures, later transformed into the foundational Christian figures, with twentieth-century Jewish figures.

11. This theme of cultural displacement is brilliantly enacted in the famous opening scene of Potok's novel *The Chosen*, which depicts an iconically American baseball game in New York between two groups of Orthodox Jewish boys, one Hasidic and one Mitnaggedic. See Potok, *The Chosen* (New York: Fawcett Crest), 1968.

12. The use of a "fisherman's" cap in Rome, at least, may be an allusion to Peter.

13. A Hasidic sect's reverence for its rebbe is customary, but in this sect's case it is also a result of their growing realization that his decision that they should leave Eastern Europe before the war saved their lives. In a Hasidic community the rabbinic leader is a charismatic dynast referred to as "the rebbe." The rebbe is consulted regarding every important decision in an individual's life, from choosing a marriage partner to changing a career.

14. See Daphna Arbel's essay in the present volume.

15. In addition to his famous paintings in which the crucifixion is a central motif, Chagall used the motif within various other works, e.g., *Message Biblique* (1956–1957). *The Creation of Man* combines Christian and Jewish motifs. See G. Sed-Rajna, *Jewish Art*, trans. S. Friedman and M. Reich (New York: Harry N. Abrams, 1997), 351; translation of *Art juif* (Paris: Editio-Éditions Citadelles & Mazenod, 1995). Other Jewish artists who have used the crucifixion motif include Chaim Gross and Motka. Elie Wiesel employed the motif more loosely in *Night*. Non-Jewish artists in the twentieth century, including Pablo Picasso, used the crucifixion motif as a metaphor for suffering.

16. Sed-Rajna, *Jewish Art*, 351.

17. I refer here to ideological orthodoxies (with a lowercase *O*) of either left or right, as well as to those not conforming necessarily to a left/right bifurcation (such as academic, hyper-nationalist, or other types of orthodoxies). I am certainly not referring here to "Orthodox Jews" to the exclusion of ideologically orthodox Jews on the left.

18. The novel thematizes other conflicts and themes as well, including Jewish-Christian polemics, European anti-Semitism, Diaspora Jewry's evolving perceptions of the Holocaust, conflicts between parents and children, generational differences within immigrant minority communities, and so forth.

19. Kremer, "Daedalus in Brooklyn," 32.

20. To cite just three examples, in *The Chosen, The Promise,* and *In the Beginning,* Potok juxtaposed particular notions of Talmudic study, Jewish theology, and biblical interpretation against, respectively, Freudian psychoanalytic theory, scientific text criticism, and biblical criticism.

21. Of course, denials of a particular cultural core, or of the possibility of identifying any core, can also be seen as gestures of power. For a selection of recent studies of colonizing discourse in the realm of religion, and critical reflections on those studies, see M. Vessey, S. Betcher, R. Daum, and H. Maier, eds., *The Calling of the Nations: Exegesis, Ethnography, and Empire in a Biblical-Historic Present* (Toronto: University of Toronto Press, forthcoming).

22. Similarly, many Christians today would argue that the core of Christianity is the death and resurrection of Jesus, but the meaning of this notion differs among Christians. Probably it goes without saying that claiming to possess an understanding of the real meaning of the death and resurrection of Jesus is unavoidably reductive and potentially hegemonic. What I wish to emphasize here is that claiming that even this is "the" core of Christian culture is also a contestable assertion. When the identification of the core of a culture appears to be (or is said to be) especially self-evident, the constructedness of such an identification calls for critical analysis. With differences in mind, this is as true of essentializing claims regarding the core of Judaism as it is of essentializing claims regarding the core of Christianity.

23. Just as the will to power characteristic of hegemonic discourse seems to require an internal, heretical Other, so too does it benefit from its explicit or implicit endorsement of the comparably hegemonic discourse of its external counterpart, perhaps even of a particular external counterpart. That is, the promotion of one's own claim to represent orthodoxy in one's own domain is strengthened by the tacit promotion or explicit endorsement of the similar claims to orthodoxy of one's counterpart. The two Orthodoxies implicitly support each other's claims to be orthodox, in part because it reinforces their own internal claims, stated or not. For a stimulating formulation and application of this approach to Jewish and Christian origins, see Boyarin, *Border Lines.*

24. Of course, these images do far more than represent Asher Lev's family's pain; the placement of these figures in a crucifixion scene enlarges the semiotic range of the figures. Likewise, the selection of Hasidic Jews as representative of the vast, differentiated mass even of only the Jewish victims of the Shoah is hopelessly reductive.

25. The reader should not misunderstand that my comments examining Potok's theme of a "core cultural clash" in this novel are intended to disparage Potok's great achievements as a writer, or the many strengths of *My Name is Asher Lev.* It is an appealing novel, as are several of the other works in his series of novels exploring the theme of a protagonist's struggle to mediate between the conflicting claims of two cultures with which s/he identifies. Moreover, like any novel, the book was a product of its time, and the author's theme was a coherent one in the 1970s.

26. For more on the various shades of difference within Jewish, Muslim, and Christian cultures at different periods and places with respect to the plastic arts, representational art, and various forms of iconography, see K. Bland, *The Artless Jew: Medieval and Modern Affirmations and Denials of the Visual* (Princeton, NJ: Princeton University Press, 2000); T. Allen, "The Arabesque, the Beveled Style, and the Mirage of an Early Islamic Art," in *Tradition and Innovation in Late Antiquity*, ed. F. M. Clover and R. S. Humphreys (Madison: University of Wisconsin Press, 1989), 209–44; and A. Grabar, *Christian Iconography: A Study of Its Origins* (Princeton, NJ: Princeton University Press, 1968).

27. C. Potok, "On Being Proud of Uniqueness," a lecture delivered at the Southern College of Seventh-day Adventists, Collegedale, Tennessee, March 20, 1986, ed. J. Gladson, http://www.lasierra.edu/~ballen/potok/Potok.unique.html.

28. There is abundant anthropomorphic imagery for the Deity in the Bible, in rabbinic literature, in liturgical texts, and in esoteric mystical literature. This imagery is supposed to be understood symbolically, of course.

29. Potok, "On Being Proud of Uniqueness."

30. See, e.g., Maimonides, Mishne Torah, *Hilkhot Melakhim* 11:4. Menachem Hameiri in Perpignan (d. 1315) followed Maimonides' approach and promoted a relatively positive view of Christianity as the ideology of "nations bound by the law." Whether legal formulations of this sort should be taken at face value is a complex question. In any event, Islam was decidely aniconic, whereas Byzantine Christianity, particularly after the defeat of the iconoclasts, certainly was not. Regarding differences between Maimonides' and Hameiri's approaches, see J. Katz, *Between Jews and Gentiles* [in Hebrew], 2nd ed. (Jerusalem: Mossad Bialik, 1960), 116–28; and Katz, *Exclusiveness and Tolerance: Studies in Jewish-Gentile Relations in Medieval and Modern Times* (New York: Schocken, 1962). Regarding the formulation '*umot hagdurot bedarkhe hadatot,* my late teacher Amos Funkenstein pointed out that "the expression itself belongs first and foremost to the philosophical tradition and is the medieval version of the 'natural religion.'" A. Funkenstein, *Perceptions of Jewish History* (Berkeley: University of California Press, 1993), 149n.

31. The classic study of the *Sefer Toldot Yeshu* is S. Krauss, *Das Leben Jesu nach jüdischen Quellen* (Berlin: S. Calvary, 1902). There are a number of different versions extant, which drew on earlier Jewish and Christian sources. Concerning medieval kabbalists' polemical characterizations of Christianity, see M. Idel, "The Attitude towards Christianity in the Book of *Hameshiv*" [in Hebrew], *Zion* 46 (1981): 77–91. See also R. Ben-Shalom, "Medieval Jewry in Christendom," in *The Oxford Handbook of Jewish Studies*, ed. Martin Goodman (Toronto: Oxford University Press, 2002), 153–92.

32. A sampling of important sources points to both aniconic ideology and resistance to such ideology. For a modest sampling, see Dt. 12:3, Judith 8:18, 2 Macc. 12:40, Philo, *De legatione ad Gaium*, 30, Midr Tann le-Dvarim Mekh 23:4, mAvoda Zara 3–5. Several of these sources are cited and treated in Efraim E. Urbach, *The Halakhah: Its Sources and Development* (trans. Raphael Posner, *Yad la-Talmud*; Tel Aviv: Modan, 1996), 208–9, 413, and Urbach, *The Sages: Their Concepts and Beliefs* (trans. Israel Abrahams, 2 vols.; Jerusalem: Magnes Press of the Hebrew University, 1979), 596. See also Vivian B. Mann, ed., *Jewish Texts on the Visual Arts* (Cambridge: Cambridge University Press, 2000) and Kalman P. Bland, *The Artless Jew: Medieval and Modern Affirmations and Denials of the Visual* (Princeton: Princeton University Press, 2000). Archaeological research of synagogues in the Byzantine period indicates that components of Galilean Jewish culture at that time manifested more positive attitudes towards the production of figurative art than Herodian policy seems to have endorsed. The fact that the Mishna prohibits particular figurative images and not all figurative art should alert us to the likely presence of resistance

to an exclusively aniconic ideology in third century Jewish Galilean towns. For an argument for early Israelite (and regional) aniconism, see Tryggve Mettinger, *No Graven Image?: Israelite Aniconism in its Ancient Near Eastern Context* (Coniectanea Biblica Old Testament Series 42; Stockholm: Almqvist and Wiksell International, 1995). See also Diana Vikander Edelman, ed., *The Triumph of Elohim: From Yahwisms to Judaisms* (Grand Rapids, Michigan: Eerdmans, 1996). For a reading of moderate aniconism in the Hellenistic period, see Joseph Gutmann, "The 'Second Commandment' and the Image in Judaism," in *No Graven Images: Studies in Art and the Hebrew Bible* (New York: Ktav, 1971). For a fine, balanced discussion of Jewish aniconism in the context of the second commandment, see Carl S. Ehrlich, "'Make Yourself No Graven Image': The Second Commandment and Judaism," in *Textures and Meaning: Thirty Years of Judaic Studies at the University of Massachusetts Amherst*, eds. L. Ehrlich, S. Bolozky, R. Rothstein, M. Schwartz, J. Berkovitz, J. Young (electronic publication; Amherst, Mass.: Department of Judaic and Near Eastern Studies, University of Massachusetts Amherst, 2004). For a nuanced analysis of aniconic attitudes as a measure of the rabbinization of Byzantine Jewish society, see Seth Schwartz, "Rabbinization in the Sixth Century," in *The Talmud Yerushalmi and Graeco-Roman Culture III*, ed. Peter Schäefer, *Texts and Studies in Ancient Judaism* (Tübingen: Mohr Siebeck, 2002).

33. It is now more or less taken for granted in the field that proscriptions and prescriptions in the canonical traditions of the Mishna are more productively read as indications of early third-century, rabbinic cultural norms than they are as historically reliable descriptions of the social practices of the majority of the population of Roman-occupied Palestine, least of all in the late first and early second centuries. Even this formulation needs to be complicated considerably, as the term "rabbinic" is far too broad a designation for the variety of figures, groups, and "schools" in different locations and time periods in *Eretz Yisrael*–Palestine and other locations in the first few centuries CE.

34. I am indebted to E. Urbach, whose discussion led me to this text in *b. Avodah Zarah* 41a (Urbach, *Halakhah*, 413n31. K. Bland's helpful analysis of this theme pointed me to Rav Kook's (1865–1935) message of dedication to the Bezalel Academy of Arts and Design in Jerusalem in 1907, while he was rabbi in Jaffa, fourteen years prior to his appointment as first chief Ashkenazi rabbi in Palestine. Kook, in Bland's words, "credited the law for legitimizing visual art and compelling Jews to produce it. He enthusiastically acknowledged the salutary powers of the visual arts" (Bland, *Artless Jew* 35). Kook's reading of halakhic approval extends, in Bland's paraphrase, "to portraits of the human face and even to complete sculptures of the human figure, as long as certain minimal precautions are observed involving the cooperation of non-Jewish helpers. The category of proscribed art, offensive to Jewish sensibilities, which may not be produced or displayed in schools or museums is wide-ranging and significant: 'The nation of Israel abhors and will not tolerate pictures specifically characteristic of idolatry, whether from the ancient and present pagan world or from the Christian world'" (33–35).

35. The notion of a "final solution" to the *perfidia iudaica* can be found already in seventh-century Christian discourse. For a careful analysis of this phenomenon, see R. G. Salinero, *Las conversiones forzosas de los judíos en el reino visigodo* (Rome: Escuela Española de Historia y Arqueología en Roma, 2000).

36. See, e.g., *b. Pesahim* 53b.

37. Of course, this is not an exhaustive list. See, e.g., Lamentations regarding the First Temple's destruction; regarding the destruction of the Second Temple, see, e.g., Josephus, *Jewish War*, 6; the Talmudic tractates *Ta'anit* and *Gittin*; and the midrash collection *Lamentations Rabba*.

38. Maimonides strongly condemned the person who chose martyrdom rather than electing to survive by committing apostasy (*Mishne Torah Hilkhot Yesodei ha-Torah*, 5:1). The

Franco-German Tosafists took the contrary position (*Tos. Avodah Zarah* 27b s. v. *yakhol*). They even required martyrdom on the part of someone compelled to commit apostasy in private (*Tos. Avodah Zarah* 54a s. v. *ha*). See "Martyrdom," *Encyclopaedia Judaica*, CD ROM ed. (Jerusalem: Judaica Multimedia [Israel], 1997). See also Maimonides, *Hilkhot Melakhim* 10:2, which exempts the minor, the *heresh* ("deaf-mute"), and the simple-minded from the requirement of *kiddush ha-Shem* altogether, as they are not subject to the performance of the commandments.

39. In his classic study *The Last Trial*, S. Spiegel traces evidence of a Jewish midrashic tradition in which Isaac is both sacrificed and resurrected. See Spiegel, *The Last Trial: On the Legends and Lore of the Command to Abraham to Offer Isaac as a Sacrifice: The Akedah*, trans. J. Goldin (New York: Pantheon, 1967). The important *unetaneh tokef* prayer in the High Holy Day liturgy is an extravagant example of a medieval Jewish liturgical text commemorating a rabbi's lurid torture and martyrdom in the context of a Christian official's demand that he commit apostasy. It is commonplace that many martyrological accounts in Jewish exegetical and liturgical texts in the Middle Ages were produced by authors familiar with aspects of Christian martyrological discourse, including the Passion narratives.

40. For an intriguing analysis of the spatial dimensions of the controversy surrounding the *David*, see D. M. Gunn, "Covering David: Michelangelo's *David* from the Piazza della Signoria to My Refrigerator Door," in *'Imagining' Biblical Worlds: Studies in Spatial, Social, and Historical Constructs in Honor of James W. Flanagan*, ed. D. M. Gunn and P. M. McNutt (New York: Sheffield Academic Press, 2002).

41. I am deferring a discussion of the "precedent" of a crucified religious Jew constituted by the Passion narrative itself.

42. Even, and perhaps especially, culturally dominant motifs are always overdetermined signs.

43. Other popular motifs in Christian figurative tradition include depictions of Mary, Mary and the infant Jesus, Mary and the dead Jesus (as in the *Pietà*), the Last Supper, saints, and a range of martyrs. The symbols of cross and of crucifixion are particularly important.

44. This can be seen in texts ranging from Exodus to Isaiah, in rabbinic sources, in liturgical texts, in Christian polemical texts, in plastic art, and in "secular" historiography. While this comparison is difficult to gauge, scholarly attempts to challenge or complicate what Salo Baron called the "lachrymose view" of Jewish history perhaps have achieved more success at the academic than at the popular level. Obviously, the Shoah shifted the ground considerably, in various respects. Nevertheless, the lachrymose narrative has been rightly unsettled. See D. Biale, *Power and Powerlessness in Jewish History* (New York: Schocken, 1986).

45. S. L. Kremer, "Interview with Chaim Potok," *Studies in Jewish Literature* 4 (1984): 85. Of course, a critical issue is whether by "who are at the very heart of their Judaism," Potok meant "*their* Judaism" or "their *Judaism*."

46. Alas, Potok is no longer with us. Some readers may find my criticism unfair or even churlish. Thoughtful readers may offer a respectable counterargument. I consider myself a fan as well, but the constructedness of any model of cultural core calls for interrogation.

9 | 'Abbās Maḥmūd al-'Aqqād's *The Genius of Christ*

An Innovative Muslim Approach to Jesus

F. PETER FORD JR.

In the mid-twentieth century, an Arabic book about Jesus written by a Muslim appeared in Cairo and immediately generated considerable interest. This was partly due to the popularity of its author. 'Abbās Maḥmūd al-'Aqqād had already gained a solid reputation in the Arab world as one of Egypt's most respected and prolific writers. He had produced dozens of books and hundreds of articles covering a vast range of historical, social, and literary themes. He was also regarded as a prominent apologist for Islam, defending the faith as valid and rational for the modern era. Arab Muslim readers had especially enjoyed his series of biographical studies on Muḥammad and other leading personalities from early Islamic history. In 1953, al-'Aqqād added to this series two titles dealing with well-known biblical figures who were also regarded as important prophets in Islam prior to Muḥammad: *Abraham: Father of the Prophets*, and the book being considered here, *The Genius of Christ* (*'Abqarīyat al-Masīḥ*).

Public interest in *The Genius of Christ* was also due to the unusual attitude portrayed in the book toward its subject. Most previous works about Christ by Muslim authors had sought to delineate a distinctly Islamic view of Jesus, while criticizing Christian beliefs. Al-'Aqqād, however, displayed a genuinely positive approach based almost exclusively on the Christian Gospels rather than Islamic sources, with virtually no anti-Christian sentiment. Both Muslim and Christian readers in Egypt reportedly spoke well

175

of the book, and some 200,000 copies were sold within the first year. Al-'Aqqād produced a second edition in 1958, entitled *The Life of Christ (Ḥayāt al-Masīḥ)*, which remains available in Cairo bookshops. However, despite the acclaim for the book given by a number of Western Christian scholars of Islam, its English translation appeared only recently.[1]

The Perspective of Jesus in Islam

To appreciate the novelty of al-'Aqqād's approach to his subject, one must first recognize the manner in which Jesus has been viewed in Islam.[2] This of necessity must begin with the Qur'ān, the foundation for Islamic faith. There Jesus is mentioned in a few dozen passages, primarily with regard to his role as one of the many prophets who appeared prior to Muḥammad and who taught the unity of God and how to worship him properly. Yet in many respects Jesus is elevated in the Qur'ān above all other prophets, such that Muslims have generally considered him to be second in esteem only to Muḥammad. Simultaneously, however, the Qur'ān challenges certain beliefs about Jesus that were perceived to be held among Christians of Muḥammad's time. Thus, the Qur'ān affirms certain Christian teachings about Jesus, while rejecting others.[3]

To begin with, the Qur'ān resolutely affirms that Jesus' mother Mary was a virgin when she gave birth to him and that she was chosen for this special role because of her purity and humble submission to God. There are strong parallels between the accounts of the Annunciation in Luke 1 and similar passages in the Qur'ān (e.g., Q.3:42–47; 19:16–26).[4] Jesus was conceived when God "breathed into her of his spirit" (Q.21:91). Nevertheless, the Qur'ān also affirms that this miraculous birth was only a sign of his special call as a prophet; it in no way implied the idea of divinity for Jesus. "The example of Jesus before God is like that of Adam: he created him from dust, then said to him, 'Be!' and he was" (Q.3:59). In other words, Jesus was no more divine than was Adam, who was also created in an unusual and miraculous manner.

The Qur'ān recognizes Jesus (*'Īsā* in Arabic) to have been a special prophet, bearing the distinctive title of "Messiah" (*al-Masīḥ*) and appointed to proclaim God's message to the Jews. As such, he was endowed with special power to perform miracles, such as healing the sick, giving sight to the blind, and even raising the dead. There is a strong emphasis, however, on the assertion that such powers were granted to him only by the permission of God (Q.5:110). Furthermore, Jesus was uniquely designated as God's "word" and "a spirit from him" (e.g.,

Q.4:171), yet Muslims have always understood these terms quite differently from Christians, as indicating a special call but not a divine status.

In fact, the Qur'ān speaks in no uncertain terms against any notion of divinity for Jesus, criticizing Christians for such pagan-like beliefs. Addressing itself to the Christian community as members of the "People of the Book" (those, including Jews, who had received a divine scripture in the past), the Qur'ān exclaims:

> O People of the Book! Do not exaggerate in your religion, nor say anything about God except the truth. The Messiah, Jesus, son of Mary, was only a messenger of God, and his word which he bestowed on Mary, and a spirit from him. So believe in God and his messengers, and do not say, "Trinity." Stop! It is better for you. For God is one God. It is far from his glory that he should have a son. (Q.4:171)

Such strong sentiment must be understood within the context of the Qur'ān's primary judgment against the polytheism that was dominant in Arabia in Muḥammad's day. The Qur'ān is replete with passages that call the Arabs to renounce their worship of a wide variety of gods, including what were considered to be the "daughters of God" *(banāt Allāh)*. They are summoned to acknowledge God as the sole deity who created and sustains the world, who mercifully provides for his creatures, and who guides humanity into following his divine will. So fundamental was this concept that it later became expressed in the first part of the *shahādah*, the central creed of Islam: "There is no god except God." This affirmation of the absolute unity of God and the rejection of associating anything alongside of him was eventually applied in the Qur'ān to Christians who insisted on speaking of Jesus as the Son of God. Some have suggested that the Christian claims in view in such passages were in fact not those of orthodox Christianity but instead represented contemporary heretical views.[5] While this may well be the case, the fact remains that the Qur'ān insists on an uncompromising distinction between God as creator and Jesus as nothing more than his human creation.

The Qur'ān also claims that Jesus brought a special message from God called the "Gospel" *(al-injīl)*, which not only confirmed previous divine revelations, such as the *tawrāt* delivered by Moses, but which was in turn confirmed by Muḥammad's own message (e.g., Q.5:46, 48). Since the source of all these messages is God, they are considered to be in full harmony with one another. The Christians addressed by the Qur'ān are said to be in possession of the written form of the Gospel (Q.4:47; 7:157), but there is no indication of the specific contents of this scripture or that it might consist of more than a single document.

One of the most important passages in the Qur'ān about Jesus con-demns the claim that he was crucified. Interestingly, though, it is not the Christians but the Jews who are judged:

> ... because of their saying, "We killed the Messiah, Jesus, son of Mary, the Messenger of God"—though they did not kill him and did not crucify him, but it appeared to them as such. Those who differ about this are in doubt, and they are without knowledge and only follow opinion. But cer-tainly they did not kill him. Rather, God raised him up unto himself. God is mighty and wise! (Q.4:157–58)

This passage raised certain questions among Muslim commentators, such as: "What caused the Jews to think that they had succeeded in cruci-fying Jesus?" or "What does it mean that Jesus was raised up to God?" Although they did not find clear answers to these questions in the Qur'ān itself, they were in no doubt concerning the assertion that Jesus did not die at the hands of the Jews. Nevertheless, in other passages Jesus *does* make reference to his future death, for example, "Peace be upon the day that I was born, and on the day that I will die, and on the day that I will be raised to life" (Q.19:33). Muslim scholars have put forth various interpretations in order to reconcile these passages.

These statements about Jesus in the Qur'ān have formed the basis for virtually all subsequent views of Jesus among Muslims. Yet in the classical era of Islam there are some variations of these themes as well as additional material. Much of this developed out of simple curiosity among Muslims to "fill in the gaps" about Jesus' vocation as a special prophet of Islam. A prime source for this information was the *hadīth* literature, that is, accounts of what Muhammad said, did, or approved that were separate from the Qur'ān. After circulating primarily in oral form for well over a century, they were finally incorporated into major collections and became, along with the Qur'ān, the key foundation for Islamic law. During the col-lection process, a great number of reports were rejected as spurious by the more prudent scholars, yet even these found their way into popular litera-ture. Included in all forms of the *hadīth* literature are numerous state-ments about Jesus that go far beyond what is found in the Qur'ān, focusing on such topics as the physical appearance of Jesus, or the rela-tionship between Jesus and Muhammad.[6] A prominent theme in this liter-ature is the descent of Jesus from heaven shortly before the final judgment. The accounts vary considerably in detail, but in general it is said that he will destroy Christian symbols of the cross, kill the swine that Christians eat, and promote the teachings of Islam. He will also kill the *Dajjāl*, the eschatological archenemy of the Muslims. Some accounts claim that following a prophetic ministry of about forty years, he will die and be buried, later to rise in the general resurrection.[7]

Jesus is further represented in another genre of Muslim literature that could be characterized as pietistic or ascetic. It originated especially among the Sufis who, to varying degrees, sought to revere God in a more mystical fashion. These stories highlight Jesus as an eminent teacher concerned with the proper way to worship God in spirit and to serve fellow people with humility. In this vein, the thirteenth-century Sufi master Ibn al-'Arabī referred to Jesus as "the Seal of the Saints," echoing the prominent title of Muḥammad as "the Seal of the Prophets."[8] A more pragmatic approach was taken by a few of the early Muslim historians, such as the ninth-century al-Ya'qūbī, who drew with surprising freedom from the New Testament Gospels in order to supply information about Jesus' life and teachings.[9]

Perhaps the most respected Muslim scholars were the commentators on the Qur'ān, who would naturally have had something to say about Jesus when seeking to elucidate those passages in which he is featured. Often drawing from the above sources, especially the *hadīth* literature, they present diverse views (of their predecessors as well as their own) concerning especially the beginning and end of Jesus' life. For example, while the commentators universally accept the virginal conception of Jesus as literally true, they produce a variety of explanations for how this might have transpired, especially through the agency of the angel Gabriel.[10] Even more prominent are the discussions concerning the attempted crucifixion of Jesus. Despite some uncertainty about what actually occurred, the commentators agree that the Jews succeeded in placing someone on the cross—only that it was not Jesus. The earliest commentators proposed that one of Jesus' disciples voluntarily took his place in order to protect his master from a terrible fate. This substitutionist theory gained general acceptance, despite reservations by some. The question of who was the unfortunate individual, however, was complicated by the more theologically problematic question of how God could have allowed an innocent person to be killed. This was resolved by promoting the view that it was Judas Iscariot who was crucified as punishment for his betrayal of Jesus. Somehow God caused him to take on the appearance of Jesus, so that he was seized by the Jews and put to death, and all who witnessed the event thought that it was Jesus who suffered this ignominy. Tied to this interpretation is the assumption that Jesus himself was rescued from the chaos by being taken up to heaven alive. As to the death of Jesus, referred to elsewhere in the Qur'ān, most commentators sought to interpret this as an event still in the future, in harmony with the various *ḥadīth* accounts concerning his eschatological return to earth.[11]

As might be expected, issues concerning Jesus also figured prominently in the polemical literature that arose on both sides of the growing Muslim-Christian divide. Muslim authors frequently sought to refute Christian claims about Jesus, most often by discrediting the Christian Bible. For this, they developed the notion of the "corruption" *(taḥrīf)* of the biblical message. This term was already present in the Qur'ān with reference to the manner in which the Jews mishandled their scripture by purposefully distorting its meaning (e.g., Q.2:75; 4:46). Although this specific term is not used in the Qur'ān against Christians, they are criticized as well for having "forgotten" part of their scripture and "hiding" other parts (Q.5:14–15). In the following centuries, as relations between Christians and Muslims deteriorated, Muslims who criticized Christianity began to apply the concept of *taḥrīf* to Christians. At first, the charge was leveled against Christian interpretation of the New Testament or against the original intent of the biblical writers; the text itself was assumed to have been reliably transmitted. But later, the eleventh-century polemicist Ibn Ḥazm accused Christians of having altered the actual wording of the text in order to support their erroneous doctrines about Jesus. Most subsequent Muslim arguments against Christians and their Bible tended to combine allegations of both faulty interpretation and also a degree of textual corruption.[12]

The classical age of Islam thus developed a distinctly Islamic view of Jesus that had been established in the Qur'ān, while broadening Muslim criticism against Christian beliefs about him. The literature produced reached its peak in the fourteenth century when the notable theologian Ibn Taymīyah produced his massive treatise entitled *The Correct Response to Those Who Changed the Religion of Christ*, summarizing the arguments of his predecessors.[13] Little subsequent material was produced among Muslims until the twentieth century, when the arguments against the Christian view of Jesus were again taken up by various Arab writers, especially in Egypt.

The scholars who led this endeavor were Muḥammad 'Abduh (d. 1905), the renowned reformer of Islam who argued that reason and faith were compatible, and his more conservative disciple Rashīd Riḍā (d. 1935). Their chief work, produced jointly, was a groundbreaking but unfinished commentary on the Qur'ān. We find there, as well as in other works that each wrote separately, several references to Jesus and Christians. On the one hand, 'Abduh demonstrates a high regard for Jesus as found in the New Testament Gospels, which he tacitly accepts as authentic documents. His complaint against Christians is that they have interpreted Jesus' sayings in an irrational manner, taking many of them literally instead of figuratively (such as his reference to God as "Father"). On the other hand, Riḍā is extremely critical of Christian beliefs about Jesus, asserting as well that the original gospel preached by Jesus had been altered due to the moral lapse of Christians. The New Testament Gospels were thus a mixture of the true gospel revealed to Jesus and additions made by their human authors. The only criterion by which to determine the true gospel was the Qur'ān.[14] Furthermore, Riḍā arranged for the Arabic translation of a controversial document known as the *Gospel of Barnabas*. Stylized as a first-century "Gospel," this work presents a distinctively Islamic perspective of Jesus; in it, Jesus explicitly denies that he is the Son of God, foretells the coming of Muḥammad by name, and escapes crucifixion when Judas Iscariot is substituted in his place. Whereas Western scholars have universally recognized this to be a sixteenth-century forgery, Riḍā accepted it as genuine, enabling its Arabic translation to gain immediate popularity.[15]

Unfortunately, it was Riḍā's approach rather than 'Abduh's that was to characterize almost all subsequent Arab Muslim writing about Jesus. Authors upheld a strictly Islamic view of Jesus, often invoking the *Gospel of Barnabas*, and regarded the Christian perspective of Jesus to be at best distorted, at worst deserving only condemnation.[16] In fact, in the years preceding al-'Aqqād's book, only a single work within this literature can be said to exhibit a more irenic approach to Jesus and the Gospels: *The Messiah, Jesus the Son of Mary*, written in 1951 by 'Abd al-Ḥamīd Gūdah al-Saḥḥār. This author actually incorporates a number of passages from the Gospels into his biographical account without denying their validity. Nevertheless, the book is primarily dependent on the Qur'ān and Islamic material, as well as the author's own imagination. The result is a portrayal of Jesus as a distinctly Islamic prophet who primarily serves as a forerunner of Muḥammad.[17]

Undoubtedly al-'Aqqād was familiar with most if not all of these writings. It is quite possible that al-Saḥḥār's book served to encourage him, in both a positive and negative sense, to produce his own study of Christ. In any case, al-'Aqqād chose to distance himself from both the method and attitude followed by his predecessors and to adopt a far more positive approach than any of them. To be sure, since the mid-twentieth century several relatively positive Muslim works about Jesus have appeared: in the Arab world,[18] in the Indian subcontinent,[19] and among Western-educated Muslim scholars.[20] Nevertheless, none of these more recent works achieves the same level of esteem for the Jesus of the New Testament Gospels as al-'Aqqād's *The Genius of Christ*.

A Closer Look at the Author

'Abbās Maḥmūd al-'Aqqād was born in 1889 in Aswan, the southernmost major city of Upper Egypt.[21] His parents were devout Muslims who passed on a strong religious heritage to their children. At an early age, he developed an interest in politics, literature, and writing and he began composing poetry at age ten. During his early years, he had considerable exposure to the Western frame of mind and learned English on his own, aided by the presence of hundreds of British carrying out the construction of the Aswan Dam. Near the end of his primary school education, one particular experience made a lasting impression on him. Muḥammad 'Abduh (whom al-'Aqqād already admired through reading his articles) was in Aswan in 1902 for the dedication of the dam, and while there he visited al-'Aqqād's class at school. After hearing the boy read one of his compositions, 'Abduh remarked that he "especially deserves to become a writer someday." Al-'Aqqād later claimed that the person who exerted the greatest influence on his life was 'Abduh, and he even wrote a biography about him.

Shortly after completing primary school, al-'Aqqād's formal education was cut short by his move to Cairo to seek employment. Yet he never ceased to collect books and be an avid reader for the rest of his life. For several years he struggled to make a living as a journalist and poet, becoming a strong critic of contemporary Arabic poetry, which he felt to be inexpressive. The first half of the twentieth century was a turbulent period in Egypt's history, as the country endeavored to gain full independence from British domination. A fervent nationalist, al-'Aqqād supported the cause of liberal democracy. Following World War I, he took over as editor for the official newspaper of the Wafd Party, which was the leading voice for autonomy. It was in this capacity that he finally gained recognition and influence, and his writing began to increase as a result.

Gradually, however, al-'Aqqād became disenchanted with politics and skeptical of the secularist approach to development that was espoused by Egypt's leading intellectuals. As a result, he left the political scene and turned to religious themes in his writing in the early 1940s. One commentator regards this new orientation as mere personal escapism due to his meager formal education.[22] Yet this view does not appreciate the genuine commitment to Islam evident in al-'Aqqād's works and his conviction that religion spoke directly to the social problems of his day. In fact, the period from 1942 to 1961 witnessed his most productive literary output, in which he published on average three books per year, one-third of which dealt with some aspect of Islam. He became one of Egypt's most popular authors and was awarded the State Appreciation Prize for Literature in 1960. Failing health finally caught up with him, and he died of a heart attack in 1964.

During his remarkable literary career, al-'Aqqād produced over one hundred books and nearly six thousand published articles, besides several works of poetry, introductions to other books, and translations of non-Arabic works. The breadth of his writing is equally amazing; one bibliographic survey lists the following topics he addressed: philosophy, religion, language, arts and literature, social sciences, Egypt and the Arab world, biographies, and music. The biographical studies in particular incorporate about thirty complete books on individual people, ranging from figures of the past, both Muslim and Western (e.g., Shakespeare and Benjamin Franklin), to contemporary leaders as diverse as Gandhi and Hitler. Meanwhile, he constantly read Western literature and was adept at synthesizing a work and conveying its essence in an article or book, along with his own critique. He frequently addressed social and ethical issues, arguing for an authentic Egyptian self-identity that nevertheless welcomed Western ideas that would enable society to advance. In many of his works, he attacked what he regarded as the traditional view of social law, which consisted merely of negative injunctions. Such an outlook, he believed, served only to shackle the human conscience. Rather, society must employ laws that work for progress and freedom.

Eventually, al-'Aqqād found in religion a new basis for these ideas, and he committed himself to serving his community as a modern Muslim apologist. About twenty-five of his books deal with some aspect of Islam or religion in general. Like his mentor 'Abduh, he defended the faith as valid and rational for the modern era. He believed that people should exercise their free will, making full use of reason rather than blindly accepting religious tradition. He also claimed that Islam formed the foundation for all aspects of public life. He argued that there was nothing in Islam that was inconsistent with modernity, and that all social and political reforms could be carried out within an Islamic framework. Al-'Aqqād was also known for emphasizing the more internal aspects of Islam and the need for the individual to develop a "cosmic consciousness" in order to ascertain divine reality. Thus, he occasionally extolled the Sufi or mystical approach to religion, although he was careful to caution against its excesses.

In addition to expounding the attributes of Islam for his fellow Arab Muslims, al-ʿAqqād believed it was necessary to defend the faith against outside attacks. Several of his books explore the theme of progressive revelation and prophetic activity, exhibiting a distinct apologetic for the supremacy of Islam over other religions, including Christianity. The various religions are treated with respect, and as precursors to Islam they comprise a degree of truth. Yet they were always incomplete and in need of further revelation, which culminated in the ministry of Muḥammad. Furthermore, the more advanced religions were those that appeared within the Semitic race, through prophets descended from Abraham. By all accounts, then, Islam is to be regarded as the pinnacle of divine activity among humanity.

As was the case with his books in general, biographies formed the largest segment of al-ʿAqqād's works on religion, comprising fourteen individual titles. First and foremost was his celebrated book on the Prophet of Islam, entitled *The Genius of Muḥammad* (1942). In the introduction, al-ʿAqqād relates the story of how, many years previously, he had been challenged to write such a book as a kind of Muslim parallel to the famous treatise on Muḥammad by the Scottish essayist Thomas Carlyle. This was the second of a series of lectures delivered by Carlyle in 1840 and published the following year as *On Heroes, Hero-Worship, and the Heroic in History*.[23] The series as a whole (which included expositions on Luther, Rousseau, Napoleon, and others) dealt with the impact of certain individuals who, despite their historical specificity, convey an authority that transcends history. In the case of Muḥammad, Carlyle's conciliatory approach—despite a few negative assertions—countered the polemical attitude that had long been current in the West, and his essay gained widespread attention both there and in the Muslim world. Al-ʿAqqād's friends who knew this work, however, questioned why they should be content with the product of someone who did not really understand Muḥammad in the Muslim manner, and they suggested that he write his own similar book. So it was that Carlyle's essay became the model for al-ʿAqqād's own work on Muḥammad, in which he praised the greatness of the Prophet and in which the term "genius" (*ʿabqarīyah*) was virtually equivalent to Carlyle's "hero."

The book on Muḥammad was soon followed by similar studies on other important leaders in early Islam, such as the first four caliphs, the military commander Khālid bin al-Walīd, and the Prophet's wife ʿĀʾishah and daughter Fāṭimah. Two works within this series deal with prophets who predate Muḥammad, namely, Abraham and Jesus. Since several of the titles incorporate the phrase "*The Genius of . . . ,*" the collection as a whole became known as the "Genius *('abqarīyah)* series," and they were later published together in a single, large volume. Meanwhile, *The Genius of Muḥammad* formed the model for al-'Aqqād in the subsequent works. He emphasized that they were not meant to be biographies as such, but that each book was a "portrait of the person's inner character." Some critics felt that this approach tended to sacrifice historical objectivity and overlook a person's faults at the expense of his or her virtues. Indeed, one can locate within these books several examples of factual inaccuracies, blatant exaggerations, and assertions made without evidence. Yet in the words of one scholar, "Al-'Aqqād has managed . . . to present an eloquent and incisive apology for Islam to those willing to accept his assumptions and conclusions."[24]

A Closer Look at the Book

By its very title, *'Abqarīyat al-Masīh—The Genius of Christ*—was clearly meant to be an integral part of the "Genius" series. And since Jesus, like Abraham, played a key role in the history of God's progressive revelation to humanity, Muslim readers would hardly question its inclusion. Yet because the person of Jesus also figures so prominently in Christianity, al-'Aqqād was undertaking a new and potentially volatile subject, one that was inextricably linked with the historical vicissitudes of Muslim-Christian relations right up to the present. What is probably most fascinating about the book is the way al-'Aqqād manages to balance the two perspectives in a single volume. Although the boundaries of what might be considered a truly Islamic view of Jesus are stretched to some extent, there is nothing here that lies outside them. At the same time, because of his general dependence on the New Testament Gospels, al-'Aqqād presents a Jesus who is familiar to Christian readers. He also makes free use of Western literature in his exposition of the context and issues surrounding Jesus' ministry. At times, he is rather careless in his quotation or use of these sources, sometimes passing on misinformation without critical analysis and sometimes offering his own speculations without proper support. From a modern scholarly perspective, the value of the book is quite limited. The significance of this work lies rather in the author's attitude regarding a topic that has historically been a point of contention between Muslims and Christians.

'Abqarīyat al-Masīh was first published in January 1953. Al-'Aqqād produced a revised edition in 1958 in which he added a brief preface and three new chapters at the beginning of the book. Some of the original

chapters also received new titles, but their content remained unchanged. The second edition also bore a new, more mundane title: *Ḥayāt al-Masīḥ*, or *The Life of Christ*. Al-ʿAqqād gives no indication as to why the change was made, and the new title hardly does justice to his approach. It could be that it reflects some disapproval concerning the book's orientation. In the case of *The Genius of Muḥammad*, al-ʿAqqād had been severely criticized by orthodox Muslims who "could not quite reconcile the concept of individual genius to the concept of divine revelation."[25] Internal evidence suggests that he was not in favor of this change, and it most likely resulted from an editorial decision in response to similar pressure (*Genius*, 45–46). In any case, references to the book here use its original title, since that much more appropriately reflects the theme of the work. The following synopsis of the book also focuses on the original work before briefly noting the additional material of the second edition.

The book begins with a poetic overture entitled "The Blessed Tree." This is probably the most "Islamic" portion of the book, with several quotations from the Qurʾān in which the olive tree is mentioned as a blessing to humanity. Al-ʿAqqād then applies this as a symbol of Christ and his mission: just as the olive tree provides needed food, oil, and wood, so Christ brought a message of light and goodness that blessed all people and that especially influenced the mission of Muḥammad.

The first main section presents various aspects of the sociohistorical context in which Christ and his message appeared. Its first three chapters begin, appropriately, with the Jewish religious context. Al-ʿAqqād discusses how the notion of "the Messiah" had been only vaguely enshrined in other religions but had received its full development in Judaism. He refers to several Old Testament passages dealing with "anointing" or God's "anointed one" (i.e., Messiah), following a traditional Christian perspective that assumed a monolithic messianic hope among the Jews of that time. (Current scholarly opinion recognizes that this concept was much more complex.) He next considers the idea of prophecy in ancient Israel and its bearing on the Jewish expectation of a coming messenger from God. He recognizes that Muslims attach great significance to the office of prophet and would understand prophets to have appeared only rarely in history. Thus, he explains the prevalence of prophets in ancient Israel by claiming that the term was used more comprehensively and by distinguishing between two levels of prophet. The superior type of prophet was indeed rare, and by the time of Christ, the Jews had high expectations that one would soon appear. Al-ʿAqqād recognizes, however, that the Jews were hardly united in their religion. So he provides rather detailed explanations of the main Jewish sects that existed in the first century CE: the Sadducees, Pharisees, Essenes, and Zealots, as well as the Samaritans. Also discussed are various aspects of first-century Jewish religion, such as the Temple, the Sanhedrin, and the more obscure Nazirites. Although al-'Aqqād's usually accurate presentation is sometimes speculative, his purpose is clear: none of the diverse facets of Jewish religious life in themselves could meet the inner spiritual needs of the people; the Jews longed for something more that could not be found in their religion as they knew it.

Al-'Aqqād then moves on to the wider context of Jesus and his message, demonstrating that the Gentile world was equally in need of and ready for that message. Thus, the deterioration of Roman society was evidenced in the slave uprisings of that period, as well as the growing disparity between rich and poor. In Palestine, the Jews suffered under the decadence of Herod's court and the burden of Roman taxation. In a chapter on the religious life of the Roman world, al-'Aqqād's focus is on the influx of deities from the East and how their attraction to Westerners is proof that their search for genuine faith could not be met by their own religions. The same was true for the various systems of philosophy current in the Roman world at that time. He ends with a long discourse on the Jewish philosopher Philo of Alexandria, claiming that his combination of traditional Judaism with Greek ideas helped prepare the way for the mission of Christ.

The next section, comprising a collection of essays that cover various historical factors with regard to Jesus, continues to set the stage for al-'Aqqād's examination of Jesus' mission. Al-'Aqqād first deals with Galilee as the specific setting in which Jesus lived and preached. He adopts the traditional view that the Galilean Jews were seriously tainted by Gentile influence and thus rejected by Jews of the south. More recent scholarship has recognized their loyalty to the faith of Jerusalem at the time of Christ and even their general acceptance in Judea. Al-'Aqqād's perspective, however, better serves to bolster his thesis: the eclectic character of Galilee, including the tolerance and syncretism of its Jewish inhabitants, made it a more fitting place of origin for the mission of Jesus, since that mission was destined to move beyond traditional Judaism and into the world at large.

In a chapter entitled "When Christ Was Born," al-'Aqqād joins most scholars in holding the date of Jesus' birth to be 5 or 6 BCE. The bulk of this chapter, however, deals with those he claims have doubted the actual historicity of Jesus. He counters such skepticism, first with a fine review of the bits of evidence from the historians Josephus, Tacitus, and Suetonius. After presenting other arguments that point to the Jesus of history, such as the rapid emergence of Christianity, he concludes that the mission of Christ is completely logical within its historical setting.

Up to this point, almost the only direct references to Jesus have been to a few of his sayings and to the event of his birth. Only one-third of the way through his book does Jesus himself come into focus. Al-ʿAqqād first presents a "descriptive portrait" of Christ but begins rather inauspiciously with a quotation from an apocryphal source allegedly describing Jesus' physical appearance, which he regards as compatible with the biblical data. Fortunately, he remains within the parameters of the Gospels when he mentions such characteristics of Jesus as his eloquence in speech, his partiality for nature, and his gentle yet resolute demeanor. This leads al-ʿAqqād into a fascinating portrayal of Jesus' determination to remain true to his mission. The faithful messenger experienced the lot of all prophets: the necessity to speak the word of truth in the face of opposition and to "venture into the struggle *(al-jihād)*" without reservation (*Genius*, 148). Yet this necessarily involved an inner struggle as well, and al-ʿAqqād draws from the scene of the garden of Gethsemane to describe the temptation Jesus faced: either to shrink back from the ordeal or to demand assurance of a successful outcome. Jesus' victory in resisting either path and his willingness to forge ahead and allow destiny to follow its course characterize for al-ʿAqqād his entire mission.

The next section forms the heart of the book, focusing on the essential message Jesus proclaimed. The title of this part is simply "The Call" *(Al-Daʿwah)*. While this term initially refers to the divine call to which Jesus himself responded, it primarily designates the call Jesus issued to his Jewish listeners—disciples and opponents alike. Al-ʿAqqād asserts that this call had a universal dimension as well, and although its proclamation was ultimately carried out by Jesus' followers, it was prefigured in Jesus' own ministry. As he had already demonstrated, both Jewish and Gentile worlds were in need of this call; Jesus' message of brotherhood and peace came to meet that need. Naturally, it met with opposition. Referring to Jesus' parable of the Great Banquet in Luke 14, al-ʿAqqād says that the Jews refused the "invitation" (using the same term *al-daʿwah* with a slightly different connotation). So the invitation instead went to others who "were more deserving of it," namely, the Gentiles. Jesus' mission thus involved "a change of course" or the start of a new "direction." The last word here is *qiblah*, normally the technical term for the direction in which Muslims face when at prayer. Al-ʿAqqād employs it here to indicate one's orientation toward the will of God. The change in direction not only represents the shift in the call of Christ from Jews to Gentiles but also the shift in attitude for anyone who would follow that call, the choice that must be made between selfish ambitions and the way of God. This leads al-'Aqqād into a brief homily in which Jesus becomes the model for making the most critical commitment in life: renouncing the way of the world and seeking the more important things that last.

Al-'Aqqād then turns his attention to the opposition that stood in the way of the call. He briefly digresses with a chapter on John the Baptist. Although John's austere lifestyle and acerbic character contrasted with Jesus' approach, the negative response John received from the Jews anticipated what Jesus likewise encountered. Al-'Aqqād continues then with the obstacles faced by Jesus in proclaiming his call. These are summed up in the word "law," meaning not just the law of Rome or even that of the Jewish authorities but the entire fabric of society and religion that was at once stratified, inflexible, and hypocritical. Jesus came neither to eliminate this "law" nor to add to it, but to bring about its required transformation. Part of that mission was his pronouncement of divine forgiveness, which would become his "greatest offence" to the Jewish leaders. Thus, when they compelled him to judge the woman caught in adultery (John 8:1–11), he sent her away without condemnation. He refused to be drawn into their traps concerning their law, for his "kingdom [was] not of this world . . . [and] had nothing to do with other kingdoms" (*Genius*, 170; cf. John 18:36).

In contrast to that inflexible and hypocritical law, Jesus brought the "law of love." It was not his intention to abolish the existing law, but to fulfill it (cf. Matt 5:17). What Christ abolished, says al-'Aqqād, were the external aspects of the law, while he instituted the law of love, which was the essence of the law itself, "the eternal principles on which the human conscience is based" (172). He offers several examples, drawn mainly from the Sermon on the Mount, that show how the law of love and conscience was even stricter in its requirements. "For the conscience is first responsible for a person's intentions and thoughts, and only then for his deeds and encounters" (176). It was the law as it was meant to be, yet radically opposed to the law as it existed; it was "new wine in an old wineskin" (177; cf. Matt 9:17). This concept also leads to a proper discernment of the stern ethical injunctions of Jesus. Al-'Aqqād believes that a more literal interpretation of his commands was appropriate for the original disciples who devoted themselves to propagating his call, but for ordinary folks who must live in the day-to-day world, Jesus' commands should be understood figuratively. For al-'Aqqād, Jesus relocated ethics to a more humane center, where the focus was a person's motives rather than meticulous compliance to the law. "Thus a person should give out of love and from his own free will" rather than under compulsion (182). Someone might own many possessions, but this is permissible as long as that person serves God rather than those possessions, for "it is more profitable to gain the soul than to gain the world" (182; cf. Matt 16:26).

In his chapter entitled "The Kingdom of Heaven," al-'Aqqād elaborates on his thesis that the call proclaimed by Jesus' was rejected by the Jews and so became a universal call to all people. He offers an intriguing comparison from early Islamic history: if the message of Muḥammad had been accepted by the Meccans at the outset, there would have been no *hijrah*, or emigration to Medina, and the history of Islam would have been fundamentally altered. In the same way that the initial rejection of the Meccans served to advance the cause of Islam, so the rejection of Jesus' message by the Jews prompted its spread throughout the world. Thus, al-'Aqqād views Jesus' mission as one that evolved from a call appropriately directed to the Jews alone, to a call that incorporated all of humanity. Here he has simplified the complex data of the Gospels, assuming that the Jewish response was negligible, and that Jesus unequivocally initiated a mission to the Gentiles. Yet if he overstates his case here, at least he captures some of the radical inclusiveness inherent in many of Jesus' sayings. He goes on to discuss Jesus' teaching about the kingdom of heaven, emphasizing its spiritual character and universal scope. Again, his selectivity of the biblical data is evident; he sets aside any future aspect of the kingdom as too ambiguous and focuses on the present dimension of the kingdom and its immediate relevance to Christ's mission. For him, Jesus' self-designation as "the Son of Man" applies only to the here-and-now, and the "kingdom of the Son of Man" exists in this world as people conduct their lives in conformity to Jesus' commands. Such a mission, he says, could never have arisen among the pagan religions; its appearance among the Jews, and its subsequent rejection by them that led to its spread, could only have been arranged by Divine Wisdom.

The remainder of the book deals with supplementary issues related to the mission of Jesus. Al-'Aqqād here explores the means by which Jesus' call was proclaimed and propagated. Most important was the remarkable teaching ability of Jesus himself, as evidenced especially through his use of parables. Another factor was the fidelity of the disciples. Al-'Aqqād notes how these men were trained by their master to carry on the mission after his own role would end. They became his special *ummah*, or "community" (201). They were ordinary men with their own frailties, but they were faithful to their call. Then—without any reference here to how

Jesus' own ministry ended—al-'Aqqād relates how they were scattered throughout the world and proclaimed the same message, primarily among the Gentiles.

Al-'Aqqād next examines the New Testament Gospels as sources for the life of Christ. His brief technical discussion concerning their authorship, date, interrelationship, and so forth, while reflecting generally accepted scholarship, would probably leave most Muslim readers somewhat bewildered. Nevertheless, he affirms the Gospels as reliable records whose minor discrepancies can be explained. Since their importance for him lies with the "personality" of Christ rather than historical details, he holds that contradictions may even support their credibility. He then explains why his work makes no reference to the miracles of Jesus. Here he draws on an argument about cause and effect by al-Ghazālī, the renowned twelfth-century Muslim theologian. Al-'Aqqād does not discount the authenticity of Jesus' miracles, but neither does he regard them as necessary in order to explain or receive the truth of Christ's message. Miracles, of themselves, never led anyone to faith. In any case, the greatest miracle was the impact Jesus had on history despite his humble origins.

In the longest chapter of his book, al-'Aqqād attempts an outline of Jesus' life based on the Gospels. It is really only here that the work becomes biographical in nature, despite the title given to the second edition. However, the presentation is uneven; some aspects are considered at length, while others are mentioned briefly or not at all. After noting Jesus' birth, childhood, and education (presumably in the local synagogue), al-'Aqqād focuses on the "turning point" of Jesus' career: his baptism by John, followed by the temptation in the wilderness. Here we are treated to another remarkable meditation concerning the inner struggles of Jesus. He would not succumb to worldly expectations of messianic privilege but would instead rest solely on divine assistance in order to carry out his mission. Furthermore, he would experience this kind of temptation—and victory—throughout his ministry. He thus embarked on his mission, which, as al-'Aqqād had stated earlier, progressed from an ethnic to a universal call. Otherwise, little is said about what this mission entailed; the Gospel accounts of Jesus' ministry of healing and exorcism are completely ignored here, as they are throughout the book. Instead, al-'Aqqād examines two of the titles that were ascribed to Jesus ("the Son of God" and "the Son of Man") in an attempt to interpret them in a manner acceptable for Muslims.

From here, al-'Aqqād jumps directly to the end of Jesus' mission and his final confrontation with Jewish leaders. During his last visit to

Jerusalem for the feast of Passover, Jesus was aware of an impending crisis. Finally, he "spent the night in prayer and confiding with his Lord, saying 'Let this cup pass from me, oh Father! Yet may it be according to your will, not according to my will'"—words taken from the Gospel accounts of Jesus in the garden of Gethsemane (224). However, what transpires following this is not the arrest, trial, and crucifixion, but rather the so-called cleansing of the temple, which, according to the Synoptic Gospels, occurred earlier in the week. For al-ʿAqqād, it was this incident that prompted the Jewish authorities to take "immediate action," yet he does not explain what that action might have been. Rather, he claims that at this point, "the role of history ends, and the role of faith begins" (226). He expresses his view here that the Gospel accounts of the events surrounding the crucifixion cannot be trusted because of certain discrepancies. Instead, he turns to a report related by a leader of the Ahmadīyah sect of Islam indicating that at the end of his mission in Palestine, Jesus traveled to India and died there. While al-ʿAqqād makes no definitive judgment on the veracity of this account, he states that it "would be improper to neglect, since it deserves particular attention" (227). In conclusion, he says, the way in which Jesus' life ended cannot be resolved with certainty, yet that by no means impinges on his affirmation of the genius of Christ and the universal nature of his call.

The epilogue bears an independent character and was reprinted on its own several times after the book was published. In it, al-ʿAqqād explores what might transpire "if Christ were to return" to the world of today. To set the stage, he recounts a famous tale from Dostoyevsky's *The Brothers Karamazov* in which Jesus suddenly yet peaceably arrives in fifteenth-century Seville. He is apprehended by "the Grand Inquisitor," who resents that Jesus has come to change the traditions of the church, claiming that the freedom of conscience offered by Jesus would create a grievous constraint for the people. In the same way, says al-ʿAqqād, if Christ were to return at this time, "he would renounce many things which are being done today in his name. He would find scribes and Pharisees among his followers, and he would reproach them for their hypocrisy" (230). Then, asks al-ʿAqqād, has the message of Christ gone out in vain? No, he says, but we must continue the struggle to gain complete freedom of conscience and to put into practice the ideals taught by the religions, despite the ongoing presence of evil. Even if Christ came today and rectified many errors, it is up to humanity, with a conscience illuminated by religion, to carry on the task.

In 1958, five years after the publication and warm reception of *ʿAbqarīyat al-Masīh*, al-ʿAqqād thought it prudent to produce a revised edition. Along with a brief preface, he appended three chapters to the beginning of the book, while leaving the rest entirely unchanged. Most likely he placed them at the front rather than at the end of the book because he saw them as part of the wider context for the life and mission of Christ, which was the focus of the first section of his work. This would especially apply to the first of these chapters, which deals with the Dead Sea Scrolls and their significance for the study of Christian origins. The scrolls had been discovered in 1947, but the political turmoil of the region had prevented any scholarly assessment until the mid-1950s. Al-'Aqqād was clearly caught up in the excitement of the potential significance of this discovery and the likely identification of the Qumran community with the Essenes. His conclusion, however, is that the Dead Sea Scrolls offer nothing that would change the focus of his book; indeed, coming as they do from a secluded and puritanical group, they only serve to confirm that the world was in need of a mission precisely such as that brought by Christ.

The remaining new material deals with significant works that had recently been published. First, al-'Aqqād considers the controversy surrounding an Old Testament passage in the newly released complete edition of the Revised Standard Version of the Bible. Conservative Christians had criticized its rendition of Isaiah 7:14, which had the phrase "young woman" in place of the word "virgin" as found in the Authorized Version. While he considers this to be a minor matter, al-'Aqqād seems to affirm both the older reading as well as the traditional Christian interpretation of the passage as a prophecy of the virgin birth of Jesus. More important for him, however, was the recent appearance of a number of works in English about Jesus. He focuses his attention on three books that rely heavily on speculative assumptions to maintain that only a strictly Jewish version of early Christianity had faithfully followed the teachings of Jesus. Naturally, al-'Aqqād criticizes this view since it counters a fundamental thesis of his book, namely, that it was the Gentiles who preserved Jesus' message when the Jews rejected it.

A Closer Look at al-'Aqqād's Approach

We are left then with a book about Jesus from the pen of a Muslim apologist that is radically unlike any Muslim book that preceded it—or that has followed it. One can only wonder at the manner in which al-'Aqqād seems to address a Muslim audience at times, and a Christian audience at other times. This becomes even clearer when specific terminology is examined. There is, on the one hand, repeated use of Islamic vocabulary; some are terms that are fundamental to the discussion, such as the recasting of the word *qiblah*, the direction for Muslim prayer, as the spiritual path toward God taken by Jesus and his followers. Additionally, Jewish religious leaders are often described as *fuqahā'* (Muslim jurists) who might issue a *fatwā* (Islamic legal pronouncement). The words *nīyah* (the intention to perform an Islamic duty) and *jihād* (struggle in the cause of Allāh) frequently appear in discussions that deal with Jesus' inner character. On the other hand, Christian terminology is also present. The disciples of Jesus are usually referred to as *al-talāmīdh*, as in the Arabic Bible, rather than by the Qur'ānic term *al-ḥawārīyūn*. The title *rasūl*, which in Islam is reserved for the chosen few who brought direct revelation from God, is used for Paul and others according to Arab Christian usage. References to God as "Father" and to "the Holy Spirit" that appear in biblical quotations and that are strictly Christian concepts are left intact without further discussion. Probably the most important observation in this regard is the manner in which al-'Aqqād refers to his main character. The name "Jesus" rarely appears; when it does, sometimes the Islamic form is given *('Īsā)* and sometimes the Christian form *(Yasū')*, although the latter is found almost exclusively in biblical quotations or summaries. Instead, al-'Aqqād consistently uses the title *al-Masīḥ*. Since this term is popular among both Muslims and Christians, he has avoided criticism from either side on this point. However, he sometimes employs the Muslim salutation "peace be upon him" (*'alayhi al-salām*), especially when he uses only a personal pronoun to refer to Christ.

A more indicative feature, however, is the matter of written sources. It must be considered one of the most significant aspects of this work that the author, as a Muslim, chooses to use the Gospels rather than traditional Islamic material as the primary basis for a presentation about Christ. Quotations from the Qur'ān are infrequent and almost never deal directly with the person of Jesus. The classical Islamic material on Jesus in the *ḥadīth* literature, the Qur'ānic commentaries, and other sources are altogether ignored. On the other hand, there are innumerable references to the Bible, and especially the Gospels. Al-'Aqqād's own comment about this in the second edition is probably not far from the truth: "We have opened the two Testaments at least a hundred times in order to investigate them in our research and to utilize them in our quotations" (80). His source was clearly the nineteenth-century Arabic translation of the Bible produced by the American missionary Cornelius Van Dyck, which has remained the standard among Protestant Arab Christians ever since. Al-'Aqqād quotes this translation verbatim, or nearly so, in several places. Yet his citations, as

Cragg notes, frequently evince "a certain casualness"[26]; words are substituted, important phrases are omitted, and occasionally his rendition considerably alters the sense of the original Arabic text. He does not usually provide the location of a passage; at most, he indicates the name of the book and occasionally the chapter number as well. Obviously he read the biblical material carefully in preparation for writing a particular segment, but it seems that when he later put pen to paper, often he simply relied on his memory without bothering to check the actual wording of the text.

Al-'Aqqād's repeated use of the Gospels to support his presentation of Christ is backed up by various comments concerning these documents as reliable sources. He insists that the disciples were not lying when they passed on the words of their Master (208) and that there is no good reason to dismiss the authenticity of the Gospels even though they were written some years after the fact and in several versions (212). Nowhere does he give any indication that there was a process of *taḥrīf* whereby "corruption" occurred either in the text of the Gospels or in their interpretation. Furthermore, *'Abqariyat al-Masīḥ* contains no reference at all to the *Gospel of Barnabas*. In fact, in an article that al-'Aqqād wrote in 1959, he explicitly rejects this document as a reliable source for the life of Jesus.[27]

This is not to say that al-'Aqqād accepts the New Testament Gospels categorically. His rejection of the accounts concerning the arrest, crucifixion, and resurrection of Jesus is clear evidence to the contrary; these cannot be regarded as historical, he says, but instead belong to "the role of faith." Undoubtedly he would include in this category other passages he mentions without comment, such as statements in Mark and John that point to the "divinity" or the "divine incarnation" of Jesus (213). Furthermore, the discriminating manner in which he selects those texts that support his argument, while leaving aside other relevant material, indicates the ambivalent approach he actually demonstrates with regard to the Gospels. Ultimately, al-'Aqqād's view of the Gospels seems to follow that of his mentor Muḥammad 'Abduh, who had accepted them as "authentic" but claimed that certain statements in them were misunderstood by the disciples or misinterpreted by later Christians.

In the end, however, al-'Aqqād is not greatly concerned with this issue. The following statement is especially revealing:

> We have relied on the Gospels in order to study the life of the Messenger . . . and we have not found any more trustworthy source than these. However, as we have examined them we have pursued a method different from that followed by those who emphasize the historicity of events and reports. . . . Rather, as we have compiled the various events and reports,

we have inquired concerning what lies behind these which would elucidate the personality of the Messenger. (213)

Since it is the personality of Christ that is most important for al-
'Aqqād, what emerges from his study is a portrait of Jesus in which many
of the historical elements of the Gospels are either left in the background
or ignored altogether.

This approach allows al-'Aqqād, for example, to omit several important features of Jesus' ministry that are prominent in the Gospels. What is
particularly striking in his presentation is the paucity of interaction
between Jesus and other people. Aside from a few references to the presence of the disciples or his opponents or some women, al-'Aqqād's portrait of Christ is mostly abstract. This contrasts sharply with the image of
Jesus in the Gospels as one who is constantly on the move, mingling with
the crowds, actively involved with admirers and adversaries alike. There
the bulk of Jesus' teaching is connected in some way with the people who
surround him, and al-'Aqqād often diminishes the impact of his quotations of Jesus by ignoring the context in which those sayings occur. The
most obvious aspect of Jesus' ministry excluded by al-'Aqqād is his miracles. The constant reference in the Gospels to Jesus' healing the sick, cast-
ing out demons, and feeding the multitudes is completely lacking in
'Abqariyat al-Masīḥ. Al-'Aqqād tries to explain his disregard for the miraculous, claiming that this is not a necessary factor in appreciating and
accepting the message of Christ (214–15). In the Gospels, however, that
message often goes hand in hand with Jesus' performance of miracles,
which serve not only to illustrate but also to effect his teaching about
divine forgiveness and reconciliation. Al-'Aqqād's approach was likely due
to his desire to find acceptance within the rationalistic worldview of modern society, an interest that is also manifest in other Arab Muslim works
about Jesus. The same tendency is found in many Western studies, yet it is
an understatement to say that such an approach does not do justice to the
full "genius" of Christ as found in the Gospels.[28]

Al-'Aqqād's rejection of the Gospel accounts concerning the end of
Jesus' life is, of course, understandable for him as a Muslim, despite the
desire among some Christian reviewers to find a more congenial attitude.[29] However, both the manner in which he discusses this topic and the
solution he proposes are noteworthy. On the one hand, he expresses his
desire not "to stir up controversy in matters . . . not connected with [our]
purpose" (228). On the other hand, the substance of his remarks runs the
risk of alienating both Christians and Muslims. Christian reviewers have
expressed their frustration by the offhand manner in which al-'Aqqād

points out various discrepancies in a few Gospel passages, with no appreciation for how these have been dealt with by Christian scholars. Equally disappointing for them is the way in which he ignores the many prior references to Jesus' passion in his sayings. This is especially true of al-'Aqqād's presentation of Peter's confession (Mark 8:29–30 and parallels; *Genius*, 203–4), where the Gospels go on to emphasize Jesus' prediction of his death.

However, orthodox Muslim readers as well are likely to be disconcerted with the report of Jesus' end that al-'Aqqād proposes in place of the Gospel accounts, namely, that he traveled to India and died there. This is the view held by the Aḥmadīyah sect of Islam, which also claims that Jesus was nailed to the cross but did not die there, that instead he lost consciousness and later revived.[30] As noted above, the view that developed historically in Islam, and is held by most Muslims today, is that Jesus was never placed on the cross but that he was rescued by God from the attempted crucifixion and taken alive into heaven, and at the end of time he will return to earth. The Aḥmadīyah sect and its views about Jesus' end have been rejected by most Muslims as unorthodox. While al-'Aqqād had never claimed to be a member of this sect, he had promoted ideas similar to theirs in a series of newspaper articles written in 1928–1929 (57). In *'Abqarīyat al-Masīḥ*, he is much more circumspect about these views, undoubtedly due to their controversial nature among Muslims and Christians alike. Nevertheless, he does not hide his partiality for the notion that Jesus somehow ended up in India and died there.

Al-'Aqqād's often casual and selective approach to the Gospels is in many ways replicated in his handling of nonbiblical material in support of his views. He makes several references to some of his favorite classical Arab writers (e.g., al-Ghazālī) and to a number of classical Greek and Latin authors (e.g., Josephus). It may well be that he used standard English translations of their works, although in most cases he probably derived these quotations from English secondary sources. However, details concerning the origin of a classical citation are never provided beyond the occasional reference to the title of a particular treatise within the work. Al-'Aqqād also makes frequent use of secondary sources, all of which (as nearly as can be determined) are English works written by Western scholars. Yet his methodology with respect to this material, from an academic perspective, is far from appropriate. Footnotes or other means of proper citation are rare. In a very few cases, he mentions the author or title of a book he used, but there were undoubtedly many others he does not name at all. As is the case for his other works, although he often used these sources well, his writing at other times displays a casual approach toward his sources that is reflected in numerous historical inaccuracies. In most cases, it is impossible to ascertain whether his imprecision or dubious claim should be traced to a faulty source or (as is more likely) to al-'Aqqād's own indiscriminate research or occasionally speculative reasoning. However, it is probably best not to overstate the importance of this matter in evaluating the book as a whole. In the final analysis, historical events are not what al-'Aqqād wishes to emphasize, but rather the message of a particular person in history.

Previous reviewers of 'Abqariyat al-Masīḥ have raised the question of whether there might have been a specific source that influenced al-'Aqqād's overall perspective of Jesus and his mission. Certainly this cannot be found among the Arabic Muslim works on Jesus that predate his book. If anything, al-'Aqqād wrote his own study as an alternative approach to those more traditionally Islamic presentations. Despite the number of references in the book to Western secondary sources regarding specific points of the discussion, there is no clue that would indicate that a more general work on Jesus was in the background. Al-'Aqqād makes a single reference to the ethical perspective of Albert Schweitzer (180), whose book *The Quest of the Historical Jesus* (1910) he might well have known. However, Schweitzer's "thoroughgoing eschatology" contrasts sharply with the way in which al-'Aqqād minimizes the eschatological aspect of Jesus' message, making Schweitzer an unlikely candidate here. Several reviewers have instead suggested that al-'Aqqād's primary source was Emil Ludwig's *The Son of Man: The Story of Jesus* (1928).[31] Although there is no mention of Ludwig or his book in 'Abqariyat al-Masīḥ, this suggestion is most likely based on the fact that al-'Aqqād had written a series of newspaper articles in 1928–1929 in response to this book. There, however, al-'Aqqād sharply criticizes Ludwig for focusing on Jesus the man without saying anything about Christ the messenger, and for limiting Jesus' message to the Jews rather than recognizing his universal mission (52). The impact of Ludwig's book on al-'Aqqād was clearly much more negative than positive. Furthermore, the articles are evidence that some of the main themes of 'Abqariyat al-Masīḥ were already forming in al-'Aqqād's mind more than twenty years before he actually wrote the book.

Rather, the source that almost certainly influenced al-'Aqqād positively was the popular work by Ernest Renan, *La vie de Jésus* (1863), whose 1927 English translation would have been available to al-'Aqqād. The author was a French Catholic who sought to portray Jesus as a romantic revolutionary, yet one who was devoid of any supernatural traits. Based primarily on the Synoptic Gospels and supplemented by his own imagination, Renan's biography is an attempt at a realistic, indeed vivid, account of Jesus' life. Evidence that al-'Aqqād knew of this work, and also thought highly of it, is another feature of his 1928–1929 articles. There he states that in contrast to Ludwig, "Renan is the most adept at creating stories and at combining the facets of the life of Christ in a manner which does not exclude research." His primary complaint is that Renan did not attempt to establish the historical existence of Jesus in his book. Yet, he asserts, if Renan were alive today, he would most likely expand it to include this issue. Al-'Aqqād also parts company with Renan regarding the end of Jesus' life, noting that the French author accepts the crucifixion, though not the resurrection (53). These remarks in these articles strongly suggest that Renan's book made a significant impression on al-'Aqqād, while they likewise show that such influence was not controlling. Several years later, he would present a portrait of Christ that was distinctly his own.[32]

In fact, despite his extensive use of biblical and Western sources, al-'Aqqād endeavors to depict Jesus as a "messenger" *(rasūl)* sent by God in the fundamentally Islamic sense of the term. Here, however, we find a certain reticence in al-'Aqqād's view of the role of God. He often uses the adjective "divine" *(ilāhī)* with reference to the mission of Christ, yet nowhere does al-'Aqqād indicate that Christ's message was direct revelation from God. Indeed, explicit references to God *(Allāh)* are rare; far more common is his use of the term "the [Divine] Mystery" *(al-ghayb)*, indicative of a more remote sense of God's involvement. Like the Old Testament book of Esther, God seems to be relegated to the background, at work behind the scenes. Some have maintained that al-'Aqqād simply equates prophetic activity with religious genius, as if God's role were inconsequential,[33] and it is true that he wishes to emphasize the human aspect of Jesus' prophetic role. Yet there is sufficient evidence of his assumption that Jesus was sent by divine will to issue a call that is ultimately God's own invitation. The reality of the divine presence in Jesus' mission is perhaps most evident in al-'Aqqād's portrayal of the inner character of Christ, when he explores the struggle Jesus faced as he sought to determine the will of God.

As God's messenger, then, Jesus set out on his mission. Having chosen the divine *qiblah* in which he would head, he called others to reject selfish ambitions and embrace the same *qiblah*. He had come not to eliminate the existing Jewish law but to transform it. Thus, his call focused on the internal dimension of the law in contrast to the external concerns current in the religion of the day. Yet because his "law of love" went beyond mere duty, it was even stricter in what it required. In order to meet that requirement, Jesus sought to relocate one's ethical center from mere outward observance to inward motivation. However, his call met with opposition by the Jewish leaders, and al-'Aqqād understands the Gospels correctly when he recognizes that this continued to increase until it reached a climax during Jesus' last visit to Jerusalem. The manner in which that climax was resolved is, of course, markedly different between the Gospels and al-'Aqqād's version, but this certainly does not negate the intensity of the opposition he describes.

Al-'Aqqād emphasizes this Jewish opposition partly because he sees in it the key to the transformation of Jesus' message from an exclusive call involving the Jews only, to a universal call that incorporated the Gentiles. Had the Jews welcomed his message, Christianity would have remained just another sect within Judaism, "an ethnic clique" (186). Their rejection prompted Jesus to make the switch. Al-'Aqqād focuses on the parable of the Great Banquet (Luke 14:16–24), where those who are summoned (the Jews) are rejected after having declined the offer, while those who actually come (the Gentiles) are welcomed. He sees this parable as exemplary of the shift Jesus himself made in his own ministry. However, al-'Aqqād fails to recognize that the parable actually envisions a significant response by the less fortunate Jews before the Gentiles are invited and respond.[34] Indeed, Jesus' entire ministry according to the Gospels was almost exclusively among his compatriots; the New Testament as a whole portrays the early church (ideally, and to a large extent in reality) as a community in which both Jews and Gentiles were equal participants. As noted above, al-'Aqqād has overstated his case with regard to the degree in which the Gentile mission was already being promoted by Jesus. Still, his point that such a mission was inherent in Jesus' message is well taken.

The Jewish opposition to the call of Christ, says al-'Aqqād, was not because the Jews had no need of it. His long review of the various sects within Judaism is meant to show that there was a longing within Israel for a new prophetic word. Yet these variations within Judaism also serve to demonstrate the legalism and hypocrisy that for him typified Jewish religion in general. The Jews' need for the new call was great, but they were not able to recognize their need and respond to that call, entrenched as they were in their own tradition. Meanwhile, the Gentile world was also in need, perhaps more so. Roman society was stratified, with the lower class languishing while the upper class lived in decadent opulence. Some people sought vainly for inner peace through the various religions and philosophies of the time, while most settled for the lifeless rituals of pagan ceremonies. Such a stark

portrayal might be considered exaggerated or even distorted by most contemporary historians, but for one such as al-'Aqqād who sought to analyze
the very soul of a society, the gravity of the situation was all too evident. He
compares it to a disease requiring medicine: the patient may be in need of
treatment but not necessarily ready to request and receive it. Whereas the
first statement applied to both Jews and Gentiles, only the Gentile world recognized its need and embraced the call of Christ.

This dichotomy between the reaction of the Jews and that of the Gentiles is carried into al-'Aqqād's remarks about how the message continued
to be spread through the disciples after Jesus' role had ended. He admits
that the Jews were included in the early mission of the church, but he
offers no indication that they made any significant response, as was indeed
the case. Instead, he emphasizes the rapid spread of Jesus' message
throughout the Gentile world. The disciples, having been trained by the
master, were scattered across the Roman Empire, where they found their
message well received. They faced opposition as well, just as their master
had. Their willingness to suffer for the sake of their message is further evidence for al-'Aqqād that they had received it directly from Christ and had
been instructed by him to carry it among the Gentiles. Throughout the
book we find a genuinely favorable attitude toward the disciples, an out-
look that contrasts sharply with most Muslim writings on Christianity,
which often blame them (especially Paul) for misunderstanding or even
falsifying the message of Jesus. They figure prominently in *'Abqariyat al-
Masīḥ*, even though the focus is on Jesus himself, because al-'Aqqād
understands that they were intimately involved in his mission. He admires
their depth of conviction and their perseverance in the face of opposition:
"We must pay attention to what they said and believe with their kind of
faith" (209). Even Paul is mentioned a number of times without any
adverse criticism, despite the statement that he exercised "a degree of
accommodation" so that the message could be more readily understood
and received by the Gentiles (207–8).

However, there are also hints in the book of a rather different view of
Christianity as it came to be expressed following the period of the disciples. Al-'Aqqād claims, for example, that as Gentiles joined the ranks of the
faithful, they brought with them certain pagan beliefs and customs; he
implies that, over time, this led to an inappropriate syncretism. In another
brief passage that anticipates the epilogue, he states that if Christ had
returned to the earth a few generations later, he would have found it necessary to preach against the manner in which his ethical injunctions had
been distorted into a crude form of asceticism. But perhaps the most

revealing insight into al-'Aqqād's perspective is found in the following statement, in which the central role of Jesus himself is emphasized:

> For surely there is no message without a messenger; there is no way to establish Christianity apart from a Christ. The origin of that spiritual message must also be its essence and core, the fundamental basis of its power and effect. Whatever particulars go beyond the original messenger are but offshoots and additions. (199)

Al-'Aqqād says nothing more in this book about what might have constituted those accretions to Jesus' teachings. In other works he is more clear, though still quite brief: There developed a belief in "the divine right of kings," leading to a misunderstanding of religious authority; Christian emperors began to mix politics and doctrine, causing hardship for the people; and various schools of thought arose and fostered serious disputes about the unity of God as understood in the Gospels (61). Yet despite his conviction that the church went astray in these matters and that Islam came to reestablish proper belief in God and to carry religion to its highest point, al-'Aqqād displays remarkable reticence in offering criticism of the manner in which Christianity developed. This is due to his equally strong conviction that Christianity still preserved the essence of Jesus' message, which even Islam has not superseded. One can still fully ascertain within the Gospels the eminent genius of Christ and the majestic power of his message—a message that, for al-'Aqqād, was as relevant for his own day as it was for the first century.

The Book's Contribution to Muslim-Christian Dialogue

There is no clear indication in *'Abqariyat al-Masīḥ* as to why al-'Aqqād wrote this book. What is obvious is his fascination with the personality of Jesus, which went hand in hand with the message he taught. The new *qiblah* proclaimed by that prophet was a radical call to a devout way of life based on the will of God for humanity, but its appeal would have been drastically diminished were it not for the fact that Jesus himself had first chosen that *qiblah*. He struggled with the calling that had been destined for him, but emerging victorious, he called others to follow the same path and taught them how to remain faithful.

Undoubtedly al-'Aqqād sought to convey this personality primarily to his fellow Muslims. The prevalence of Islamic terminology, the occasional reference to passages from the Qur'ān, and above all the presentation of a Jesus who remains within the parameters of Islamic prophethood all point to a Muslim audience. Furthermore, he was writing (as he did with all his works) on a popular level; he did not bother to provide proper footnotes or to verify the accuracy of his statements. Yet, as one reviewer says, "what [the book] lacks in scholarship it makes up for by sympathy and warmth."[35] Jesus was a prophet, asserts al-'Aqqād, who continues to speak with authority and eloquence to the masses of today. At the same time, there is a word from Jesus to the religious elite in Islam who would emphasize rituals and interpretations that only serve to stifle true faith. It is clear that al-'Aqqād was no less patient with the merely external forms of his own religion than he found Jesus to be with his.

On the other hand, al-'Aqqād must surely have had Christian readers in mind as well. His use of the Gospels as his primary source speaks volumes in this regard. Traditional Islamic interpretations of Jesus are all but abandoned while he instead borrows from Western scholarship. He seeks to avoid issues of controversy between the two faiths, and for the most part he succeeds. He has thus endeavored, as a Muslim, to comprehend the founder of Christianity, and to appropriate for himself the substance of his life and teaching from within a Christian framework. In the process, he has discovered much that he has in common with Christian believers.

So it would seem that part of al-'Aqqād's purpose was to build a bridge across the Muslim-Christian divide: to help Muslims hear the Christ of the Gospels speaking to their own religious convictions, while also to help Christians appreciate the degree to which Islam can genuinely embrace the founder of their faith. Al-'Aqqād was probably all too aware of the dearth of material on Jesus from either side that sought to encourage a dialogue. Despite its weaknesses, *'Abqarīyat al-Masīḥ* succeeds in breaking new ground for interreligious conversation. Among the many points of contact in this regard are the following key issues that arise from this book, which continue to be relevant.

1. No other Muslim work about Jesus has focused on the New Testament Gospels as sources meriting general acceptance, as well as extensive utilization, as has *'Abqarīyat al-Masīḥ*. While al-'Aqqād's blanket recognition of their validity does not manifest itself completely, and although he frequently misreads or misapplies the biblical text, he has made a laudable effort at investigating the Bible for himself with respect and even admiration. Muslim readers are thus escorted by one of their own from familiar and safe territory "into the deeper waters of the New Testament."[36] As a result, this book serves as a sincere challenge for Muslims to move even beyond al-'Aqqād's interpretation of Jesus, to read the Gospels for themselves and examine what they have to say about Jesus' mission as he himself understood it. At the same time, the book is a sincere challenge to

Christians regarding their treatment of the Qur'ān, in which the Scripture of Islam is often either dismissed as irrelevant to Christian faith, or rein-terpreted as a semi-Christian text misunderstood by traditional Islam. *'Abqarīyat al-Masīḥ* invites Christians to mirror al-'Aqqād's approach to the Bible and to appropriate for themselves some measure of the Qur'ān's religious, even spiritual, significance.[37]

2. Both Muslims and Christians have long regarded ethics as an appro-priate arena for dialogue and cooperation, and here al-'Aqqād offers fresh motivation. He especially succeeds in comprehending the radical nature of Jesus' ethical teaching present in the Gospels. Against the inflexibility of conventional Jewish law (as he saw it), he highlights Jesus' emphasis on eternal principles:

> Christ fulfilled the established law, because he instituted the law of love; and the law of love goes beyond the established law. For that law had com-mitted a person to carry out his duty. But love goes beyond duty; it does not wait to be commanded nor does it wait to be compensated. (172)

It would seem that al-'Aqqād wished to apply this truth to the situation he found in the Egypt of his day. With Islamic traditionalism on the one hand, and Western secularism on the other, he found that the message of Jesus as presented in the Gospels provided a solid religious foundation on which Muslims and Christians could together build a just and peaceful society. Yet this would require a drastic reorientation to the path of God by following the *qiblah* that Jesus introduced. His use of this term, with its original focus on prayer, captures the sense of movement toward God through absolute dependence on the divine will that is fundamental to both faiths.

3. Not only did Jesus call others to follow the *qiblah* of God, but he himself became the model as well. In this regard, al-'Aqqād more than once ventures into the inner recesses of Jesus' character, exploring the mystical depths of Jesus' soul as he wrestled with his divine calling. Tempted as he was to succumb to worldly expectations of messianic privi-lege, Jesus found himself "standing on the pinnacle of faith and on the brink of hell at the same moment" (220). Here we see Jesus the Sufi, engaged in "spiritual exercises" (148, 220), plunging into the recesses of his conscience as he seeks to ascertain the will of God. Yet we also see Jesus the prophet, beset with the temptation to avoid the difficult and uncertain path, but emerging victorious through the struggle by way of his utter reliance on the God who is in control. Such a portrayal, despite its empha-sis on human genius more than divine determination, lies firmly within the Muslim concept of prophethood. At the same time, al-'Aqqād has

surely grasped here a fundamental dimension of the Jesus portrayed in the Gospels, who was "tempted in every way, just as we are" (Heb. 4:15).

4. Christians have invariably affirmed that the divine will to which Jesus faithfully submitted finally led him all the way to the cross. Although al-'Aqqād deals graciously with this issue, preferring to leave open the question of the end of Jesus' mission, there is little doubt that he rejects the historicity of the crucifixion. Although he is in agreement with the Gospels that the opposition Jesus faced from the Jewish leaders reached its climax in his last visit to Jerusalem, and that the "cleansing of the temple" was a key event that induced the Jews into resolute action against him, he insists that what happened next cannot be historically determined. The disappointment with this stance among Christian reviewers can be epitomized in the following:

> From a simple critical point of view, the most inexplicable weakness [of al-'Aqqād] . . . is his categorical judgment concerning the . . . death of Jesus. No impartial critic would be able to retract his reliance on the Gospels when dealing with the most established event of the life of Christ: his death on the cross.[38]

Dialogue with al-'Aqqād on this issue, at least from the historical perspective, would seem to be futile.

Nevertheless, *'Abqariyat al-Masīḥ* does provide material for considering the *theological* dimension of the cross of Christ. In recounting the struggle of Jesus to affirm and pursue the will of God, al-'Aqqād in some measure captures what Christians call the "passion" of Christ, that is, the intense emotional and spiritual anguish he experienced during the events surrounding the crucifixion. In particular, he twice alludes to Jesus' request to his Father that the cup of suffering might pass from him but that God's will be done in any case. He does not admit that Jesus spoke those words, according to the Gospels, during his agony in the garden of Gethsemane just prior to his arrest. This is understandable, given that this event occurred after the "role of history" ended for al-'Aqqād. Yet he sees in this prayer Jesus' determination to face the ultimate trial, one that the disciples would interpret as utter defeat but one that God would bring to victory. On the one hand, al-'Aqqād implies that God answered Jesus' prayer and indeed took away the cup of suffering. On the other hand, he seems to envision some kind of final confrontation not unlike that which the Gospels say actually took place, and that Christians have subsequently interpreted to be the heart of the Christian message. Although the event of the cross is absent from *'Abqariyat al-Masīḥ*, something of its essence still remains.

Al-'Aqqād readily admits that his book is not the final word regarding the person and message of Christ: "There is room for others to offer their own presentations and illuminations from various points of view" (227–28). Thus, he offers an invitation, evidently to both Muslims *and* Christians, to continue the conversation about the prominent role Jesus has for Islam as well as for Christianity. Notwithstanding its limitations, *'Abqarīyat al-Masīḥ* continues to deserve consideration from readers who are willing to listen to each other—as well as to the book's main character.

NOTES

1. See A. M. al-'Aqqād, '*The Genius of Christ*, trans. and ed. F. P. Ford Jr., Studies in Contemporary Philosophical Theology (Binghamton, NY: Global Publications, 2001). The translation itself takes up about one-third of this book, with the rest comprised my introduction, appendixes, and endnotes. My comments here about the book and its author are largely drawn from this material, along with a subsequent article (Ford, "Al-'Aqqād's *The Genius of Christ* Re-visited," *Muslim World* 91 (2001): 277–92). The published translation of al-'Aqqād's book is a revised form of my PhD dissertation (Ford, "A Modern Muslim Assessment of Jesus: A Translation and Analysis of 'Abbās Maḥmūd al-'Aqqād's *The Genius of Christ*," 2 vols. [PhD diss., Temple University, 1998]). All references or quotations to al-'Aqqād's original work, as well as to my own more extensive analysis, are to the published English version, abbreviated here as *Genius*. Further investigation, especially concerning primary Arabic sources, can best be made by consulting that work.

2. The most important works in English devoted to the general study of Jesus in Islam are O. Leirvik, *Images of Jesus Christ in Islam: Introduction, Survey of Research, Issues of Dialogue*, Studia Missionalia Upsaliensia 76 (Uppsala: Swedish Institute of Missionary Research, 1999); and N. Robinson, *Christ in Islam and Christianity* (Albany, NY: SUNY Press, 1991). Other useful studies that include some aspect of this subject are G. Parrinder, *Jesus in the Qur'ān* (London: Sheldon, 1965); H. Algar, *Jesus in the Qur'an: His Reality Expounded in the Qur'an* (Oneonta, NY: Islamic Publications International, 1999); T. Khalidi, *The Muslim Jesus: Sayings and Stories in Islamic Literature*, Convergences: Inventories of the Present (Cambridge, MA: Harvard University Press, 2001); K. Cragg, *Jesus and the Muslim: An Exploration* (London: George Allen & Unwin, 1985); H. Goddard, *Muslim Perceptions of Christianity*, CSIC Studies on Islam and Christianity (London: Grey Seal, 1996); D. A. Kerr, "Christology in Christian-Muslim Dialogue," in *Christology in Dialogue*, ed. R. K. Berkey and S. A. Edwards, 201–20 (Cleveland: Pilgrim, 1993); and D. Marshall, "Christianity in the Qur'ān," in *Islamic Interpretations of Christianity*, ed. L. Ridgeon, 3–29 (New York: St. Martin's Press, 2001). The popular book by M. Ata ur-Rahim, *Jesus: Prophet of Islam*, 1977 (Repr., Alexandra, Singapore: Omar Brothers, 2001) is quite polemical in nature. The most important works in French and German are M. Borrmans, *Jésus et les musulmans d'aujourd'hui*, Collection "Jésus et Jésus-Christ" (Paris: Desclée, 1996); and O. H. Schumann, *Der Christus der Muslime: Christologische Aspekte in der arabisch-islamischen Literatur*, 2nd ed., Kölner Veröffentlichungen zur Religionsgeschichte (Cologne: Böhlau Verlag, 1988).

3. For further analysis on the concept of affirmation/rejection in the Qur'ān concerning Jesus, see D. A. Kerr, "The Problem of Christianity in Muslim Perspective: Implications for Christian Mission," *International Bulletin of Missionary Research* 5 (1981): 152–62.

4. References to the Qur'ān begin with "Q" followed by the number of the *sūrah* (or chapter), then the number of the verse(s). The verse numbering follows what is referred to as the "Egyptian" text of the Qur'ān, which is now recognized as the standard. Many older English translations followed a text in which the verse numbering varied slightly, although there is no difference in the wording of the Arabic. When using certain translations, the reader may need to locate the passage a few verses before or after the verse number given here. Translations provided here, however, are my own.

5. See W. M. Watt, "The Christianity Criticized in the Qur'ān," *Muslim World* 57 (1967): 197–201; and Goddard, *Muslim Perceptions of Christianity*, 11–16.

6. O. Leirvik, *Images of Jesus Christ in Islam*, 42–45.

7. Ibid., 45–47.

8. Ibid., 81–102; Khalidi, *The Muslim Jesus: Sayings and Stories in Islamic Literature*, 26–45.

9. Leirvik, *Images of Jesus Christ in Islam*, 66–69; Robinson, *Christ in Islam and Christianity* (Albany, NY: SUNY Press, 1991), 43–45.

10. Leirvik, *Images of Jesus Christ in Islam*, 74–75; Robinson, *Christ in Islam and Christianity*, 160–66.

11. Leirvik *Images of Jesus Christ in Islam*, 72–73; Robinson, *Christ in Islam and Christianity*, 117–41; M. Ayoub, "Towards an Islamic Christology, II: The Death of Jesus, Reality or Delusion (A Study of the Death of Jesus in Tafsīr Literature)," *Muslim World* 70 (1980): 91–109.

12. Robinson, *Christ in Islam and Christianity*, 46–49; Goddard, *Muslim Perceptions of Christianity*, 34–38.

13. Michel, T. F., ed. and trans. *A Muslim Theologian's Response to Christianity: Ibn Taymiyya's Al-Jawab Al-Sahih*. Delmar, NY: Caravan Books, 1984.

14. M. Ayoub, "Muslim Views of Christianity: Some Modern Examples," *Islamochristiana* 10 (1984): 50–60; Leirvik, *Images of Jesus Christ in Islam*, 140–43; *Genius*, 11–13. Since much of the material in this section is drawn from my analysis of original Arabic works, as well as from secondary sources, references to my discussion in *Genius* are also provided here. For recourse to the Arabic text, see the notes and list of references in *Genius*.

15. Leirvik, *Images of Jesus Christ in Islam*, 127–39; Goddard, *Muslim Perceptions of Christianity*, 57–58.

16. Ayoub, "Muslim Views of Christianity," 61–70; Goddard, *Muslim Perceptions of Christianity*, 59–84; *Genius*, 13–14.

17. Cragg, *Jesus and the Muslim*, 54–56; Goddard, *Muslim Perceptions of Christianity*, 118–20; *Genius*, 14.

18. Goddard, *Muslim Perceptions of Christianity*, 95–140; Leirvik, *Images of Jesus Christ in Islam*, 176–207; *Genius* 15–18. One particular Arab Muslim work, published in Cairo only a year after the first edition of *The Genius of Christ*, has received considerable attention among Western Christian scholars: Muḥammad Kāmil Ḥusayn's *Qaryah Ẓālimah*, translated into English by K. Cragg as *The City of Wrong* (Hussein 1959 [1954]). This work is an imaginative portrayal of the people who were involved in the events surrounding the crucifixion of Jesus. While leaving open the question of what actually happened regarding the crucifixion itself, the author explores the way in which individuals, despite their recognition that a particular action is wrong, allow themselves to go along with the majority in their intention to carry out that action while seeking to justify their own minor role. While it is significant that Ḥusayn chose a dominant Christian theme in order to explore the matter of communal guilt, it should be noted that the book does not deal directly with the person of Jesus, who is present only behind the scenes.

19. H. Goddard, "Modern Pakistani and Indian Muslim Perceptions of Christianity," *Islam and Christian-Muslim Relations* 5 (1994): 173–79; Leirvik, *Images of Jesus Christ in Islam*, 155–58.

20. W. A. Bijlefeld, "Other Faith Images of Jesus: Some Muslim Contributions to the Christological Discussion," in *Christological Perspectives: Essays in Honor of Harvey K. McArthur*, ed. R. K. Berkey and S. A. Edwards (New York: Pilgrim, 1982), 205–15; Kerr, "Christology in Christian-Muslim Dialogue," 207–12; *Genius*, 19–20.

21. There exists no biography of al-ʿAqqād in English. A short overview of his life is found in L. Awad, *The Literature of Ideas in Egypt*, part 1, *Selection, Translation, and Introduction*, Vol. 3 Arabic Writing Today, Studies in Near Eastern Culture and Society 6 (Atlanta: Scholars Press, 1986), 166–71, but this is marred by some technical inaccuracies. Other brief summaries are in R. Allen, "al-Akkād, ʿAbbas Mahmūd" in *The Encyclopaedia of Islam*, 2nd ed., ed. H. A. R. Gibb et al., Supplement 57–58 (Leiden: Brill, 1980); N. Safran, *Egypt in Search of Political Community: An Analysis of the Intellectual and Political Evolution of Egypt, 1804–1952*, Harvard Middle Eastern Studies 5 (Cambridge, MA: Harvard University Press, 1961), 135–37; and M. M. Badawi, *A Critical Introduction to Modern Arabic Poetry* (Cambridge: Cambridge University Press, 1975), 86. However, there are numerous Arabic biographical studies of al-ʿAqqād, as well as a few unpublished English works that draw from these. In addition, al-ʿAqqād wrote two autobiographical books. See the overview and notes in *Genius*, 26–35, of which this section is a summary.

22. Safran, *Egypt in Search of Political Community*, 136–37.

23. T. Carlyle, *On Heroes, Hero-Worship, and the Heroic in History*, ed. C. Niemeyer (Lincoln, NE: University of Nebraska Press, 1966), 42–77.

24. B. K. Nijim, "ʿAbbās Mahmūd al-ʿAqqād: A Modern Muslim Apologist" (MA thesis, Hartford Seminary, 1970), 123.

25. Awad, *Literature of Ideas in Egypt*, 169.

26. K. Cragg, "'The Genius of Christ'—A Muslim Estimate" (review of *ʿAbqariyat al-Masīh* by ʿAbbās Mahmūd al-ʿAqqād), *East and West Review* 20 (1954): 89.

27. See *Genius*, 264n74 for details regarding al-ʿAqqād's article on the *Gospel of Barnabas*. This article was translated into English by K. Cragg, who also added his own comments (Cragg, "The Gospel of Barnabas," *News Bulletin of the Near East Council of Churches* (Eastertide 1961): 9–12).

28. One noted scholar about Jesus, after spending some 350 pages in a detailed analysis of the accounts of his miracles in the Gospels, concludes, "Any historian who seeks to portray the historical Jesus without giving due weight to his fame as a miracle-worker is not delineating this strange and complex Jew, but rather a domesticated Jesus reminiscent of the bland moralist created by Thomas Jefferson" (J. P. Meier, *A Marginal Jew: Rethinking the Historical Jesus*, vol. 2, *Mentor, Message, and Miracles*, Anchor Reference Library (New York: Doubleday, 1994), 970.

29. Most Christian reviewers of *ʿAbqariyat al-Masīh* have especially indicated their concern, and sometimes disappointment, at the manner in which al-ʿAqqād handles the end of Jesus' life. See B. ʿAbd al-Malik, review of *ʿAbqariyat al-Masīh*, by ʿAbbās Mahmūd al-ʿAqqād, *Muslim World* 43 (1953): 218; G. Anawati, "La personne du Christ d'après deux livres récents d'auteurs musulmans," in *ATTI: dell'VIII Congresso Internazionale di Storia delle Religioni (Roma 17–23 Aprile) 1955* (Florence: G. C. Sansoni, 1956), 444; Borrmans, *Jésus et les musulmans d'aujourd'hui*, 167; Cragg, "Genius of Christ," 91, 96; Cragg, *Jesus and the Muslim*, 54; G. Farès, "Le Christ et l'Islam contemporain," in *Mediterranée, Carrefour des religions*, Recherches et débats du centre catholique des intellectuals français, n. s. 28 (Paris: Librairie Arthème Fayard, 1959), 45–46; H. Goddard, "An Annotated Bibliography of Works about Christianity by Egyptian Muslim Authors (1940–1980)," *Muslim World* 80 (1990): 257; and Teissier 1959: 30, 35.

30. The details of the Aḥmadīyah view of the crucifixion were spelled out by the founder of this sect, Ghulam Aḥmad (d. 1908), in *Masīh Hindustān Men*, which has been translated from Urdu (Ahmad, *Jesus in India: Being an Account of Jesus' Escape from Death on the Cross and of His Journey to India* [London: London Mosque, 1978]). A comprehensive account of the Aḥmadīyah sect is given in S. Lavan, *The Ahmadiyah Movement: A History and Perspective* (Delhi: Manohar Book Service, 1974). For details about al-'Aqqād's treatment of this issue, see *Genius*, 227 and 364n74–76.

31. See K. Schoonover, "Contemporary Egyptian Authors," *Muslim World* 45 (1955): 36; Goddard, *Muslim Perceptions of Christianity*, 120; Borrmans, *Jésus et les musulmans d'aujour-d'hui* 164.

32. Only one reviewer briefly suggests a parallel between the respective works of Renan and al-'Aqqād: A.-F. el-Didi, *Jesus und der moderne Islam*, Arabische Kulture 1, ([Bonn]: n. p., 1956), 11). El-Didi simply observes that for both authors, the real miracle of Jesus was that he transformed the world.

33. R. Wielandt, "'Abbās Maḥmūd al-'Aqqād (1889–1964): Nutzen und Nachteil religions-geschichtlicher Studien für den Glauben," Akademie der Wissenschaften und der Literatur, die orientalische Komission, vol. 25 (Wiesenbaden: Franz Steiner, 1971), 105.

34. J. A. Fitzmyer, *The Gospel according to Luke (X–XXIV): Introduction, Translation, and Notes*, Anchor Bible (Garden City, NY: Doubleday, 1985), 1053–54.

35. N. A. Faris, "The Muslim Thinker and His Christian Relations," *Muslim World* 47 (1957): 70.

36. Cragg, "'The Genius of Christ'—A Muslim Estimate," 91.

37. See my own survey and analysis of this subject in Ford, "The Qur'ān as Sacred Scrip-ture: An Assessment of Contemporary Christian Perspectives," *Muslim World* 83 (1993): 142–64.

38. Teissier, "Des écrivains musulmans," 35.

10 | Christology in the Dark

The Da Vinci Code and *The Passion of the Christ*—What They Tell Us about American Religion Today

Alan F. Segal

In this essay I will compare two very unusual films in American cinema. They are unusual in several ways. First, they were extremely successful. According to the Internet Movie Database, *The Da Vinci Code* has grossed over $749,536,138, putting it at number 21 worldwide, and *The Passion of the Christ* is at number 31 with $604,370,943.[1] The *Passion of the Christ* was largely self-financed by Mel Gibson, as the advanced word was that it would be a very controversial film. Both films were critical failures, or at best mixed successes, but both films' financial backers have laughed at the critics on their way to the bank. *The Passion of the Christ* was criticized for its unremitting violence, while other aspects of the film were praised. Most critics and moviegoers expressed some disappointment at the way the novel *The Da Vinci Code* was translated to the screen. It placed second at the box office in its opening week. *The Passion* went to the top of the charts immediately and stayed there for an extended period. But *The Da Vinci Code* was based on one of the most successful trade books ever, with some 40 million copies in world circulation, which virtually guaranteed high revenue for the screen version. The novel itself might even have outsold the Bible during some of the months that it has been on the market. These two films, then, are important not just as films but because they were huge mass phenomena, in some way touching the interests and deep feelings of Americans and people around the world.

The two films are also especially unusual in that they both deal with biblical themes. Of course, the Bible is a mass phenomenon all by itself. It is the best-selling book of all time and continues to get the largest book sales in virtually every year.[2] It is the most constantly demanded, the most bought, the most read, and arguably the least heeded book of all time. Many homes have several copies. These films deal with biblical subjects in extremely provocative ways. They both claim to be faithful to their scriptural, literary, and historical sources. But faced with charges of historical irresponsibility—*The Da Vinci Code*'s author was sued for plagiarism; *The Passion* was cribbed almost entirely from the writings of Anna Emmerich—they both retreated to the defense of artistic freedom, not historical accuracy. Mel Gibson's film company, Ikon Films, has claimed that his film was accurate to the New Testament as well, but when questioned about it on TV, he also pointed out that he had an artist's rights to artistic freedom.[3]

Both films are also unusual in that neither one depicts any graphic sex, although they both contain graphic violence. They each portray bizarrely ritualized and eroticized violence, especially *The Passion*. *The Da Vinci Code* begins with a fully depicted murder, followed by self-inflicted ritualized body abuse, followed by a fully depicted scene featuring naked flagellation and the use of a cilice bound to the thigh. Unlike in *The Passion*, where the pain is endured by Christ as a redemptive atonement for the human race, all of the eroticized pain in *The Da Vinci Code* is caused by the evil forces in the film. It is not too much to suppose that *The Da Vinci Code* takes as the enemy the very kind of eroticized-pain spirituality that is at the center of *The Passion of the Christ*.

Violence has a long and very respectable tradition in American cinema. However, sex is a different question. Sex in film is highly regulated. For Jesus, sex is strongly forbidden in the eyes of religious America. The last film to combine sex with Jesus was *The Last Temptation of Christ*, which was a heady financial lesson to Scorsese and all the studios. It occasioned enormous controversy and a huge backlash, which included, on the day I saw it, nuns praying the rosary outside the theatre at a weekday early afternoon matinee and huge numbers of people picketing. There were far more people outside the theatre than in it on the day I saw it. David Sterritt almost lost his job at the *Christian Science Monitor* (of all places) simply for saying that one ought to see the film and make up one's own mind.[4]

Sterritt was not the only one. Scorsese will probably never get the chance to make another religious film. I know this because before the film opened, Elaine Pagels was talking to Scorsese about the possible sequel—a film on Paul, and I spoke to him by cell phone for a long time as well. This would have been a perfect subject for him. He likes violence, and Paul certainly had a violent life. After *The Last Temptation*'s opening, it was clear that we were not soon going to see any sequel, though the film was frequently judged a critical success.

What was the problem? Jesus was blond and blue eyed, but that was not the reason. The culture of Palestine was depicted as if it were North African, but that was not the reason. There was no doubt throughout that Jesus was the Christ, which is always ambiguous in Kazantzakis's novel, but that was not the reason. The problem was that Jesus was naked on the cross (male frontal nudity was and is a film problem for sure, though historically accurate for crucifixion) and, even worse, he was shown in fantasy having a marital and sexual relationship with Mary Magdalene. That was a bombshell. No such scene appeared in *The Da Vinci Code*, so most of the critique of the work was limited to conceptual matters, and a great deal of that critique was limited to the medium of books. Writing books about *The Da Vinci Code* has become something of a cottage industry.[5]

The pattern of likes and dislikes with *The Passion* and *The Da Vinci Code* is important because of the behavior of the conservative press. The Fox Network treated the two films in exactly the same way it treated the national election. Right after the 2000 election that brought George W. Bush to power, the Fox Channel turned on a dime. Instead of constantly criticizing the Clinton administration, it began broadcasting praise for the Bush administration. The same contrast was visible with Fox's treatment of *The Passion* and *The Da Vinci Code*. *The Passion* garnered positive reviews from Fox. No surprise there, since Fox's parent company had already bought the rights to the DVD. It was a natural plug for their core viewership as well. But *The Da Vinci Code* was the source of unremitting scorn.

The response from conservative Christians to *The Passion* was consistent with Fox's. Evangelicals, fundamentalists, and Catholics were huge fans of *The Passion*. Their churches provided sell-out crowds for showings of the film. It was arguably a love feast of conservative ecumenism.

There were, of course, legitimate spiritual reasons to like the film. Especially if you are my age (early sixties) or older and grew up Catholic, the film contained imagery and piety that you likely haven't seen since Vatican II. But there were also suspiciously anti-Semitic sections of the film, and huge parts of it followed the writings of Sister Anna Katharina Emmerich, an anti-Semitic nun of the eighteenth and nineteenth centuries.[6] Evangelicals were particularly offended by the charge of anti-Semitism. Pat Robertson denied the anti-Semitism: "It's about Jews. All Jesus' followers were Jewish so how could it be anti-semitic?"[7] And he recommended that people as young as 13 should go to see it without fear, in spite of the violence.[8]

"It is as it was" was the word from Steve McVeety, the coproducer of the film, quoting the pope. That was later retracted and replaced with the name of Monsignor Dziwisz, whose job at the Vatican was to seek reconciliation with schismatic Catholics, which is the official name for the kind of pre–Vatican II Catholicism that Mel Gibson propounds. Peggy Noonan, who reported in the *Wall Street Journal* about the quotation from Msgr. Dziwisz, thereafter decided that the pope might have said it, that there was no anti-Semitism in the film, and that the film was marvelous, though she noted sadly that the Vatican treated the film, thereafter, as a kind of "car crash."

It was extremely strange that the Protestant right found this film so interesting, because it was chock full of nostalgic Catholic piety. It contained everything from the "stations of the cross" to "the veil of Veronica" and everything that conservative Protestants had vociferously opposed in the heyday of the 1950s. But just as completely did Catholics and the Protestant right wing denounce *The Da Vinci Code*. Why such a great yes about one religious film and such a great no about a film that was about the New Testament period, at least in part, but didn't depict Jesus in any detail? (There were flashbacks to some scenes.) My theme, of course, is that it was about the culture wars of the far right Christian movement.

In the case of *The Da Vinci Code*, an extremely popular and controversial book was the basis for the film, so in a way the reaction has been against the book as well. Catholic bishops urged parishioners to boycott the film, as they previously had asked them not to read the book. In spite of the opposition of Catholics and Protestants and despite decidedly mixed reviews, *The Da Vinci Code* gradually built up huge numbers at the box office. One of the most anticipated films of 2006, it opened at the Cannes Film Festival on May 17, 2006, and the next week in the United States.

The basic scandal of *The Da Vinci Code* is the same as *The Last Temptation of Christ*: the marriage of Mary Magdalene and Jesus. In contrast to *The Last Temptation*, *The Da Vinci Code* presents this as fact, not a fantasy of Jesus from the cross. But not only does *The Da Vinci Code* treat the claim as true, it further maintains that the church engaged in a conspiracy to hide the truth and that a secret organization in the church will even commit murder to keep the secret from emerging. The film also contends that Constantine retailored the New Testament to fit his view of Christianity. To dispel the truth of her marriage to Jesus, Mary was vilified by the male-dominated church as a prostitute. It may seem strange that the backlash was stronger against *The Last Temptation*, a film that only suggested that Jesus could have been tempted to have an ordinary life. But *The Last Temptation of Christ* actually depicted Jesus and Mary in bed together, whereas *The Da Vinci Code* only describes him as a normal householder with a wife and children. Flashbacks only show a pregnant Mary Magdalene fleeing Jerusalem for her life. Meanwhile, a film that spends 80 percent of its time depicting the torturing of a human being was acclaimed by many of the people who reacted so strongly against *The Last Temptation*.

But let us examine the claims of *The Da Vinci Code*. Mary Magdalene's depiction as a prostitute actually did happen centuries after the New Testament was written. Specifically, it happened in the sixth century in a sermon by Pope Gregory the Great, which is extant. But it is another thing to show that this was a deliberate attempt to vilify Mary Magdalene, who is a saint of the church. It rather seems like an attempt to dramatize and romanticize her to fit a pattern of sin and atonement. In short, her life was recast to offer as an example of the power of repentance.

Mary Magdalene was never depicted as a prostitute in the Gospels. She was cured of seven demons, according to Mark 16:9. This story also appears in Luke 8:2, but immediately after a story in which Jesus forgives the many sins of the woman who has washed his feet with her tears. She has also been associated with the unnamed woman taken in adultery in John 8:2–11. But this association cannot be ancient, because the story itself is not to be found in the earliest Gospels. It is a medieval addition to the Gospel tradition, though it may be the perfect Christian fable. The story of the woman taken in adultery moved around a bit in the manuscript tradition and was only put into the Gospel of John quite late.

It is true that Gnostic documents such as the *Gospel of Mary*, found in Egypt in 1896, and the *Gospel of Philip*, found at Nag Hammadi in Egypt in 1947, contain very favorable traditions about Mary Magdalene. The texts say that Jesus used to kiss Mary, but where he kissed her has been effaced by time. Likely, it was on her head, as this was a custom of respect among teachers at that time. She is described as Jesus' "companion" several times, using the term *koinonos*, a word borrowed from Greek into Coptic but once in the native Coptic equivalent *hotre*. This term can also mean "consort." She is acclaimed as Jesus' favorite disciple and even more privileged than the men. But perhaps this is only meant to instill modesty in the men.

If I had to guess, I would say that the actual Mary Magdalene had a close relationship with Jesus but that she was not his sexual companion. The Gospel of John does say that she was the first person to see Christ risen, but also that she had to bring Peter before her report was believed. The Synoptics also include her among those present at the tomb. However, Paul's report in 1 Corinthians of those in the earliest church who were married does not include Jesus. One would think that if Paul knew about Jesus' marriage he would have said so, even if it was against his own teachings favoring celibacy over marriage, though accepting both.

There is no evidence, however, that Mary Magdalene was the so-called beloved disciple of the Gospel of John. There is considerable evidence that she was not, since Mary runs to tell the beloved disciple Simon Peter in John 20 that the stone has been rolled from the tomb. Contrary to Dan Brown, Leonardo Da Vinci did not depict her that way. Leonardo identified that beloved disciple in the Gospel with John the Evangelist, as does the church tradition. (It is just as likely that the beloved disciple is actually Lazarus, because he is the only one identified as the one whom Jesus loved in the Gospel.)

As far as we know, the first person to call Mary a prostitute was Pope Gregory the Great who used the example of Mary in a sermon around 530 CE to demonstrate the power of repentance and conversion. As a prostitute redeemed, Mary Magdalene became a very powerful figure. In the thirteenth century this picture of Mary as a prostitute was used to castigate the Manichaean Catharii. Apparently she had previously been identified with a legendary fourth-century Mary called Mary of Egypt, who visited Jerusalem, became an ascetic, and lived naked, protecting her modesty with her long hair (a predecessor to the Lady Godiva legend and the story of Eleanor of Aquitaine, who scourged the Muslims while on crusade with her husband by baring her breast on horseback).

According to the legend, Mary Magdalene arrived naked in a boat in the south of France to found the Merovingian dynasty. Of course, extravagant foundation legends are *de rigeur* in French royal houses. The Angevine dynasty of the Langue d'Oc, from which Eleanor came, believed they were descended from "the fair Melusine," the inspiration for Mendelssohn's great concert piece. Eleanor is remembered as the great beauty who grew a fishtail on Saturday nights, a variation on the animal groom folktale, such as the story of the frog prince or Amor and Psyche.

My operant hypothesis is this: one way to analyze these two films is to begin with their depiction of Christ, noting their very different Christologies (their way of depicting the "christness" of Jesus) and realizing that the nature of the body of Christ is being debated. The body of Christ not only designates Jesus himself but also the church, so these films are actually debating what the nature of the church should be.

The Passion of the Christ follows the Passion narrative in the Gospel of John, adding material from the Synoptics, from later Catholic tradition, and, especially, from the aforementioned writings of Anna Katharina Emmerich. It contains a "high" Christology, because it depicts Jesus as God more than man. Of course, the Nicene Creed stresses that Jesus was both truly God and truly man—both together in equal parts. But most conservatives in America favor a high Christology, one that stresses Jesus' divine nature over his human nature. One might think that a film that depicts Jesus' suffering in such detail would have a "low" Christology. But the torture of Jesus is so intense and so unbearable that it becomes clear immediately that Jesus is no ordinary man.

But *The Da Vinci Code* also has a Christology, even if it turns out to be almost the anti-Christology of *The Passion of the Christ*. The Christology starts with the very open secret at the center of the film—that Jesus was an ordinary man with a wife who was pregnant when he was crucified. This is certainly a low Christology. However, the idea that Jesus was actually married and fathered a child is, I think, rather far-fetched. *The Da Vinci Code* misinforms us about the historical credibility of the *Gospel of Mary* and the *Gospel of Philip*, which are fascinating documents but rather late (no earlier than the second century and likely a bit later). In the end, *The Da Vinci Code* is only entertainment, no matter how much is being claimed for it as a grail legend. It does indict the church and seems to blame Opus Dei for a myriad of terrors in the world. What is at stake for Protestant conservatives is the high Christology. Jesus must be shown to be God, not man. The question is why?

Even *The Da Vinci Code* admits that it is not the divinity of Christ that matters but the faith of those who believe in him, that is, the church. But that is exactly the religious right's point: for them, the divinity of Christ is the crucial issue in the modern world. It is amazing how far the religious right will go to preserve the absolute divinity of Jesus—but that is not the only point of their opposition. Anything that questions the inerrancy of the Bible or its miraculous nature as truth in this scientific age is inherently threatening. Thus, the right has to preserve the literal truth of the garden of Eden and fight against evolution. It is not the monkeys in our past that frighten the religious right. It is the idea that the Bible is not literally true. Right behind that logically comes the recognition that Jesus did not rise from the dead and that, hence, Christ is not divine and that we are not saved if we believe in him. In the past, one could have human as well as divine depictions of Jesus. But for evangelicals and fundamentalists, the divinity of Jesus is what separates them from the rest of humanity. One can, after all, claim that Jesus was human and be anything, including a Jew or a secular humanist.

It certainly seems like the two films developed along two different audiences. The one hit the evangelical crowd, and the other the secular and mainline religious crowd—or even just the people interested in being rebellious to the received story. The distinction in audience between the two films exactly parallels the religious dichotomy between the mainline and the fundamentalists, which is absolutely central to the religious life in modern America now.

The Christology of *The Passion of the Christ* is very high. Rarely in the film is there a trace of the human in this Christ. Even his suffering is divine. It is the suffering of God in his greatest of all sacrifices; he is making atonement for all. It is a vivid portrait of an atonement theology, certainly a notion with a proud history in Christianity, though not particularly recently. The release of this film saw a resurgence of the Catholic practice of religious processions in public with the consecrated host held aloft in a monstrance. Catholics used to anger Protestants with this practice during the Counter-Reformation. It used to be a statement of the prerogatives and theology of Catholicism. Now it is the symbol of a God who endured every suffering so that those who believe in him could have eternal life. More than that, it is a symbol of a God who commands that sometimes a human must make that same sacrifice that the faith should stay true. Those who believe in this Christ know what the original one did and know that they may be called upon to give their lives for the faith. They also know that what they get in return is resurrection at the end of days. All of this is inherent in high Christology. And the evangelical community knows that resurrection, not immortality of the soul, is what the New Testament teaches.

The Christology of *The Da Vinci Code* is the converse, of course. It is described as a deep secret, one that the church is apparently willing to kill for. It has in it not just a person who eroticizes pain and murders out of religious motives, but the book essentially says that in a less obvious form, this eroticization of pain is characteristic of the whole Opus Dei movement within Catholicism due to its use of the cilice. It also suggests that the church has known throughout the centuries that Jesus was only a man but has persecuted any who discovered the secret. One might imagine this a liberal Protestant variety of anti-Catholicism, but it is amazing how many Catholics also trooped to this film. Of course, any secular person would say that this is an open secret, hardly anything worth killing over. But it does make for a mildly amusing trashy novel.

The Christology of *The Da Vinci Code* is simple: Jesus was an ordinary man who had a wife and an ordinary child. He had but a few direct heirs throughout all the centuries, down to the last living heir. That person is the last heir to the line of Jesus and the Merovingian line and is unknowingly the central concern of an amazing organization, the purpose of which is to protect the bloodline. The idea is that the church wants to wipe it out, lest people realize that Jesus was ordinary? But why? If Jesus were God, he could still have had a family and he could still have had natural descendants who were even disbelievers. That would not endanger Jesus' divinity.

And what is the Christology? Or in lay terms, Who is this Christ? He is an ordinary guy who married and who produced a child and whose friends saw to it that the child could survive when he was martyred. It is a Christology with no afterlife or, at best, an afterlife of the soul that returns to its heavenly abode. This is certainly what the *Gospel of Mary*, the *Gospel of Peter*, and the other Gnostic Gospels that use the word "resurrection" but mean "immortality of the soul" have in mind. Immortality of the soul means that the soul goes to heaven but the body stays on earth and rots. It goes with the Gnostic intuition. But that is what a majority of Americans actually believe today, including the conservative faithful.

But the conservative faithful also have an additional belief. They believe that Jesus was resurrected in the flesh and that this is the sign that all those who believe in him will also be resurrected in the flesh at the end of time. This was, in fact, the belief of the early church. Only gradually did the notion of immortality of the soul creep into Christianity. The church fathers eschewed it with the Gnostic heresy. Immortality of the soul was known in Judaism before Christianity, but only among wealthy Jewish aristocrats who had been in contact with Platonism, from which this belief comes in antiquity. Resurrection of the body came from a martyrdom tradition in Judaism and was quintessentially the reward of martyrs and only incidently the reward of the rest of us. This can be seen clearly in early Christian beliefs. Jesus' resurrection was expected precisely because he was a martyr. The innovation of the church was to say that it had happened and that this means the end of days is upon us. Resurrection of the body goes with *The Passion* issue, even today, as it was in the first centuries of our era.

Immortality of the soul was the characteristic and rational notion of the afterlife among the Greco-Roman aristocracy. So if Christianity was going to encounter the Greek world, it was going to have to come to terms with immortality of the soul somehow. The first attempt at combination perhaps can be seen in the Gnostic texts that valorize Mary Magdalene. In Gnostic Gospels, Christianity was synthesized with Greek philosophy, as well as with some esoteric Jewish traditions. Although some Gnostics called the Christian afterlife "resurrection," they meant that the soul left the body behind as unclean and ascended to the heavens, a belief that is more properly called "immortality of the soul."

So anything material, like Mary's feminine gender, is secondary and irrelevant. It is merely the clothing of the soul. The whole Gnostic religion was about the return of the soul to its heavenly abode after discovering its immortality and leaving behind the evil, demon-possessed earth. *Gnosis* means "knowledge," and the saving knowledge is that one is divine in a demonic world. It often appeals to elitist groups.

Of course, neither film has really respected accepted historical facts with regard to Jesus. Gibson's movie includes the most brazen anachronisms taken from Catholic piety, including a huge amount of anti-Semitic imagery. *The Da Vinci Code*, on the other hand, is based on a totally fantastic and unsupported notion that Jesus was married and had natural offspring. They are equally guilty of ignoring history. *The Da Vinci Code* has the advantage of being original, while *The Passion* has the advantage of being traditional. But they are both huge fictionalizations of what the Gospels contain.

The New Testament has in fact more evidence for a high Christology than for a low one.[9] *The Da Vinci Code* has a certain appeal to secular people, non-Christians, and liberal Christians. It is hard for an academic not to side with the more secular side here, and I do. After all, there is more fun in *The Da Vinci Code* story, as difficult as it may be to square with the facts. It is interesting and innovative and is based on a gripping conspiracy theory. And everyone likes a good conspiracy theory—even Mel Gibson, who named one of his films *Conspiracy Theory*.[10] With *The Da Vinci Code* and *The Passion*, the film industry has helped define the two basic camps in American civil and political life. Now that the audiences have been defined, they have been appealed to by several new films: the *Left Behind* series and the *Tip of the Spear* on one side, *An Uncomfortable Truth* and *Fahrenheit 9/11* on the other. *The Da Vinci Code* and *The Passion of the Christ* are merely the flagships of a bifurcation both of artistic taste and religious belief in American society.

But just pointing out the different Christologies is not enough. Both films invite an enormous amount of participation in the film by the viewers. The camera practically never leaves Jesus in *The Passion*. The violence may be pleonastic, but it feeds into a participatory mysticism as in the Gospel of John. *The Passion* is a film in which Jesus becomes the Way and the Vine and the Gate as well as the Paschal Lamb. So the Christology is not just a declaration that Jesus is God and Christ (and in that order). The film, as much as the Gospels, invites the viewer to become the Christ, to undergo his suffering, to ascend to heaven with him, and to return on the day of judgment. Indeed, *The Passion of the Christ* takes the viewer where no canonical Gospel takes us—right into the tomb when Jesus is resurrected. There is no direct description of the resurrection and no eyewitness to it in the New Testament. There is nothing wrong with this except perhaps the martial music as Jesus awakes and marches out. It is perfectly good Christianity, and it has inspired many believers. I mention it only to compare it with *The Da Vinci Code*.

The Da Vinci Code takes the perspective of Robert Langdon, Harvard symbologist, who goes through the film solving problems and figuring out mysteries. In this respect, he is superhuman or mythological too, and so, in identifying with him, the viewer is actually internalizing the role of reasonable adventurer, rational human being taken to its limit. Each film defines its hero and invites us through the participation of the film to become the hero.

So what is the significance of this dichotomized bimodal distribution of moviegoers? It seems to me that it merely confirms what the Gallup Organization has been predicting since 1989. In his book *The People's Religion*, George Gallup predicted that the big religious news of the twenty-first century would be a new fissure in American life.[11] No longer would the biggest gaps be between Judaism, Christianity, Islam, Hinduism, Buddhism, and Jainism. The big news of the twenty-first century was going to be the polarization of American religion. Right-wing Christians, Jews, and Muslims especially would be on one line, stressing literal resurrection, perseverance in the face of the world's hostility, and readiness for martyrdom. The other side—composed of mainline Christian groups as well as similarly minded followers of other religions—would stand for cultural pluralism, making room for others, tolerance, rational inquiry, and, after death, normally the heavenly journey of the soul, that is, the reward of the intellect for having developed itself on this earth. In this scenario, the body is left behind. That is still the preferred afterlife of mainstream Americans, whether they be Christian or not. Looking at the mass reaction to *The Da Vinci Code* and *The Passion of the Christ*, we can see that the dichotomy has already formed.

NOTES

1. The Internet Movie Database, http://www.imdb.com/boxoffice/alltimegross?region =world-wide).

2. See D. Radosh, "The Good Book Business," *New Yorker*, December 18, 2006, 54–59.

3. Mel Gibson, interview by Diane Sawyer, ABC Prime Time Special Event, Spring 2004.

4. He said this in an address to the Columbia University Faculty Religion Seminar in October 2006.

5. For some scholarly examples, see B. D. Ehrman, *Truth and Fiction in* The Da Vinci Code: *A Historian Reveals What We Really Know about Jesus, Mary Magdalene, and Constantine* (New York: Oxford University Press, 2004); B. Witherington III, *The Gospel Code: Novel Claims about Jesus, Mary Magdalene, and Da Vinci* (Downers Grove, IL: InterVarsity Press, 2004); J. E. Komoszewski, M. J. Sawyer, and D. B. Wallace, eds., *Reinventing Jesus: What* The Da Vinci Code *and Other Novel Speculations Don't Tell You* (Grand Rapids: Kregel, 2006); R. Eisenman, *The New Testament Code: The Cup of the Lord, the Damascus Covenant, and the Blood of Christ* (London: Watkins, 2006).

6. Recent books written about Mel Gibson's film include K. E. Corley and R. L. Webb, *Jesus and Mel Gibson's* The Passion of the Christ: *The Film, the Gospels, and the Claims of History* (London: Continuum, 2004); J. S. Landres and M. Berenbaum, eds., *After* The Passion *Is Gone: American Religious Consequences* (New York: Altamira, 2004); and T. K. Beal and T. Linadelt, eds., *Mel Gibson's Bible: Religion, Popular Culture, and the Passion of the Christ* (Chicago: University of Chicago Press, 2006).

7. Pat Robertson, interview by Sean Hannity, *Hannity & Colmes*, Fox Network, March 3, 2004.

8. Rikk Watts and I held an interesting discussion and argument over the film in the *Journal for the Study of the Historical Jesus* 2 (June 2004): 158–229. He maintained that the film was justifiable artistically, that it was not anti-Semitic, and that it was the basis of faith. I maintained the opposite. Neither one of us accused Mel Gibson personally of anti-Semitic feelings. Time has shown both of us to have been naive. In my mind, there is now little doubt that Gibson encouraged the anti-Semitism in the film.

9. See, e.g., L. Hurtado, *How on Earth Did Jesus Become a God? Historical Questions about Earliest Devotion to Jesus* (Grand Rapids: Eerdmans, 2005).

10. It begins with the antihero, a cab driver, spouting a whole bunch of crazy conspiracies. The scuttlebutt is that this was completely unscripted and that Gibson just ad-libbed it out of the stories he and his father have told each other over the years.

11. G. Gallup Jr. and J. Castelli, *The People's Religion: American Faith in the 90s* (New York: Macmillan, 1989).

Bibliography

PRIMARY TEXTS UNDER DISCUSSION

Amichai, Y. "Jerusalem 1967." In *Poems of Jerusalem: A Bilingual Edition*. By Y. Amichai. Translated by S. Mitchell. New York: Schocken, 1987.

Al-'Aqqād, 'A. M. *The Genius of Christ*. Translated and edited by F. P. Ford Jr. Studies in Contemporary Philosophical Theology. Binghamton, NY: Global Publications, 2001.

Asch, S. "In a Carnival Night." In *From the Shtetl to the Wide World*. Edited by S. Rozansky. Buenos Aires: Musterverk fun yiddisher Literature, 1972.

Boulton, J., et al, eds. *The Letters of D. H. Lawrence*. Cambridge: Cambridge University Press, 1991.

Brown, Dan. *The Da Vinci Code*. New York: Doubleday, 2003.

Bulgakov, M. *The Master and Margarita*. Translated by M. Ginsburg. New York: Grove, 1967.

———. *The Master and Margarita*. Translated by M. Glenney. London: Collins Harville, 1967.

Dante Alighieri. *The Divine Comedy*. Translated by C. H. Sisson. Oxford: Oxford University Press, 1998.

Dor, M. *Crossing the River: Selected Poems*. Translated by D. Johnson. Oakville, Ontario: Mosaic Press, 1989.

———. *Sirpad umatekhet*. Ramat Gan: Massada, 1965.

Greenberg, U. Z. "Uri Zvi in Front of the Cross." [In Yiddish.] *Gezamlte verk* 1 (1926–36): 304–7.

Kazantzakis, N. *The Last Temptation of Christ*. Translated by P. A. Bien. New York: Simon & Schuster, 1960.

Lawrence, D. H. *The Man Who Died*. London: Martin Secker, 1931.

———. "The Risen Lord." In *The Complete Poems of D. H. Lawrence*, edited by V. de Sola Pinto and W. Roberts. New York: Viking, 1971.

Mailer, N. *The Gospel according to the Son*. New York: Random House, 1997.

Orpaz, Y. *Masa' Daniel*. Tel Aviv: Am Oved, 1969.

Oz, A. *Ad Mavet*. Tel Aviv: Am Oved, 1969.

Potok, C. *The Chosen*. New York: Fawcett Crest, 1968.

———. *My Name Is Asher Lev*. New York: Knopf, 1972.

———. *On Being Proud of Uniqueness*. Lecture delivered at Southern College of Seventh-Day Adventists, Collegedale, Tennessee, March 20, 1986. Edited by J. Gladson. http://www.lasierra .edu/~ballen/potok/Potok .unique.html.

Ricci, N. *Testament*. Toronto: Scarborough: Doubleday, 2002.

Sadeh, P. *Hahayim Kemashal*. 1957. Reprint, Tel Aviv: Shoken, 1984.

Saramago, J. *The Gospel according to Jesus Christ*. Translated by G. Pontiero. New York: Harcourt Brace, 1994.

Saramago, J., T. Crosfield, and F. Rodrigues. "The 1998 Nobel Lecture." *World Literature Today* 73 (1999).

Shapiro, L. "The Cross." In *The Jewish Government and Other Stories*, edited and translated by C. Leviant. New York: Twayne Publishers, 1971.

Shevili, B. *Ha-Yeridah min ha-Telav*. Jerusalem: Schocken, 2000.

Wiesel, E. *Night*. Translated by S. Rodway. New York: Hill & Wang, 1960.

PRIMARY PAINTINGS AND FILMS UNDER DISCUSSION

Chagall, M. (a) *White Resurrection, Yellow Resurrection, The Martyr, The Crucified*.

(b) *Revolution, Resistance, Resurrection by the River, Exodus*.

(c) *Calvary, Descent of the Cross, The Soul of the Town, Self Portrait with Wall Clock*.

Holman Hunt, W. *Light of the World*.

Rouault, G. *The Passion*.

Gibson, M., director. *The Passion of the Christ*. 2004.

Howard, R., director. *The Da Vinci Code*. 2006.

Scorsese, M., director. *The Last Temptation of Christ*. 1988.

OTHER TEXTS AND CRITICAL DISCUSSIONS

'Abd al-Malik, B. Review of *'Abqariyat al-Masīḥ*, by 'Abbās Maḥmūd al-'Aqqād. *Muslim World* 43 (1953): 218–19.

Abrams, M. H. *The Correspondent Breeze: Essays in English Romanticism*. New York: Norton, 1984.

Adams, P-L. "The Gospel according to the Son." *Atlantic* 279 (June 1997).

Agel, H. *Le Visage du Christ a l'ecran*. Paris: Desclee, 1985.

Ahmad, G. *Jesus in India: Being an Account of Jesus' Escape from Death on the Cross and of His Journey to India*. 1899. Reprint, London: London Mosque, 1978.

Alexander, S. *Marc Chagall: A Biography*. New York: Putnam's Sons, 1978.

Algar, H. *Jesus in the Qur'an: His Reality Expounded in the Qur'an*. Oneonta, NY: Islamic Publications International, 1999.

Allen, R. "al-Aḳḳād, 'Abbas Mahmūd." In *The Encyclopaedia of Islam*, 2nd ed., edited by H. A. R. Gibb et al., Supplement 57–58. Leiden: Brill, 1980.

Allen, T. "The Arabesque, the Bevelled Style, and the Mirage of Early Islamic Art." In *Tradition and Innovation in Late Antiquity*, edited by F. M. Clover, R. S. Humphrys. Madison: University of Wisconsin Press, 1989.

Alter, R., and F. Kermode. *The Literary Guide to the Bible*. Cambridge, MA: Harvard University Press, 1987.

Amishai-Maisels, Z. *Depiction and Interpretation: The Influence of the Holocaust on the Visual Arts*. Oxford: Pergamon, 1993.

———. "The Jewish Jesus." *Journal of Jewish Art* 9 (1982): 86–99.

Anawati, G. "La personne du Christ d'après deux livres récents d'auteurs musulmans." In *ATTI: dell'VIII Congresso Internazionale di Storia delle Religioni (Roma 17–23 Aprile 1955)*, 443–46. Florence: G. C. Sansoni, 1956.

Arnal, E., and M. Desjardins, eds. *Whose Historical Jesus?* Waterloo, Ontario: Wilfrid Laurier University Press, 1997.

Aschheim, S. *The Nietzsche Legacy in Germany 1890–1990*. Berkeley: University of California Press, 1992.

Ata ur-Rahim, M. *Jesus: Prophet of Islam*. 1977. Reprint, Alexandra, Singapore: Omar Brothers, 2001.

Aulén, G. *Christus Victor: An Historical Study of the Three Main Types of the Idea of the Atonement*. London: SPCK, 1931.

Awad, L. *The Literature of Ideas in Egypt, Part I: Selection, Translation, and Introduction*. Vol. 3 in *Arabic Writing Today*. Studies in New Eastern Culture and Society, no. 6. Atlanta: Scholars Press, 1986.

Ayoub, M. "Muslim Views of Christianity: Some Modern Examples." *Islamochristiana* 10 (1984): 49–70.

———. "Towards an Islamic Christology, II: The Death of Jesus, Reality or Delusion (A Study of the Death of Jesus in Tafsīr Literature)." *Muslim World* 70 (1980): 91–121.

Babington, B., and P. W. Evans. "The Lives of Christ: The Greatest Story Ever Screened." In *Biblical Epics: Sacred Narrative in the Hollywood Cinema*, 98–109. Manchester: Manchester University Press, 1993.

Badawi, M. M. *A Critical Introduction to Modern Arabic Poetry*. Cambridge: Cambridge University Press, 1975.

Baird, W. *History of New Testament Research*. Vol. 1, *From Deism to Tübingen*. Minneapolis: Fortress, 1972.

Barclay, J., and J. Sweet, eds. *Early Christian Thought in Its Jewish Context*. New York: Cambridge University Press, 1996.

Barr, J. "History of Interpretation: Modern Biblical Criticism." In *Oxford Companion to the Bible*, op. cit., 318–24.

Barratt, A. *Between Two Worlds*. Oxford: Clarendon, 1987.

Barrett, W. *Irrational Man: A Study in Existential Philosophy*. Garden City, NY: Doubleday, 1955.

Barth, K. *The Humanity of God*. Richmond, VA: John Knox, 1960.

Baugh, L. *Imaging the Divine: Jesus and Christ Figures in Film*. Communication, Culture, and Theology Series. Kansas City, MO: Sheed & Ward, 1998.

Beal, T. K., and T. Linadelt, eds. *Mel Gibson's Bible: Religion, Popular Culture, and the Passion of the Christ*. Chicago: University of Chicago Press, 2006.

Beauvoir, S., de. *The Second Sex*. Translated and edited by H. M. Parshley. New York: Vintage, 1989.

Ben-Chorin, S. *Brother Jesus: The Nazarene Through Jewish Eyes*. Translated by J. S. Klein and M. Reinhart. Athens, GA: University of Georgia Press, 2001.

———. *Bruder Jesus: Der Nazarener in jüdischer Sicht*. Munich: List, 1967.

Ben-Porat, Z. "Saramago's *Gospel* and the Poetics of Prototypical Rewriting." *Journal of Romance Studies* 3 (2003): 93–105.

Ben-Shalom, R. "Medieval Jewry in Christendom." In *The Oxford Handbook of Jewish Studies*, edited by M. Goodman, 154–92. Toronto: Oxford University Press, 2002.

Berry, D. "Buber's View of Jesus as Brother." *Journal of Ecumenical Studies* 14 (1977): 203–18.

Biale, D. "A Journey between Worlds: East European Jewish Culture from the Partitions of Poland to the Holocaust." In *Cultures of the Jews: A New History*, edited by D. Biale, 799–854. New York: Schocken, 2002.

———. *Power and Powerlessness in Jewish History*. New York: Schocken, 1986.

Bien, P. A. *Kazantzakis: Politics of the Spirit*. Princeton, NJ: Princeton University Press, 1989.

Bijlefeld, W. A. "Other Faith Images of Jesus: Some Muslim Contributions to the Christological Discussion." In *Christological Perspectives: Essays in Honor of Harvey K. McArthur,* edited by R. K. Berkey and S. A. Edwards, 200–15, 293–302. New York: Pilgrim, 1982.

Bland, K. *The Artless Jew: Medieval and Modern Affirmations and Denials of the Visual.* Princeton, NJ: Princeton University Press, 2000.

Bloom, H. *Genius: A Mosaic of One Hundred Exemplary Creative Minds.* New York: Warner, 2002.

———. "The One with the Beard Is God, the Other is the Devil." *Portuguese Literary and Cultural Studies* 6 (2001): 155.

Boero, M. "La cristología de José Saramago." *Cuadernos Hispanòamericanos* 528 (1994): 134–37.

Booth, W. C. *A Rhetoric of Irony.* Chicago: University of Chicago Press, 1974.

Borg, M. J. *Conflict, Politics, and Holiness in the Teachings of Jesus.* New York: Edwin Mellen, 1984.

———. *Jesus: A New Vision.* San Francisco: Harper & Row, 1987.

Bornkamm, G. *Jesus of Nazareth.* Translated by I. McLuskey, F. McLuskey, and J. M. Robinson. New York: Harper & Row, 1960.

Borrmans, M. *Jésus et les musulmans d'aujourd'hui.* Collection "Jésus et Jésus-Christ." Paris: Desclée, 1996.

Boyarin, D. *Border Lines: The Partition of Judaeo-Christianity.* Philadelphia: University of Pennsylvania Press, 2004.

Braun, W. "Social-Rhetorical Interests." In *Whose Historical Jesus?* Edited by W. E. Arnal and M. Desjardins. Waterloo, Ontario: Wilfrid Laurier University Press, 1997.

Bultman, R. *Jesus and the Word.* London: A & C Black, 1910.

Burkert, W. *The Creation of the Sacred: Tracks of Biology in Early Religions.* Cambridge, MA: Harvard University Press, 1996.

Burridge, R. A. *What Are the Gospels? A Comparison with Graeco-Roman Biography.* 2nd ed. Grand Rapids: Eerdmans, 2004.

Byatt, A. S. *Wordsworth and Coleridge in Their Time.* London: Nelson, 1970.

Calder, L. "The Militant Magician," *Guardian,* December 28, 2002.

Camus, A. *The Myth of Sisyphus and Other Essays.* Translated by J. O'Brien. New York: Knopf, 1955.

Capps, Donald. *Jesus: A Psychological Biography.* Santa Rosa, CA: Polebridge, 2003.

Carlyle, T. *On Heroes, Hero-Worship, and the Heroic in History.* Edited by C. Niemeyer. Lincoln, NE: University of Nebraska Press, 1966.

Carrol, P. J. "*Playboy* Interview with Norman Mailer," *Playboy.* January 1968, 74.

Cassou, J. *Chagall.* London: Thames & Hudson, 1965.

Chadwick, O. *Secularization of the European Mind in the Nineteenth Century.* Cambridge: Cambridge University Press, 1975.

Charlesworth, J. H. *Jesus within Judaism.* Garden City, NY: Doubleday, 1988.

Chatelain, J. *The Biblical Message: Marc Chagall.* New York: Tudor, 1973.

Chattaway, P. T. "Jesus at the Movies." *Books and Culture* 6 (March/April 2000): 10–14.

———. "Jesus in the Movies." *Bible Review* 14 (February 1998): 28–35, 45–46.

Chazun, R. *Fashioning Jewish Identity in Medieval Western Christendom.* Cambridge: Cambridge University Press, 2004.

Chesterton, G. K. "What's Right with the World?" In *A G. K. Chesterton Anthology.* Edited by P. J. Kavanagh. San Francisco: Ignatius, 1985.

Corley, K. E., and R. L. Webb, eds. *Jesus and Mel Gibson's* The Passion of the Christ: *The Film, the Gospels, and the Claims of History.* London: Continuum, 2004.

Costa, H. "The Fundamental Re-Writing: Religious Texts and Contemporary Narrative." *Daedalus* 6 (1996): 250.

Cousland, J. R. C. *The Crowds in the Gospel of Matthew.* Novum Testamentum Supplements 102. Leiden: Brill, 2002.

Cragg, K. "'The Genius of Christ'—A Muslim Estimate" (review of *'Abqarīyat al-Masīḥ* by 'Abbās Maḥmūd al-'Aqqād). *East and West Review* 20 (1954): 88–96.

———. "The Gospel of Barnabas." *News Bulletin of the Near East Council of Churches* (Eastertide 1961): 9–12.

———. *Jesus and the Muslim: An Exploration.* London: George Allen & Unwin, 1985.

Cross, J. E., ed. and trans. *Two Old English Apocrypha and Their Manuscript Source: The Gospel of Nicodemus and the Avenging Saviour.* Cambridge: Cambridge University Press, 1996.

Crossan, J. D. *The Historical Jesus: The Life of a Mediterranean Jewish Peasant.* San Francisco: HarperSanFrancisco, 1991.

Daniel-Rops, H. *Jesus and His Times.* 2 vols. Garden City, NY: E. P. Dutton & Co., 1958.

Daum, R. "Describing Yavneh." PhD diss., University of California, Berkeley, 2001.

Dearborn, M. V. *Mailer: A Biography.* Boston: Houghton Mifflin, 1999.

de Beauvoir, S. *The Second Sex,* ed. and trans. H. M. Parshley. New York: Vintage, 1989.

de Boer, E. *Mary Magdalene: Beyond the Myth*. Harrisburg, PA: Trinity Press International, 1997.

Deleuze, G., and F. Guaterri. *A Thousand Plateaus*. Translated by B. Massumi. Minneapolis: University of Minnesota Press, 1987.

Denham, E., ed. *Northrop Frye Unbuttoned: Wit and Wisdom from the Notebooks and Diaries*. Toronto: Anansi, 2004.

Dewender, T., and T. Welt. *Imagination—Fiktion—Kreation: Das kulturschaffende Vermögen der Phantasie*. Munich: K. G. Saur, 2003.

Edelman, D. V., ed. *The Triumph of Elohim: From Yahwisms to Judaisms*. Grand Rapids: Eerdmans, 1996.

Ehrlich, C. S. "'Make Yourself No Graven Image': The Second Commandment and Judaism." In *Textures and Meaning: Thirty Years of Judaic Studies at the University of Massachusetts Amherst*, ed. L. Ehrlich, S. Bolozky, R. Rothstein, M. Schwartz, J. Berkovitz, and J. Young (electronic publication; Amherst, MA: Department of Judaic and Near Eastern Studies, University of Massachusetts Amherst, 2004).

Ehrman, B. D. *Lost Christianities: The Battles for Scripture and the Faiths We Never Knew*. Oxford: Oxford University Press, 2003.

———. *Lost Scriptures: Books That Did Not Make It into the New Testament*. Oxford: Oxford University Press, 2003.

———. *Truth and Fiction in* The Da Vinci Code: *A Historian Reveals What We Really Know about Jesus, Mary Magdalene, and Constantine*. New York: Oxford University Press, 2004.

Eisenman, R. *The New Testament Code: The Cup of the Lord, the Damascus Covenant, and the Blood of Christ*. London: Watkins, 2006.

El-Didi, A.-F. *Jesus und der moderne Islam*. Arabische Kulture 1. [Bonn]: n.p., 1956.

Ericson, E. C., Jr. *The Apocalyptic Vision of Bulgakov's* The Master and Margarita. Lewiston, ME: Edwin Mellen, 1991.

Esqueda, O. J. "El Jesús de Endo y Saramago: La cristología de *Jesús y El evangelio según Jesucristo*." *Kairos* 31 (2002): 95–97.

Evans, C. A. *Jesus and the Victory of God*. London: SPCK; Minneapolis: Fortress, 1996.

Evans, C. A., and B. D. Chilton. *Jesus in Context: Temple, Purity, and Restoration*. Arbeiten zur Geschichte des antiken Judentums und des Urchristentums 39. Leiden: Brill, 1997.

Evans, S. C. *The Historical Christ and the Jesus of Faith: The Incarnational Narrative as History*. Oxford: Oxford University Press, 1966.

Evans, J. "The Militant Magician." *Guardian*, December 28, 2002.

Falk, H. *Jesus the Pharisee: A New Look at the Jewishness of Jesus*. New York: Paulist Press, 1985.

———. "Rabbi Jacob Emden's Views on Christianity." *Journal of Ecumenical Studies* 19 (1982): 107–8.

Farès, G. "Le Christ et l'Islam contemporain." In *Mediterranée, Carrefour des religions*, 31–52. Recherches et débats du centre catholique des intellectuals français, n. s. 28. Paris: Librairie Arthème Fayard, 1959.

Faris, N. A. "The Muslim Thinker and His Christian Relations." *Muslim World* 47 (1957): 62–70.

Farrar, F. W. *Life of Christ*. London: Cassel, 1874.

Finkel, A. *The Pharisees and the Teacher of Nazareth*. AGSJU 4, 1964; Reprint, Leiden: Brill, 1974.

Fitzmyer, J. A. *The Gospel according to Luke (X–XXIV): Introduction, Translation, and Notes*. Anchor Bible. Garden City, NY: Doubleday, 1985.

———. *Scripture and Christology: A Statement of the Biblical Commission with a Commentary*. New York: Paulist Press, 1986.

Fleishmann, J. *The Problem of Christianity in Modern Hebrew Thought*. Jerusalem: Magnes Press, 1964.

Flusser, D. *Jesus*. Translated by R. Walls. New York: Herder & Herder, 1969.

———. *Jesus in Selbstzeugnissen und Bilddokumenten*. Rowohlts monographien. Reinbek bei Hamburg: Rowohlt, 1968.

Ford, F. P., Jr. "Al-'Aqqād's *The Genius of Christ* Re-visited." *Muslim World* 91 (2001): 277–92.

———. "A Modern Muslim Assessment of Jesus: A Translation and Analysis of 'Abbās Maḥmūd al-'Aqqād's *The Genius of Christ*." 2 vols. PhD diss., Temple University, 1998.

———. "The Qur'ān as Sacred Scripture: An Assessment of Contemporary Christian Perspectives." *Muslim World* 83 (1993): 142–64.

Forshey, G. E. "The Jesus Cycle." *American Religious and Biblical Spectaculars*, 83–121. Media and Society Series. New York: Praeger, 1992.

Franks, J. *Revisionist Resurrection Mythologies: A Study of D. H. Lawrence's Italian Works*. New York: Lang, 1994.

Fredriksen, P. "Love." In *The Oxford Companion to the Bible*, edited by B. Metzger and M. Coogan. New York: Oxford University Press, 1993.

Freedman, M. S. *Martin Buber: The Life of Dialogue*. New York: Harper, 1955.

Freud, S. *Civilization and Its Discontents*. In *The Standard Edition of the Complete Psychological Works*, vol. 21. London: Hogarth Press, 1953.

Frier, D. G. "José Saramago's *O Evangelho Segundo Jesus Cristo*: Outline of a Newer Testament." *Modern Language Review* 100 (2005): 368.

Frye, N. *The Great Code: The Bible and Literature*. New York: Harcourt Brace Jovanovich, 1982.

Funk, R. W., and R. W. Hoover. *The Five Gospels: What Did Jesus Really Say?* New York: Macmillan, 1993.

Funkenstein, A. *Perceptions of Jewish History*. Berkeley: University of California Press, 1993.

Furst, L. *Romanticism in Perspective*. 2nd ed. London: Macmillan, 1979.

Gallup G., Jr., and J. Castelli. *The People's Religion: American Faith in the 90s*. New York: Macmillan, 1989.

Garrett, S. *The Demise of the Devil: Magic and the Demonic in Luke's Writings*. Minneapolis: Fortress, 1989.

Geiger, A. *Judaism and Its History*. Translated by M. Mayer. London: n.p., 1866.

Gibson, M. Interview by Diane Sawyer, ABC Prime Time Special Event, Spring 2004.

Goddard, H. "An Annotated Bibliography of Works about Christianity by Egyptian Muslim Authors (1940–1980)." *Muslim World* 80 (1990): 251–77.

———. "Modern Pakistani and Indian Muslim Perceptions of Christianity." *Islam and Christian-Muslim Relations* 5 (1994): 165–88.

———. *Muslim Perceptions of Christianity*. CSIC Studies on Islam and Christianity. London: Grey Seal, 1996.

Goethe, W. von. *Goethe's Faust*. Translated by W. Kaufmann. New York: Viking, 1967.

Goldstein, M. *Jesus in the Jewish Tradition*. New York: Macmillan, 1950.

Goodacre, M. "The Synoptic Jesus and the Celluloid Christ: Solving the Synoptic Problem through Film." *Journal for the Study of the New Testament* 80 (2000): 31–43.

Goodier, A. *The Passion and Death of Our Lord Jesus Christ*. London: Burns, Oates & Washbourne, 1933.

———. *The Public Life of Our Lord Jesus Christ: An Interpretation*. 2 vols. London: Burns, Oates & Washbourne, 1930.

Gordon, M. "Jesus Christ, Superstar." *Nation*, June 23, 1997, 27.

Grabar, A. *Christian Iconography: A Study of Its Origins*. Princeton, NJ: Princeton University Press, 1968.

Graetz, H. *History of the Jews*. Philadelphia: Jewish Publication Society of America, 1956.

Graham, D. "Images of Christ in Recent Film." In *Images of Christ: Ancient and Modern*, edited by S. Porter, M. Hayes, and D. Tombs. Sheffield: Sheffield Academic Press, 1997.

Gray, P. "Using the Lord's Name." *Time* April 28, 1997. http://www.time. com/time/magazine/article/0,9171,986263,00.html (accessed March 26, 2007).

Grossegesse, O. "José Saramago: *O Evangelho Segundo Jesus Cristo* (1991)." In *Portugiesische Romane der Gegenwart: neue Interpretationen.* Ed. R. Hess (Frankfurt am Main: TMF/Domus Editoria Europaea, 1993), 126.

Guignon, Ç. and D. Pereboom, eds. *Existentialism: Basic Writings.* Indianapolis: Hackett, 2001.

Gunn, D. M., and P. M. McNutt, eds. *"Imagining" Biblical Worlds: Studies in Spatial, Social, and Historical Constructs in Honor of James W. Flanagan.* New York: Sheffield Academic Press, 2002.

Gutmann, J. "The 'Second Commandment' and the Image in Judaism." In *No Graven Images: Studies in Art and the Hebrew Bible.* New York: Ktav, 1971.

Haight, R. *The Future of Christology.* London: Continuum, 2005.

———. *Jesus Symbol of God.* Maryknoll, NY: Orbis, 1999.

Halton, B. "Listen Carefully." *SouthCoast Today,* January 3, 1999. http:// www.s-t.com/daily/01-99/01-03-99/e05ae172.htm (accessed March 7, 2005).

Hanger, D. *The Jewish Reclamation of Jesus.* Grand Rapids: Zondervan, 1984.

Harris, J. H. *The Short Fiction of D. H. Lawrence.* New Brunswick, NJ: Rutgers University Press, 1984.

Harshav, B., ed. *Marc Chagall on Art and Culture.* Stanford, CA: Stanford University Press, 2003.

Harvey, A. E. *Jesus and the Constraints of History.* London: Duckworth, 1982.

Heidegger, M. *Ontology: The Hermeneutics of Facticity.* Trans. J. van Buren. Bloomington, IN: Indiana University Press, 1999.

Heschel, S. *Abraham Geiger and the Jewish Jesus.* Chicago: University of Chicago Press, 1998.

Hinz, E., and J. Teunissen. "Savior and Cock: Allusion and Icon in Lawrence's *The Man Who Died." Journal of Modern Literature* 5 (1976): 279–96.

Hirshman, M. *A Rivalry of Genius: Jewish and Christian Biblical Interpretation in Late Antiquity.* Translated by B. Stein. Albany, NY: SUNY Press, 1996.

T. Honderich, ed., *The Oxford Companion to Philosophy.* Oxford: Oxford University Press, 1995, 483.

Hoover, R. W., ed. *Profiles of Jesus.* Santa Rosa, CA: Polebridge Press, 2002.

Hurtado, L. *How on Earth Did Jesus Become a God? Historical Questions about Earliest Devotion to Jesus.* Grand Rapids: Eerdmans, 2005.

Hussein, M. K. *City of Wrong: A Friday in Jerusalem.* Translated by K. Cragg. Amsterdam: Djambatan, 1959.

Idel, M. "The Attitude towards Christianity in the Book of Hameshiv." [In Hebrew.] *Zion* 46 (1981): 77–91.

Internet Movie Database, http://www.imdb.com/boxoffice/alltimegross ?region=world-wide).

Jacob, W. *Christianity through Jewish Eyes.* Cincinnati: Hebrew Union College, 1974.

Jocz, J. *The Jewish People and Jesus Christ.* Grand Rapids: Baker, 1981.

Johnson, E. *Consider Jesus: Waves of Renewal in Christology.* New York: Crossroad, 1990.

Jones, M. V. "The Gospel according to Woland and the Tradition of the Wandering Jew." In *Bulgakov: The Novelist-Playwright,* edited by L. Milne, 115–24. Luxembourg: Harwood Academic Publishers, 1995.

Kafka, F. *Stories 1904–1924.* Translated by J. A. Underwood. London: Abacus, 1995.

Kagan, A. *Marc Chagall.* New York: Abbeville, 1989.

Kahof, A. *Chagall to Kitaj: Jewish Expedience in 20th Century Art.* New York: Praeger, 1990.

Kakutani, M. "Gospel according to the Son: Mailer's Perception of Jesus." *New York Times,* April 14, 1997.

Kasser, R., M. Meyer, and G. Wurst. *The Gospel of Judas.* Washington, DC: National Geographic Publications, 2006.

Katz, J. *Between Jews and Gentiles.* 2nd ed. [In Hebrew.] Jerusalem, 1960.

———. *Exclusiveness and Tolerance: Studies in Jewish-Gentile Relations in Medieval and Modern Times.* New York: Schocken, 1962.

Kaufman, H. "Evangelical Truths: José Saramago on the Life of Christ." *Revista Hispánica Moderna* 47 (1994): 450–52.

Kaufmann, W. *Existentialism: From Dostoevsky to Sartre.* New York: Penguin, 1975.

———. *Nietzsche: Philosopher, Psychologist, Antichrist.* Princeton, NJ: Princeton University Press, 1974.

Kazantzakis, H. *Nikos Kazantzakis: A Biography Based on His Letters.* Translated by Amy Mims. New York: Simon & Schuster, 1968.

Kazantzakis, N. *The Greek Passion.* Translated by J. Griffin. New York: Simon & Schuster, 1953.

Kelber, W. H. *The Oral and the Written Gospel.* Philadelphia: Fortress, 1983.

Kermode, F. "Advertisement for Himself." *New York Review of Books*, May 15, 1997, 4–8

———. *The Genesis of Secrecy: On the Interpretation of Narrative.* Cambridge, MA: Harvard University Press, 1979.

Kerr, D. A. "Christology in Christian-Muslim Dialogue." In *Christology in Dialogue*, edited by R. K. Berkey and S. A. Edwards. Cleveland: Pilgrim, 1993, 201–20.

———. "The Problem of Christianity in Muslim Perspective: Implications for Christian Mission." *International Bulletin of Missionary Research* 5 (1981): 152–62.

Khalidi, T. *The Muslim Jesus: Sayings and Stories in Islamic Literature.* Convergences: Inventories of the Present. Cambridge, MA: Harvard University Press, 2001.

Kierkegaard, S. *Fear and Trembling.* Translated by V. Howard and E. H. Hong. Princeton, NJ: Princeton University Press, 1983.

———. *Fear and Trembling, and The Sickness unto Death.* Translated by W. Lowrie. Princeton NJ: Princeton University Press, 1954.

Kinnard, R., and T. Davis. *Divine Images: A History of Jesus on the Screen.* New York: Carol Publishing, 1992.

Klassen, W. *Judas: Betrayer or Friend of Jesus?* Minneapolis: Fortress, 1996.

Klausner, J. *Jesus of Nazareth: His Life, Time, and Teaching* Translated by H. Danby. London: Macmillan, 1925; 3rd ed., 1952.

———. *Yeshu ha-Notzri.* 2 vols. Jerusalem: Stybel, 1922.

Klausner, Y. *A History of Modern Hebrew Literature.* Jerusalem: Ahiasaf, 1952.

Klobucka, A. "An Interview with Nobel Prize-Winning Portuguese Novelist José Saramago." *Mass Humanities* 1 (Spring 2002): 4–5.

Kloppenborg, J. S. *Excavating Q: The History and Setting of the Sayings Gospel.* Minneapolis: Fortress; New York: Citadel, 2000.

Koester, H. *Ancient Christian Gospels: Their History and Development.* London: SCM Press; Philadelphia: Trinity Press International, 1990.

Koester, H., and T. O. Lambdin. "The Gospel of Thomas." In *The Nag Hammadi Library in English*, edited by J. Robinson, 124–38. San Francisco: Harper & Row, 1978.

Komoszewski, J. E., M. J. Sawyer, and D. B. Wallace, eds. *Reinventing Jesus: What* The Da Vinci Code *and Other Novel Speculations Don't Tell You.* Grand Rapids: Kregel, 2006.

Krauss, S. *Das Leben Jesu nach jüdischen Quellen.* Berlin: S. Calvary, 1902.

Kremer, S. L. "Daedalus in Brooklyn: Influences of *A Portrait of the Artist as a Young Man* on *My Name Is Asher Lev.*" *Studies in American Jewish Literature* 4 (1984): 26–38.

————. "Interview with Chaim Potok." *Studies in Jewish Literature* 4 (1984): 85.

Krugovoy, G. *The Gnostic Novel of Mikhail Bulgakov: Sources and Exegesis* Lanham, MD: University Press of America, 1991.

Lampe, P. *From Paul to Valentinus: Christians at Rome in the First Two Centuries.* Translated by M. Steinhauser. Minneapolis: Fortress, 2003.

Landres, J., and M. Berenbaum, eds. *After the Passion Is Gone: American Religious Consequences.* New York: Altamira, 2004.

Lavan, S. *The Ahmadiyah Movement: A History and Perspective.* Delhi: Manohar Book Service, 1974.

Lawrence, D. H. *Women in Love.* Oxford: Oxford University Press, 1998.

Layton, B. *The Gnostic Scriptures: A New Testament with Annotations and Introductions.* New York: Doubleday, 1987.

Leirvik, O. *Images of Jesus Christ in Islam: Introduction, Survey of Research, Issues of Dialogue.* Studia Missionalia Upsaliensia 76. Uppsala: Swedish Institute of Missionary Research, 1999.

Lennon, J. M. *Conversations with Norman Mailer.* Jackson: University Press of Mississippi, 1988.

————. "Mailer's Cosmology." In *Critical Essays on Norman Mailer*, edited by J. M. Lennon, 145–56. Boston: G. K. Hall, 1986.

Levenson, J. D. *The Death and Resurrection of the Beloved Son: The Transformation of Child Sacrifice in Judaism and Christianity.* New Haven, CT: Yale University Press, 1993.

Ludwig, E. *The Son of Man: The Story of Jesus.* Translated by E. and C. Paul. New York: Boni & Liveright, 1928.

Mack, B. *The Lost Gospel: The Book of Q and Christian Origins.* San Francisco: HarperSanFrancisco, 1993.

————. *A Myth of Innocence: Mark and Christian Origins.* Philadelphia: Fortress, 1988.

————. *Who Wrote the New Testament? The Making of Christian Myth.* San Francisco: HarperSanFrancisco, 1995.

Mackey, J. P. "Jesus on Our Screens." In *New Image of Religious Film*, edited by J. R. May, 57–91. Communication, Culture, and Theology Series. Kansas City, MO: Sheed & Ward, 1997.

————, ed. *Religious Imagination.* Edinburgh: Edinburgh University Press, 1986.

Mailer, N. *The Armies of the Night: History as a Novel and the Novel as History.* New York: New American Library 1968.

————. *The Executioner's Song.* Boston: Little, Brown, 1979.

————. *Marilyn: A Biography.* New York: Grosset & Dunlop, 1973.

————. *The Naked and the Dead*. New York: Rinehart, 1948.

———— *Some Honorable Men: Political Conventions 1960–1972*. Boston: Little, Brown, 1976.

————. *St. George and the Godfather*. New York: New American Library, 1972.

————. *Why Are We in Vietnam?*. New York: G. Putnam's Sons, 1967.

Mailer, N. *Advertisements for Myself*. New York: Putnam's, 1959.

Malone, P. *Movie Christs and Antichrists*. New York: Crossroad, 1988.

Mann, V. B., ed. *Jewish Texts on the Visual Arts*. Cambridge: Cambridge University Press, 2000.

Marshall, D. "Christianity in the Qur'ān." In *Islamic Interpretations of Christianity*, edited by L. Ridgeon, 3–29. New York: St. Martin's Press, 2001.

Marx, K. "Critique of the Gotha Programme." In *Selected Works in Two Volumes*, by K. Marx and F. Engels, 2:24. Moscow: Foreign Languages Publishing House, 1955.

May, John R. "Art: Shaping Images of Christ." In *Imaging Christ: Politics, Art, Spirituality*, edited by F. Eigo, 73–103. Villanova, PA: Villanova University Press, 1991.

McDonough, B. T. *Nietzsche and Kazantzakis*. Washington, DC: University Press of America, 1978.

McGann, J. *The Romantic Ideology: A Critical Investigation*. Chicago: University of Chicago Press, 1983.

McLeod, H. *Secularization in Western Europe: 1848–1914*. New York: Macmillan and New York: St. Martin's Press, 2000.

Meier, J. P. *A Marginal Jew: Rethinking the Historical Jesus*. Vol. 2, *Mentor, Message, and Miracles*. Anchor Reference Library. New York: Doubleday, 1994.

Mendelssohn, M. *Jerusalem, or On Religious Power and Judaism*. Translated by A. Arkush. Hanover, NH: University Press of New England, 1983.

Mettinger, T. *No Graven Image? Israelite Aniconism in Its Ancient Near Eastern Context*. Coniectanea Biblica Old Testament Series 42. Stockholm: Almquist & Wiksell International, 1995.

Metzger, B. M., and M. D. Coogan, eds. *The Oxford Companion to the Bible*. Oxford: Oxford University Press, 1993.

Meyer, B. F. *The Aim of Jesus*. London: SCM Press, 1979.

Meyer, F. *Marc Chagall: Life and Work*. Translated by R. Allen. New York: Harry Abrams, 1963.

Michel, T. F., ed. and trans. *A Muslim Theologian's Response to Christianity: Ibn Taymiyya's Al-Jawab Al-Sahih*. Delmar, NY: Caravan Books, 1984.

Miles, J. "Mailer's Gospel." *Commonweal*, July 18, 1997.

Miller, R. J. *Born Divine: The Births of Jesus and Other Sons of God*. Santa Rosa, CA: Polebridge, 2002.

———. *The Complete Gospels*. Sonoma, CA: Polebridge, 1992.

Milton, J. *Complete Poems and Major Prose*. Edited by Merritt Y. Hughes. New York: Odyssey Press, 1957.

Natov, N. *Mikhail Bulgakov*. Boston: Twayne, 1985.

Nietzsche, F. *The Birth of Tragedy*. Translated by W. Kaufmann. New York: Random House, 1967.

———. *Nietzsches Werke in zwei Banden*. Salzburg: Das Bergland-Buch, 1952.

———. *On the Genealogy of Morality*. Translated by M. Clark and A. J. Swensen. Indianapolis: Hackett, 1998.

———. *Thus Spoke Zarathustra*. Translated and edited by W. Kaufmann. New York: Viking, 1967.

———. *Twilight of the Idols*. Translated by R. J. Holingdale. Middlesex, England: Penguin, 1968.

Nijim, B. K. "'Abbās Maḥmūd al-'Aqqād: A Modern Muslim Apologist." MA thesis, Hartford Seminary, 1970.

Oates, J. C. *The Hostile Sun: The Poetry of D. H. Lawrence*. Los Angeles: Black Sparrow, 1973.

Pacoud-Reme, E. "Resistance, Resurrection, Liberation." In *Marc Chagall*, 172–75. New York: Harry Abrams, 2003.

Pannenberg, W. *Jesus: God and Man*. Translated by L. L. Wilkins and D. A. Priebi. Philadelphia: Westminster Press, 1968.

Parrinder, G. *Jesus in the Qur'ān*. London: Sheldon, 1965.

Pelikan, J. *Jesus through the Centuries: His Place in the History of Culture*. New Haven, CT: Yale University Press, 1985 (reprinted in 1999 with a new preface).

———. *Mary through the Ages: Her Place in Culture*. New Haven, CT: Yale University Press, 1996.

Pires-O'Brien, J. "A Novel View of the Gospels." *Contemporary Review* 274, no. 1599 (1999): 187–91.

Pittman, R. H. "Dreamers and Dreaming in M. A. Bulgakov's *The Master and Margarita*." In *Bulgakov: The Novelist-Playwright*, edited by L. Milne. Luxembourg: Harwood Academic Publishers, 1995.

———. *The Writer's Divided Self in Bulgakov's* The Master and Margarita. Oxford: Macmillan, 1991.

Provoyeur, P. *Marc Chagall, Biblical Interpretation*. New York: Alpine Fine Arts Collection, 1983.

Radosh, D. "The Good Book Business." *New Yorker*, December 18, 2006, 54–59.

Rahner, K. "Dogmatic Reflections on the Knowledge and Self-Consciousness of Christ." In *Theological Investigations* 5, 193–215 (Baltimore: Helicon, 1966).

Reinhartz, A. "Jesus of Hollywood." In *The Historical Jesus through Catholic and Jewish Eyes*, edited by L. Greenspoon, 131–46. Valley Forge, PA: Trinity Press International, 2000.

———. *Scripture on the Silver Screen*. Louisville, KY: Westminster John Knox, 2003.

Renan, E. *The Life of Jesus*. London: Trübner & Co., 1865.

———. *The Life of Jesus*. Everyman's Library. London: J. M. Dent & Sons, 1927.

———. *Vie de Jésus*. Paris: Culman-Lévy, 1863.

Ricci, N. "On Writing Testament." http://ninoricci.com.

Riesner, R. *Jesus als Lehrer: Eine Untersuchung zum Ursprung der Evangelien-Überlieferung*. 3rd ed., Wissenschaftliche Untersuchungen zum Neuen Testament 2/7. Tübingen: Mohr, 1988.

Riley, R. *Film, Faith, and Critical Conflict: The Case of Martin Scorsese's* The Last Temptation of Christ. Westport, CT: Praeger, 2003.

Robertson, P. Interview by Sean Hannity, *Hannity & Colmes*, Fox Network, March 3, 2004.

Robinson, J. M. *The Nag Hammadi Library in English*. New York: Harper & Row, 1978.

Robinson, J. M. *The Secrets of Judas: The Story of the Misunderstood Disciple and His Lost Gospel*. San Francisco: HarperSanFrancisco, 2006.

Robinson, N. *Christ in Islam and Christianity*. Albany, NY: SUNY Press, 1991.

Rollyson, C. *The Lives of Norman Mailer: A Biography*. New York: Paragon, 1991.

Rosenbloom, N. H. "Theological-Historical Conflict with Christianity in Uri Zvi Greenberg's Poetry." *Perakim: Organ of the American Hebrew Academy* 4 (1966): 263–320.

Roskies, D. G. *Against the Apocalypse: Responses to Catastrophe in Modern Jewish Culture*. Cambridge, MA: Harvard University Press, 1984.

Ryken, L. "The Bible as Literature." In *Oxford Companion to the Bible*, edd. Metzger, B.M., and Coogan, M.D. (New York/Oxford: Oxford University Press, 1993), 460–63.

Safran, N. *Egypt in Search of Political Community: An Analysis of the Intellectual and Political Evolution of Egypt, 1804–1952*. Harvard Middle Eastern Studies 5. Cambridge, MA: Harvard University Press, 1961.

Salinero, R. G. *Las conversiones forzosas de los judíos en el reino visigodo.* Rome: Escuela Española de Historia y Arqueología en Roma, 2000.

Sanders, E. P. *Jesus and Judaism.* Philadelphia: Fortress, 1985.

Sandmel, S. *We Jews and Jesus.* New York: Oxford University Press, 1965.

Saramago, J., T. Crosfield, and F. Rodrigues. "The 1998 Nobel Lecture." *World Literature Today* 73 (1999).

Saramago, J. "Is It Time to Return to the Author? Between Omniscient Narrator and Interior Monologue," trans. R. Deltcheva, *CLCWeb: Comparative Literature and Culture: A WWWeb Journal,* September 2000, http://clcwebjournal.lib.purdue.edu/clcweb00-3/saramago00.html. Accessed June 30, 2005).

Sartre, J.-P. *Basic Writings.* Edited by S. Priest. London: Routledge, 2001.

Schäfer, Peter. *Jesus in the Talmud.* Princeton: Princeton University Press, 2007.

Schillebeeckx, E. *An Experiment in Christology.* New York: Crossroad, 1981.

Schoeps, H.-J. *Das Leben Jesu: Versuch einer historischen Darstellung.* Frankfurt: Eremiten, 1954.

Schoonover, K. "Contemporary Egyptian Authors." *Muslim World* 45 (1955): 26–36.

Schumann, O. H. *Der Christus der Muslime: Christologische Aspekte in der arabisch-islamischen Literatur.* 2nd ed. Kölner Veröffentlichungen zur Religionsgeschichte. Cologne: Böhlau Verlag, 1988.

Schwartz, Y. "The Person, the Path, and the Melody: A Brief History of Identity in Israeli Literature." *Prooftexts* 20, no. 3 (2000): 318–39.

Schweitzer, A. *The Quest of the Historical Jesus.* Translated by W. Montgomery. New York: Macmillan, 1968.

———. *The Quest of the Historical Jesus: Critical Study of Its Progress from Reimarus to Wrede.* Translated by W. Montgomery. London: A & C Black, 1910.

Sed-Rajna, G. *Jewish Art.* Translated by S. Friedman and M. Reich. New York: Harry N. Abrams, 1997.

Segal, A. F., and R. Watts. "Gibson's *The Passion.*" *Journal for the Study of the Historical Jesus* 2 (June 2004): 158–229.

———. "Jesus, the Jewish Revolutionary." In *Jesus' Jewishness: Exploring the Place of Jesus within Early Judaism,* edited by J. H. Charlesworth, 199–225. New York: Crossroad, 1991.

Sobrino, J. *Christology at the Crossroads: A Latin American Approach.* Maryknoll, NY: Orbis, 1978.

Solomon, J. "The New Testament and Tales of the Christ." In *The Ancient World in the Cinema,* rev. and expanded ed., 176–223. New Haven, CT: Yale University Press, 2001.

Spiegel, S. *The Last Trial: On the Legends and Lore of the Command to Abraham to Offer Isaac as a Sacrifice: The Akedah*. Translated by J. Goldin. New York: Pantheon, 1967.

Stanislawski, M. "Eastern European Jewry in the Modern Period: 1750–1939." In *The Oxford Handbook of Jewish Studies*, edited by M. Goodman, 396–411. Toronto: Oxford University Press, 2002.

Stanton, G. N., and G. Strousma, eds. *Tolerance and Intolerance in Early Judaism and Christianity*. Cambridge: Cambridge University Press, 1998.

Stern, R. C., C. Jefford, and G. DeBona. *Savior on the Silver Screen*. New York: Paulist Press, 1999.

Strauss, D. F. *Das Leben Jesu*. Tübingen, Germany: C.F. Osiander, 1835–1836.

Sweeney, J. J. *Chagall*. New York: Museum of Modern Art, 1946.

Tatum, W. B. *Jesus at the Movies: A Guide to the First Hundred Years*. Santa Rosa, CA: Polebridge, 1997.

Teissier, H. "Des écrivains musulmans d'aujourd'hui nous parlent du Christ." *Cahiers religieux d'Afrique du Nord* (Algiers) 10 (1959): 28–36.

Telford, W. R. "Jesus Christ Movie Star: The Depiction of Jesus in the Cinema." In *Explorations in Theology and Film*, edited by C. Marsh and G. Ortiz, 115–39. Malden, MA: Blackwell, 1997.

———. "The New Testament in Fiction and Film: A Biblical Scholar's Perspective." In *Words Remembered, Texts Renewed: Essays in Honour of John F. A. Sawyer*, edited by J. Davies, G. Harvey, and W. G. E. Watson, 360–94. Sheffield: Sheffield Academic Press, 1995.

Teshuva, J. B. *Chagall, A Retrospective*. Westport, CT: Hugh Lauter Levin Associates, 1995.

Tesser, C. C., ed. "A Tribute to José Saramago, 1998 Nobel Literature Laureate." *Hispania* (1999): 1–2.

Van Biema, D. "A Kiss for Judas," *Time*, February 27, 2006, 37.

Vermes, G. *The Authentic Gospel of Jesus*. London: Allen Lane, 2003.

———. *Jesus and the World of Judaism*. London: SCM Press, 1983; Philadelphia: Fortress, 1984.

———. *Jesus in His Jewish Context*. Minneapolis: Fortress, 2003.

———. *Jesus the Jew: A Historian's Reading of the Gospels*. London: Collins; Philadelphia: Fortress, 1973.

———. *The Religion of Jesus the Jew*. London: SCM Press; Minneapolis: Fortress, 1993.

Vessey, M., S. Betcher, R. Daum, and H. Maier. *The Calling of the Nations: Exegesis, Ethnography, and Empire in a Biblical-Historic Present.* Toronto: University of Toronto Press, forthcoming.

Walsh, R. *Reading the Gospels in the Dark: Portrayals of Jesus in Film.* Harrisburg, PA: Trinity Press International, 2003.

Watson, Gerard, "Imagination and Religion in Classical Thought." In *Religious Imagination*, ed. J. P. Mackey (Edinburgh: Edinburgh University Press, 1986): 35.

Watt, W. M. "The Christianity Criticized in the Qur'ān." *Muslim World* 57 (1967): 197–201.

Webb, R. L. *Jesus and Mel Gibson's* The Passion of the Christ: *The Film, the Gospels, and the Claims of History.* London: Continuum, 2004.

Weidemann, L. "Saramago, José: *O Evangelho Segundo Jesus Cristo*," in Tesser, "Tribute to José Saramago," 24.

Weinberg, D. H. *Between Tradition and Modernity: Haim Zhitlowski, Simon Dubnow, Ahad Ha-Am, and the Shaping of Modern Jewish Identity.* New York: Holmes & Meier, 1996.

Wielandt, R. "'Abbās Maḥmūd al-'Aqqād (1889–1964): Nutzen und Nachteil religionsgeschichtlicher Studien für den Glauben." Akademie der Wissenschaften und der Literatur, die orientalische Kommission, vol. 25. Wiesbaden: Franz Steiner, 1971.

Willmes, B. *Die sogenannte Hirtenallegorie Ex 34: Studien zum Bild des Hirten in Alten Testament.* Frankfurt: Peter Lang, 1984.

Witherington, B., III. *The Gospel Code: Novel Claims about Jesus, Mary Magdalene, and Da Vinci.* Downers Grove, IL: InterVarsity Press, 2004.

Witherington III, Ben. "The Wright Quest for the Historical Jesus," *Christian Century*, November 19–26, 1997, 1075–78.

Wright, A. C. "Bulgakov, Stalin, and Autocracy." In *Bulgakov: The Novelist-Playwright*, edited by L. Milne, 38–49. Luxembourg: Harwood Academic Publishers, 1995.

Wright N. T. *Christian Origins and the Question of God: The New Testament and the People of God.* Minneapolis: Fortress, 1992.

———. *Jesus and the Victory of God.* Minneapolis: Fortress, 1996.

Yueh-Han Yieh, J. *One Teacher: Jesus' Teaching Role in Matthew's Gospel Report.* Beihefte zur Zeitschrift für die neutestamentliche Wissenschaft 124. Berlin: Walter de Gruyter, 2004.

Zerubavel, Y. *Recovered Roots: Collective Memory and the Making of Israeli National Tradition.* Chicago: University of Chicago Press, 1995.